The
Reluctant
Psychic

A MEMOIR

Suzan Victoria Saxman

WITH

Perdita Finn

ST. MARTIN'S GRIFFIN ♏ NEW YORK

www.stmartins.com

Designed by Meryl Sussman Levavi

The Library of Congress has cataloged the hardcover edition as follows:

Saxman, Suzan.
  The reluctant psychic: a memoir / Suzan Saxman, with Perdita Finn.—First Edition.
    p. cm.
  ISBN 978-1-250-04771-7 (hardcover)
  ISBN 978-1-250-04779-3 (e-book)
  1. Saxman, Suzan.   2. Psychics—United States—Biography.   I. Title.
  BF1027.S29A3 2015
  133.8092—dc23

                                                              2014032172

ISBN 978-1-250-07934-3 (trade paperback)

Our books may be purchased in bulk for promotional, educational, or business use. Please contact your local bookseller or the Macmillan Corporate and Premium Sales Department at (800) 221-7945, extension 5442, or by e-mail at MacmillanSpecial Markets@macmillan.com.

First St. Martin's Griffin Edition: February 2016

10 9 8 7 6 5 4 3 2 1

For

Gavin Albion,

for putting up with a mother who lives between the worlds

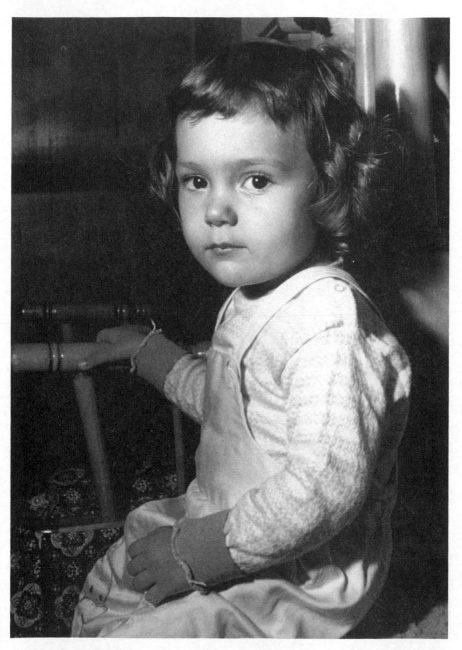

Pretending to be a child

No matter where I move or how many times I change my name or what color I dye my hair, people find me. I don't advertise. I don't have a Web site. I don't even answer the phone. And still when I arrive at my used-clothing store in town, there are people lurking in the parking lot hoping to get a reading with me. "It's urgent," they tell me. "I'm desperate," they plead. "I've heard what you can do."

They show up with photographs, locks of hair, bloody shirts ripped apart by bullets, and so many questions, hundreds of questions, about the other side.

And it's not just the living who are insistent. The dead pursue me, too. They always have. Even before the living knew what I could do, the dead were getting in line, crowding close, and demanding that I carry their messages across the veil. "I'm sorry." "I love you." "Why did you buy that car?" "Tell Bobby he's a piece of shit." "Don't throw away my stuff!"

The other day a couple came to me because they were worried about their kid who had been sick for months with some mysterious illness. I ushered them into my reading room, a little alcove near the Victorian dresses I sell to the steampunk crowd. I sat them down on stools opposite a table with Tarot cards and crystals.

I don't need anything special to communicate with the other side. But it calms people down to have something to touch or do when I'm giving them a reading, sort of like teddy bears to hold in a therapist's office. But before I could even ask these people to pick *a card, the spirit of a tall, thin man with a scraggly beard had staggered into the room. He looked incredibly uncomfortable, embarrassed even.*

"Who's Paul?" I asked.

"Paul?"

"Paul?"

The couple exchanged glances, confused. The name didn't ring a bell.

But now I was seeing more about this man. "Paul tells me he lives in a cardboard box in your living room."

The woman gasped and clutched her husband's hand. The man's face had gone white.

"Why does he live in a cardboard box in your living room?" I asked. It's often hard to make sense of what I see. "Oh," I realized all at once. "He's dead."

It turned out that almost a year earlier the woman had agreed to hold on to the ashes of her sister's ex-husband, a terrible drunk who had died indigent and utterly alone. "I didn't really know what to do with him," she said. "I put the urn, it's in a cardboard box, behind the bookcase and I guess we kind of forgot about it."

"Well, Paul wants to be out of your house, that's for sure," I told them. "He hates it. He knows you always disapproved of him. He feels very ashamed. He doesn't care where you bury his ashes, though; just get rid of them. He needs to move on. He really does."

"Is that why our daughter's sick?" asked the man, concerned.

"Oh no," I said, remembering why they'd come in the first place. "That's something else. Something small. A tick." I could see it crawling up a young girl's leg. "Lyme disease?"

"I knew it!" said the woman. "I told the doctor that's what it was, but he wouldn't believe me."

"There's a test," I told the woman. "Not the one the doctor gave her, but another one. Ask him for the other test."

"How do you know that?" asked the man. "What are you anyway? An intuitive? A medium? A clairvoyant? A psychic?"

I shrugged. I don't really know what I am. I never have. But I've always been like this. I see the things no one else seems to see—bits and pieces of the future, past lives, forgotten stories, hidden secrets, an angel or two, some demons, and the dead. The dead are everywhere. Now and then I can hide from the living, but I can never hide from the dead. What am I? I don't know. But in between cleaning up after my pets and selling jewelry in my shop, I talk to the living, I talk to the dying, I talk to the dead.

1

This Is What a Psychic's Invisible Friends Look Like

As soon as I began speaking, I knew I couldn't let anyone hear my real voice. How old was I? A little older than one? Maybe two? But I knew that I was not a child.

I felt like I was awakening from a dream and didn't know where I was. I didn't know what life I was in. I didn't even know who I was. Suzan? Was that my name? Really? I was an old woman, older than anyone in my family. What was I doing on Staten Island when I should be living in a cottage somewhere in England or walking the streets of London? I was an old British woman. That's what I sounded like to myself—the voice I heard in my own head. I certainly wasn't a child.

Instinctively, I knew that if anyone discovered who and what I really was, I would be in danger. Even as a toddler I was on my guard. I knew I could not trust anyone, not even my parents, especially my parents. Especially my mother.

What would happen if she found me out? Would she put me up for adoption? Would she leave me in a basket on someone's doorstep? Would she report me to the authorities? Would she bring in the priests and the exorcists? Would she burn me at the stake?

All of these were barely understood possibilities, left over, I suppose, from lives I had lived where all of these things had happened. I was an old, melancholy baby right from the beginning. Who would possibly want me?

In my earliest memory, my mother walked into the living room and said, "Who left the radio on?"

I was clutching my favorite doll, a Casper the Friendly Ghost toy, and I had been talking to it. In my real voice. My old-lady English voice. I started babbling when my mother came into the room, because I knew I had to pretend to talk like a baby.

The radio wasn't on. I pulled the string on my toy and made Casper talk. That seemed to get me off the hook. This time.

But I could not always hide the things I knew and saw. They slipped out and they got me in trouble.

I was very young when I began telling my mother the things I knew about her. I saw her, in my mind, as a little girl pulling my aunt Mary, disabled from polio, in a child's red wagon. They were down by the train tracks with a group of other children, and my mother was wearing a red dress. They were putting pennies on the tracks and waiting for a train to come and crush them flat.

I told my mother what I had seen.

"I never told you that," she said. "How did you know I was wearing a red dress?"

"I saw it," I said innocently. "In my head."

"What do you mean, *in your head?*"

"You were mean to Aunt Mary. I saw that, too."

"I was not. How can you say that? I had to help her go everywhere because she couldn't walk because of the polio. I've told you that. I did everything for my sister."

I was beginning to feel anxious and frightened. My mother was angry at me and I didn't understand why. I started to cry, but I couldn't hold back from describing what I was seeing. It was too powerful. And I knew that it was true. "But you threw that big shell at her," I said. "You made that scar on her forehead."

My mother stared at me in astonishment. "How do you know that?"

"I saw it," I said, which was the truth.

I had been in the room with my mother, and while my eyes had focused on a single object, on a chair, the eye inside my head had witnessed a scene unscrolling across my brain. The world around me had blurred, while the movie inside my head appeared before my inner eye with absolute clarity.

The children by the tracks, the blue of the sky, my mother's red dress, the conch shell in her hand—I had seen them as if they were right before my eyes. The little girl scarcely resembled my forty-three-year-old mother, but I could feel that she was the same person. Every being has a unique vibration, whatever its current physical appearance, and I can sense it in that place that opens up just below my heart.

My mother's bossiness, her restlessness, and her rage—I'd recognized her essence at once. But I couldn't articulate any of that as a child. "I saw it in my head," was all that I could say.

I knew at once that I had said something wrong, that I wasn't supposed to see these things. What I'd said terrified my mother in some way that I couldn't understand. It made her angry at me. But I couldn't seem to stop myself.

My mother wanted our family to look as normal as possible. This was the 1960s, and we lived in a colonial suburban house on Staten Island. Daddy went to work every day to the hospital in New Jersey where he was the director of environmental services. My mother plucked her eyebrows and put on makeup and a camel-hair coat to walk the dog. We didn't have plastic covering on the furniture, but we might as well have. No one lived in the living room. No one ever came over.

My mother slept in my parents' bedroom by herself. Daddy slept in the TV room on a pull-out bed. My sister, ten years older than me, slept in a blue room, and I was supposed to sleep in a room decorated all in pink. But I couldn't.

Every night I would sleep for a few minutes—at the most an hour—and then startle awake. Looming over me was the giant dark shadow of a man. He had long white hair, a wide-brimmed black hat, and beneath it eye sockets that sometimes were empty and sometimes blazed with fire. Other than his eyes, he looked like the Quaker Oats man from the cereal box, which really isn't that frightening when he's on a cereal box, but when he's at the end of your bed in the middle of the night and he has holes where his eyes should be, it's scary as hell.

My blood turned to ice in my veins when he appeared. That's how frightening he was.

All my life, very little has frightened me. Most horror movies amuse me. I find Stephen King's novels fascinating, but they don't give me goose bumps. But even the thought of the man in the black hat made me shudder for years. And as a child to actually see him? It was beyond terrifying.

I don't remember the first time I saw him, because I was *always* seeing him. I never had one night's sleep when he wasn't in the room. I'd clutch Casper the Ghost close and shut my eyes, immobilized with terror, but I knew I was being watched. I'd open my eyes, and there the man would be. He wanted something from me. I didn't know what. He was no ephemeral, translucent being—he was as real as my mother and father. Still, I knew he was a spirit, that he came from somewhere else, that he was an intruder in our house.

How do I know someone is a spirit when they look as solid as a real person to me? It's like those pictures where you have to spot the thing that does not belong. A spirit always has a tell, a way I know they don't quite fit into the picture of reality. Something is off-kilter. It could be very subtle, but the man in the black hat was not subtle at all. He had no eyes. He came from the world of death; his entire essence was of death.

"The man in the hat! The man in the hat!" I would finally scream, finding my voice. My mother, annoyed, would run into my room, sure I was being murdered. But no one was ever there. He was always gone by the time my parents arrived. My father would look for an intruder and check the doors. "It's nothing," they'd say. "Go back to bed."

But I couldn't. Because he'd come back as soon as they were gone.

Once I was alone again and the house was quiet, he would reappear like a vision from hell. Finally, when I couldn't endure my terror any longer, I would crawl out of bed and run to my mother's room.

She endured my arrival. She didn't hold me or touch me or soothe me with caresses. She lay on one side of the bed, and I lay on the other. My mother had long blond hair that she wore down at night, which made her look wraithlike and terrifying. She, too, scared me, but where else could I go? I couldn't be alone, or the man with the black hat would appear. I chose my mother's coldness over the cold terror he awoke in me.

Children are alert to the spiritual world in a way that grown-ups have learned not to be. A woman whose daughter had an invisible friend came to see me for a reading. The child demanded the invisible boy be given a plate of food at dinner and room beside her in the car. Naturally, the boy wasn't visible to the mother and the whole thing had become exasperating. But he wasn't invisible to me. He was the spirit of a boy from the girl's neighborhood who'd died many years before and was lonely for a friend.

There are spirits all around us, and children can see them. Children's parents tell them the sprits aren't real, that they don't matter, and so slowly the kids learn to ignore them and finally they forget how to see them altogether.

Are there monsters under the bed? Sometimes there really are.

Surprisingly, I didn't have an invisible friend who was another child, just my demonic Quaker Oats man. It figures.

My mother never tried to explain away his appearance as other mothers might have, nor did she acknowledge him and try to explore who he might be. Still, she would whisper to my aunts when she thought I wasn't listening, "Suzan saw the man with the hat again."

I knew my older sister wasn't having these experiences. I knew my parents weren't. I knew instinctively that if I tried to talk about what I saw, they would roll their eyes and shake their heads as if it were all silliness. But I could feel their fear each night when I called to them. My first lesson as a child was not to speak about what I was experiencing because it made my mother frightened, too.

One night I was feverish and I threw up in my mother's bed. "You puked in the bed!" she screamed at me in disgust. "I was trying to sleep. What's the matter with you anyway? You puked!"

I was ashamed and humiliated. I did everything wrong. But there was nowhere else I could go.

Perhaps it would have helped if my dog had been allowed to sleep in my room. But Muffet was permanently exiled to the basement. I used to go down there and sit beside her on the cement floor. I could feel her thoughts. She was furious and confused. She couldn't understand why she'd been rescued from the pound just to end up living in the cellar. I knew how she felt.

I also was a different species. If my mother could have, she would have locked me away as well. I used to wrap my arm around my face and suck on my skin. I had mouth-shaped sores in the crook of each arm. I never had a bottle, a pacifier, or even my thumb. My mother didn't believe in thumb sucking. I never remember anyone holding me. I held myself like a bat. I was an upset animal worrying a hot spot, trying desperately to comfort myself.

My heart raced all the time. I had so many secrets inside of me that wanted to come out. Sometimes I would just burst into tears with the frustration of it all.

"Oh, Suzan, just stop it," my mother would say. "Stop it right now."

My mother imagined herself pious, but she never prayed with me or even took me to church or offered me any of the solaces of religion. She'd been raised Catholic and in her room was a statue of the Virgin Mary. She was always going on and on about the Blessed Mother, how perfect she was, how chaste.

I resented the Virgin, all covered up in her blue and white robes like she was hiding something. There was something false about her. Or maybe I had her confused with my own mother.

"Isn't there another Mary?" I asked.

"What are you talking about?"

"I like the other Mary."

"Mary Magdalene?"

"That's her," I said. "That one."

I recognized her name. I saw her in my mind, a woman with long dark hair, naked and dancing in the woods. She was of the forest; she was part of nature; she *was* nature, the essence of nature. She was freedom and laughter and music. I didn't see any of that when I looked at my mother's statue. That Mary was bound beneath her chaste blue and white robes, controlled by men. She was what men wanted women to be. My heart yearned for the other Mary, the untamed one. But all of these sensations were trapped inside of me and I had no idea how I was supposed to express them. My thoughts were too big for my little head, and they were dark and deep and wild.

"Mary Magdalene wasn't a very nice lady. How do you know about her?" My mother's eyes narrowed.

"The TV," I lied. I had no idea how I knew that there was another Mary, but I did.

"You don't need to know anything at all about Mary Magdalene," said my mother. I could tell she didn't like her.

I also knew my mother didn't like children. She told me so. Sometimes she remembered to add as an afterthought that she did like my sister and me, and sometimes she didn't. She decorated our house with Hummel figurines of rosy-cheeked Alpine girls and boys. They were frighteningly cheerful in their frozen state of happiness. I thought they were hideous. Was this who I was supposed to be? A von Trapp family singer?

She made me wear velvet dresses and gold shoes—outfits so fanciful that the other kindergartners called me Princess Suzan when I went to school—but I never remember her once telling me that she loved me.

In kindergarten, the teachers realized that I was practically blind. I had always been used to the world being blurry and unfocused, but now I couldn't see the blackboard. My mother took me to the optometrist, and he told us I needed thick corrective lenses.

My mother let me pick out pastel pink plastic frames that made me feel pretty. When we got home, however, she told me how ugly I looked in them. "They don't do anything for you. I hope you're not going to let people see you in them."

I immediately lost them, and everything became fuzzy again. I could read print, but the wider world didn't exist for me. It's amazing I never got hit by a car. I was that blind.

I could see the dead around me, though, with perfect clarity. Everything else was fuzzy, but the spirits had edges, detail, brilliance. I was seeing them with my third eye, and that eye, apparently, did not need glasses. Even today I like to do blind readings. My eyes are open, but I take out my contacts and let the real world blur so I can bring the spiritual realm into focus.

In bed with my mother at night, I'd often wake up to find three spirits watching over me. They were the hooded figures of men dressed in robes. I knew they were holy and wise; they radiated peace and made me feel perfectly serene. The man in the middle was tall, with a black beard. He would nod at me; I would nod back. He smiled when I acknowledged him, but we never spoke to each other. I would wake up and see them, usually around three o'clock: the witching hour, the hour of God.

All throughout the day I would look forward to that moment when I would see my three men, and I would panic if for some reason I didn't see them. But they came almost every night until I was ten years old, which is around the age when even ordinary kids stop seeing their invisible friends. My mother was always asleep when they arrived. I knew they wouldn't come if she was awake. Even today I don't know for certain exactly who they were. But I sensed I had known them for lifetimes, and somehow I knew that they were my guardians. Somehow I also knew that they had given me the gift of prophecy.

Later I would realize that these men were probably the keepers of the Akashic Records. According to Hinduism everything that is destined to happen to us is contained within the Akashic Records, and my sweet little monks were giving me access to them. What a blessing that turned out to be!

Given what my life has been like as a psychic, I probably should have been more frightened of the Three Amigos than the man in the black hat. Thanks, guys! What a gift. They gave me an instrument to play and the skill to play it, but I can't tell you how many times I've stuck it in the closet and tried to ignore it. But that's the way it is for a lot of people, not just me. You've got a destiny, and no matter how hard you try, you can't run from it. You've got to do what you've got to do.

I'm sure that's why I got so sick when I was six years old. I came down with a severe case of rheumatoid arthritis—an old person's disease invading a young person's body. My fever soared and the family brought me to the hospital. The doctors were getting ready to immerse me in an ice bath when the fever miraculously broke. Still, they kept me in the hospital for days.

My family behaved appropriately, arriving with a stuffed rabbit for me to cuddle. But I knew that something was missing from my mother when she looked at me—some kind of honest affection. She didn't touch me, but just stared at me from the end of the bed. Hers was a masquerade of concern.

I knew I might die when I was in the hospital, but I wasn't afraid. I thought about death all the time: not in any particularly morbid way, but with a simple, clear awareness that it might happen at any moment. I recognized the likelihood of death the way old people often do. It was right around the corner. It was no big deal.

I knew I might ascend to the next level. I can remember thinking about it just that way, *ascend to the next level*, and it certainly wasn't something I'd heard talked about in Catholic kindergarten. It wasn't the way most little girls thought; I knew that. The problem was, I didn't feel connected to anything around me. I wasn't of this time, of this country, of this family. Maybe I could die and come back and find my true place. I was the thing in the picture that didn't belong. What's wrong with this picture? Me.

But I didn't die.

I did get left back that year and had to do kindergarten all over again. I returned to school older than the other kids and unable to play at recess or run around in gym because my joints would swell and hurt. I couldn't see the ball to play games anyway. I couldn't see the kids.

I was embarrassed and I wanted to fit in, and at the same time I knew that I wasn't a kid anyway. When the other children teased me or ignored me, I accepted it as my lot in life. I was supposed to be separate and different. That's the way it had always been for me, right? I was a blind, crippled old lady. The child's body was just a disguise. And it didn't surprise me that it didn't fool the other kids.

I continued to have high fevers, which I actually looked forward to and enjoyed. Dazed and delirious in bed, I would gaze up at the ceiling at tiny winged beings hovering in the corner of my room. They had the ugly, pointed faces of rodents, a twitchy sweetness, and they gazed at me with affection. These Beatrix Potter characters gone wrong were my real friends. Even today, I keep pet rats in memory of them. They were emissaries, but I didn't understand yet the message that they were bringing to me.

I know now that people like me often have illnesses as children that separate them from the world. Many of the psychics I would meet later on had experienced debilitating viruses and strange life-threatening infections. Lots of artists, musicians, and writers also got really sick when they were kids. Shamans almost always suffered through some kind of disease before they were identified. Perhaps there was something about the fever that changed the workings of my brain, but I don't think that's really it. I was as open to the spirits before my illness as I was after it. What my rheumatism did was make it impossible for me to participate in ordinary life. Like my blindness, it turned me in on myself, and that's what enhanced my psychic powers. I've read that young racehorses are confined to their stalls except when they're training. They're not allowed to play in the fields with the other foals. They might hurt themselves. They might waste their energy. They don't get to play reindeer games. They're different.

Even within my own family I was alone, and that loneliness left me to explore the only world I could really see, the world that was invisible to everyone else. If I had grown up in a nice family, an ordinary family with warmth and love, I might have forgotten who I was and become, well, if not ordinary, then more ordinary than I was. But that never happened. I was born knowing that these people were not my real family and theirs was not my home. Home was somewhere else—only it would be many, many years before I would figure out where that home really was.

A soldier came to see me. He'd been in Afghanistan. He had shark eyes, blank and dead. His girlfriend had made the appointment and she dragged him into the store. He slouched in the chair opposite me, his arms crossed protectively around his middle. He wouldn't look me in the eye.

"You've fathered a lot of kids," I noted. "I can see them all over."

"Yeah," he muttered. "Whatever."

"Do you want to know where they are?"

"Nope."

"Really?"

"I said no."

As he was talking to me, I saw him with a stick in his hand, bashing in someone's head. He was brutal, violent, out of control. "You're a tough guy," I said. "Where do you work now?"

"Maximum-security prison," he said.

"You hurt the prisoners," I said.

"I give them what they deserve." He shifted in his chair uncomfortably and looked at the door.

"But you used to be a sniper," I said. "You killed a lot of people."

"Something like that." The lack of emotion in his face was disturbing.

A young girl had come into the room and was standing beside him. About four years old and tiny, with long brown hair, she was touching his arm protectively, as if she loved him.

"I see a little girl beside you," I said. "She has long brown hair. Beautiful green eyes."

"I don't want to talk about that," he snapped. His whole body had suddenly become tense. He started rocking back and forth, back and forth.

"She says it wasn't your fault. She wants you to know that. Your parents should never have left you in charge of her in the first place. You were too young. Much too young."

"I don't want to talk about this. Can we please not talk about this?"

"Your sister wants you to know that she loves you. It's not your fault she drowned in the pool. She's never blamed you. You were only a year older than she was. You couldn't swim either. She loves you so much. So much."

"Please," he begged me. "Can we not talk about this?"

He wasn't crying or showing any emotion, but at least I knew why he was such a monster. I don't know if it changed him or not. But a whole slew of corrections officers started calling me for appointments after that.

2

Tales from the Crypt

As a little girl, I was small and dark, with deep brown eyes and two black braids that hung on either side of my face. I didn't look like anyone else in the family. My mother was blond with blue eyes. My sister was blond with blue eyes. Daddy, too, was Nordic and blond.

"Whose daughter are you?" relatives would ask me at get-togethers.

"Anne's," I'd answer, catching the confused expression on their faces.

I just didn't look like any of them. I looked like Wednesday Addams.

I looked like Steve.

Steve was the man who came over every day after Daddy left for work.

Steve was a pirate, a madman, a failed actor, a womanizer, a merchant marine, and a homeless man who lived under the

Verrazano Bridge in his car like a troll. He was also my real father.

Every morning, Daddy drove off in his green Renault and Steve drove up in his car, also—coincidentally, strangely, confusingly—a green Renault. He always parked it down the street, just a little bit away from our house, and then walked up to the front door. From the time I was very little, I was the lookout. I'd peer out the window watching Daddy's car disappear around the corner, hoping I wouldn't see it again that morning, that he hadn't forgotten anything, that he wouldn't be coming back. I'd let my mother know when I saw Steve in his trench coat, a cigarette dangling from his mouth, a smile on his lips, approaching our front door. He had to be let in quickly, before the neighbors could see.

This daily craziness made me totally neurotic. I was on edge all the time. *What if someone sees? What if Daddy comes home? What if someone figures out Steve is really my father?* I always knew I was his daughter. Even if he hadn't told me, hadn't whispered to me that when I was twenty-one I could change my name to his, I still would have known. Steve and I were kindred spirits, and I adored him.

Daddy was a pleasant face behind the newspaper. He was very kind, but in my whole life we never had any kind of conversation. He was there. He was a constant. He was a part of the furniture. He must have known I wasn't his daughter, but he never once spoke of it. In fact, years later, long after he was dead, he visited me and told me he'd known everything and it didn't matter, adding that I should stop cooking with Teflon pans because they caused cancer. He did play catch with me in the backyard sometimes, but I couldn't see the ball, of course. He worked. He read the paper. He golfed.

If I were casting the movie of my life, he'd be played by Henry Fonda.

And for my real father, for Steve, I would cast Errol Flynn.

In fact, Steve used to dress up as Robin Hood. I have a photo of him in the real Sherwood Forest. He used to like to frolic through the woods in full costume—in tights, wearing a little Robin Hood hat, carrying a real bow and arrow. He loved dressing up and always wanted his costumes to be as historically accurate as possible. The jerkin and the belt were made from real leather. He had swords he claimed came from the set of *Robin Hood*, and, well, they might have. He'd been in Hollywood for a time.

Before my sister was born, when my mother was still a newlywed, she was working at Wanamaker's in Manhattan, in the cosmetics department. One day, at lunch, she was walking up Fifth Avenue when this incredibly handsome man in a trench coat approached her. She was sure he was a movie star, maybe Tyrone Power. He was smiling at her.

My mother was very blond and very pretty.

"Excuse me, my dear," the stranger said smoothly. "Can you tell me how to get to Carnegie Hall?"

Dazzled already, my mother offered to show him the way. She knew she'd seen this man in a movie. She just couldn't think which one.

"Why don't you take my arm?" he asked her as they walked along.

She placed her arm in his, and as she did so she noticed a strange rustling noise coming from his feet. She looked down and saw wadded-up newspapers poking out from the soles of the man's shoes. She realized that the trousers he was wearing were torn and dirty and that beneath the trench coat was not a dapper suit but remnants and rags. But he had this charm about him. That's what she told me later, how she explained it. He had this charm about him.

And she was right. He did.

So my mother, married and Catholic and pious, began a twenty-year affair with a homeless man she met on the streets of New York. And I was the child who came of it.

She fixed him eggs and bacon every morning while I kept guard from the living room. Later they'd disappear into my mother's bedroom. "If Daddy comes home, we have to hide Steve," my mother had explained to me, and I was very anxious about my two fathers running into each other. Any number of times they almost did.

I felt like my head was going to explode. The world was filled with things I wasn't supposed to talk about. I saw spirits I wasn't supposed to see. I saw real people I had to pretend I didn't know about. If I made a mistake, if I mentioned to Daddy that Mommy and I had gone to the department store or a showing of the movie *Doctor Dolittle*, my mother would grab my arm, pinching it hard, digging her fingernails into my skin, and glaring at me with her eyebrows raised. She didn't drive, you see.

"How did you get there?" Daddy would ask.

Everything had to be hidden from him, every single activity, every toy and book that Steve brought to me. I had no idea what was safe to talk about and what wasn't. I learned not to talk about anything, but it made me feel insane.

I began falling into mirrors. I would go into the bathroom to brush my teeth and two hours later I would hear my mother screaming at me, "Where are you? What are you doing?" My toothbrush would be in the sink. Where had I been? What had I been doing?

Mirrors, for me, are like portals to other worlds. Maybe there's some truth to the reflective power of crystal balls, although I've certainly never used one. As an adult I often had to keep the mirrors covered so they wouldn't pull me in and even today I don't look in them, but as a child I couldn't tell anyone what was happening.

It would begin as a buzzing sound that emanated from the reflected images inside the mirrored world. They were voices, so many voices, hundreds of voices, in languages I sometimes recognized but usually didn't, and they were all clamoring for my attention. They needed me to hear them. They had things to say. So many urgent, desperate things to say. I couldn't move; I was trying with every cell of my body to listen to them and I'd completely lose track of time. The voices were mesmerizing. And always, somewhere behind them, among them, hidden in the shadows, was the man in the black hat. Was he tormenting me? Was he trying to make me crazy? *Was* I crazy? I worried that I was. Even as a little girl I knew that only crazy people heard voices in the mirrors.

Every other kid in the United States in the 1960s was glued to the television, but I was hypnotized by the bathroom mirror. I only wish the reception had been better.

I became very compulsive. I counted the steps it took me to walk from the front door to the window. I snapped my fingers three times whenever I sat down. I checked lights; I twisted doorknobs. I had to have my little rituals to make me feel in control. Because, clearly, everything in my life was out of control.

"Get down here! Right this instant!" my mother would screech.

But I had to do my whole little Macarena of tics before I

was ready to do anything. This toxic mix of frustration and rage percolated inside of me and made my heart race. I had no way other than my counting to manage it. Nothing could be discussed. I had no friend to share what was happening. I was a nervous wreck.

I remember seeing Daddy's car turning into our driveway one day and panicking. Was it really Daddy's car? Steve had already arrived, hadn't he? Oh no, he was in Mommy's room and Daddy was already getting out of the Renault! I flew upstairs so fast I tripped over the hassock in the living room, sprawling as I shouted, "He's coming! He's almost here."

"Oh God, oh God, oh God!" I heard Steve shouting.

My mother pushed past me on the stairs, straightening her hair. Already out of breath, I staggered up to the second-floor hallway and grabbed Steve, dragging him to my toy-filled closet, shutting the door, and sitting on my bed, my heart pounding.

I still have dreams of hiding Steve and I still have dreams of Daddy, but even in my dreams I never let them meet each other.

Aunt Mary came over from time to time, too. Crippled by polio as a little girl, my mother's sister lived nearby with my grandmother. Aunt Mary claimed to see things. If a bird flew into the house, she was sure someone was going to die. She had a lot of the old superstitious folk beliefs that she'd whisper to me when my mother was out of the room. Aunt Mary said she'd once seen a black-hooded figure floating through her house. She said that my grandfather, who was from Yugoslavia, had seen a man turn into a dog. She hinted that there was an old curse on our family. I wondered if I wasn't that curse.

She said later that she always knew that there was something different about me.

Not long after my illness, we were playing cards together (I think it was the children's game Concentration) when she noticed that I wasn't remembering which cards were which, but that I seemed to know what they were before they were turned over. She began testing me. She'd take a deck out and lay the cards facedown on the table. She would point to a card and ask me what color it was, red or black. I'd tell her. Then she would ask me to tell her the suit of the card she was pointing to. "It's a club," I'd know. "It's a heart." It got to where I could tell what number the card was—an ace or a queen or a ten.

Unfortunately, I can't do this anymore. As I got older, it wasn't a skill that I thought was particularly interesting or important, so I never cultivated it. Believe me, I've tried at casinos, but if it has to do with money, I'm useless. Don't come to me if what you want are the winning lottery numbers. I don't know them. But when I was a little kid, reading cards was the only talent I had and I clung to it. I didn't take dance classes, I didn't draw, I didn't play sports, and I couldn't even ride a bike. But I could win at Concentration without even trying.

"She got forty of them right this time," I heard Aunt Mary whispering to my mother. But it was all kept very hush-hush. I knew this information upset my mother. She'd shake her head, make Aunt Mary put away the cards, make her promise not to test me again. My mother certainly never praised me or even talked to me about what had happened.

I knew enough not to show off my abilities at school, but

even so I didn't fit in. I was both older than the other children and smaller than them. I couldn't run or play sports on the playground. I didn't watch the right TV shows or listen to the right music. I didn't know what I was allowed to talk about and what I wasn't. The other little girls were obsessed with babies, but when I visited Daddy at the hospital where he worked, I used to ride the elevator down to the basement in the hopes that I'd see a dead body being wheeled into the morgue. I had never seen an actual corpse, but I wanted to. I wondered if I might be able to detect its soul still lingering close. I had no idea how to be a child. No wonder I was teased and bullied at my Catholic school.

The other kids didn't play with me. They'd grab my lunch on the playground and throw it around. They'd shout at me, "Are you retarded? Is there something the matter with you?" And they would start chanting, "Suzan is a retard. Suzan is a retard."

I balled my hands into fists and dug my fingernails into my palms. I was genuinely scared of these kids. I thought they might hurt me. At the same time, I was desperate for a friend and I had no idea how to have one. I was scared to go to school. I hated being at home. It felt like there was no place in the world where I belonged or where I was safe.

I'd run away at recess to the steps of St. Theresa's Church. But I didn't sit on them. I climbed through a hole underneath them into a small crypt-like space next to the graveyard. You'd think a little kid would be scared and lonely in a place like that, but I wasn't. I was comfortable. Happy even. That dark and dirty cobwebbed lair was the only place I felt any comfort and security. And I wasn't really alone.

Often, when I was sitting in the crypt, I would look up and

see a woman in black walking by. I don't think she was dressed in modern clothes. She never said anything or stopped to peer into where I was hiding, but I felt like she knew I was there. Sometimes an old nun would crawl under the stairs and sit beside me. She was ancient, with a face like a dried-apple doll, and she wore an old-fashioned habit with rosary beads hanging from her belt. The nuns at school wore skirts, and for some reason I couldn't really explain, I didn't approve. Nuns were supposed to dress like this, like my nun, Sister Agatha.

Sometimes Sister Agatha would gently ask how I was, but other than that she didn't say anything that I remember. She just sat there with me, the way few adults know how to be with children. Once when I was very upset after my classmates' teasing, she patted me on the arm reassuringly. Her touch was as real and soothing as that of any living human being, although she was probably dead because she wore an old-fashioned habit. I don't really know. I never saw her in the school or the convent and I knew enough not to ask who she might be. She was a lot nicer than the living nuns at my school, in any case.

It's very hard for the dead to fully materialize in our world so that they can be seen by the naked eye, and if they can get here from their dimension we should treat them with respect and affection. It's easy for them to be around us, but it's hard for them to assume a form that we can recognize. Ghosts don't have to be scary. They can comfort us. We can comfort them.

At home no one knew what was going on, that I spent much of each day in a crypt like a vampire.

I was frightened to tell my mother what was happening. She would assume that I was doing something to the other children, that I was the problem. Still, one of the nuns must have called her and told her that I wasn't fitting in, because one day she showed up on the playground as a monitor.

She arrived wearing a leopard fur coat, penciled-in eyebrows, and bright red lipstick. She stood on the edge of the playground with her arms crossed, glaring at the children like she was Joan Crawford or Eva Braun. The kids were all whispering to one another.

"Who's the scary lady?"

"There's a mean lady, Sister, staring at us!" screamed one of the kids to a passing nun.

"Who is she?"

"Who is she?"

"That's my mother," I finally admitted.

"That's Suzan Ellzer's mother!" The word spread like wildfire. For weeks after her appearance, kids were still teasing me about her. Luckily, she never came back.

My mother never talked to me about the other children. She never let me invite anyone over. There were no birthday parties. If I did befriend some little girl as hopeless as myself, my mother would mock her until I dropped her.

At one point in elementary school, a small Italian girl befriended me. She used to offer to ride me home on her bike. I loved riding double with her. I didn't have a bike of my own. But each day when I came inside, my mother would be staring out the window. "She's so unkempt," my mother said. The next day she commented, "What a big nose that girl has." One day she just sighed. "That girl's family . . ." Her voice trailed. Whatever was the matter with them was too terrible to speak out loud.

The next time I briefly befriended another girl, my mother

kept pointing out how ugly her hair was. "Have you noticed how matted it is in the back?" my mother said. Even worse was when she would tell me that the girl wasn't really my friend, that she couldn't be. "She doesn't really like you, you know." I believed my mother, too. I accepted that there was something fundamentally unlikeable about me.

I think Steve knew that life wasn't always easy for me. After one of his trips with the merchant marines, he brought me a Dracula statue that I loved. Steve told me that his mother was Transylvanian and that we were related to Vlad the Impaler, who was, in Steve's imagination, a hero in Romania.

Steve traveled to England, Australia, Greece, and all over the world and brought me fairy-tale books with beautiful illustrations. He told me the stories of the Arthurian knights and took me out into the woods to learn how to duel. We'd thrust and parry, plastic swords in our hands. He taught me how to use a rope swing. When my mother got angry at him (and that happened a lot because she was very jealous of his other girlfriends), she'd throw away all the things he'd given me, banging pots and pans, screaming that I was just like him. "I can't even look at you! You look like your father!"

I loved my father's stories. He'd traveled all over the world; he loved music and film and literature. He'd been an actor for a while in Hollywood and said he'd kissed Marilyn Monroe and been friends with Boris Karloff and gotten somebody famous pregnant. My father said that's why he'd had to leave L.A.

Steve loved taking my mother and me to the movies, even if sometimes he fell asleep, a cigarette in his mouth, and his hair caught on fire. Sometimes we'd meet him at night at the army base on Staten Island to catch a film and he'd drive us home. Once our green Renault passed Daddy's green Renault and my mother screamed, "Quick! Hit the ground!" and she and I ducked down in the bottom of the car. My mother made up some lie about how we got home.

Can little children have heart attacks? I used to worry that I might. I was always in the midst of some pulse-pounding, adrenaline-fueled state of high alert.

Steve brought my mother a talking mynah bird. He'd belonged to a friend of Steve's who'd had to get rid of him. The bird, black with an orange beak, could say, "Hello, Sue!" and, "Hi, chum!"

Daddy and my mother got into one of the few fights I ever remember them having about that bird.

"Where'd you get the bird?" he yelled when he got home, his voice filled with suspicion.

I was sitting on the steps, eavesdropping.

"A friend of Suzan's gave it to us," said my mother.

"Yeah, a friend of mine gave me the bird," I said, coming into the room.

"Which friend?" asked my father suspiciously. I couldn't blame him. No one ever came over. I never went to birthday parties or sleepovers. I didn't have any friends.

I shrugged. "You don't know her." I made up a name. "Agatha." I knew I existed to cover up my mother's lies. I *was* my mother's lie. Still, we all loved that bird, even Daddy. When the bird died, eight years later, Daddy took off from work for the day, he was so upset.

I loved that if you told the bird you had to go, he'd answer, "What's the use of going?"

I liked, too, that it was like having my real father in the house even when he wasn't there.

Once in fifth grade when I was hiding in my crypt, a mass of the worst school bullies came over to the church steps and started taunting me. They were huge bulldozer girls. One of them yelled, "C'mon out, kid, 'cause I want to break your arm!" The other kids were egging her on with shouts of "Weirdo!" and "Retard!"

Usually I would have cowered and done nothing, but on this day the frustration and rage inside of me erupted at last. I couldn't take it anymore. I just couldn't. I wasn't going to be a victim anymore.

I leapt out like a lunatic on fire. I wasn't thinking at all as I took a fencing stance, in my outstretched hand an invisible sword.

"Bring it on!" I shouted at the startled kids. "My father's Robin Hood."

I don't know where the words had come from, but at that moment I felt my father beside me. He was my defender. He was my champion. He wouldn't let these kids hurt me. I stared them all down as I waved a sword only I could see in their faces.

No one said anything. They looked completely stunned and more than a little horrified. But I didn't move, and one by one the kids backed down, muttering that I was even weirder than they thought, a ticking time bomb. I didn't cry that day. I never cried anymore. Why should I?

That was the day my father picked me up at school. I'll never forget it, because Steve showed up dressed in his Robin Hood costume. He got out of the Renault in his tights, sword dangling from his waist, and held the door open for me as I walked down the school steps, head held high, knowing the other kids were watching me, amazed. I was Robin Hood's daughter, and even if my sword was invisible, it was sharp. I suppose it must have been some psychic intuition that had fueled my bravery that day. Or maybe my father was psychic, too.

Dueling with Steve, my beloved Robin Hood

I had to mention the snake. I could see him coiled and floating above this man's head. The snake was emitting a golden light and flicking his tongue in and out. I often see people's dead pets close to them, but this was stranger than that, almost mystical. It was very weird.

"Excuse me, did you ever have a boa constrictor?" I asked tentatively.

This man, he must have been in his early sixties, a good-looking guy, a businessman; he just stared at me for a moment, dumbfounded. "Henry?" he whispered, and tears started welling up in his eyes.

"Henry, Henry, Henry," he sobbed. He'd covered his face with his hands.

The snake was looking down on him and I knew what Henry wanted to tell this man. "He forgives you for what you did," I said.

The man was bawling now, blubbering.

It turned out that thirty years ago he'd had this snake, Henry, and one day the man had accidentally left the heat rock turned on and burned him up. The man had lived with the guilt all these years. It had been terrible.

The Christian church thinks snakes are the most diabolical of all life-forms, but nothing in nature is evil. I think God created everything in his image, even snakes. Everything is capable of forgiveness.

3

Quick! Call an Exorcist!

I asked too many questions for Catholic school. My problems began in kindergarten when I argued with Sister Patricia about the souls of animals. She tried to tell me that they didn't have souls, but I knew that they did.

"Only people have souls," said Sister Patricia.

"But God created dogs and cats, right?"

"God created human beings in His image," she said. "He did not create the animals in His image." Her face was getting redder with every word. She was puffing up like a blowfish.

"But what about when we come back? What if we come back as an animal? Don't we still have our same soul? Isn't that what keeps coming back? Our souls? Can't we come back as lots of different things? As people? As dogs? Don't dogs have souls then?" I'd never heard the word *reincarnation*, but I knew all about it just the same.

Sister Patricia was staring at me, astounded, over her double chin. "What are you talking about, Suzan Victoria Ellzer?"

How could I tell her that I could feel the essences of animals and that they were no different from what I sensed from people? I could feel the fear coming from the beating life force of the earthworms the children would pull apart on the playground. I could feel how wrong it was when the neighborhood kids trapped lightning bugs in jars. How could you not know that every living thing had a soul?

When I was barely five, my mother had tried to serve me lamb chops, and I had refused to eat them. How could anyone eat a baby lamb, a child just like me? I had a toy chest with white wooly lambs painted on it.

"Lamb chops don't come from animals," said my mother. "Meat's just meat."

I knew she was lying and I wrote a poem. "Lamb of God, Lamb of God I do not wish to eat this thing that lies upon my plate, this thing the world calls meat." Except for a few months during pregnancy, I have never touched meat since then.

When I met the nuns in kindergarten, I felt sure they would understand about the Lamb of God. I thought the point of the nuns and the priests was that at last I could talk to someone about the spiritual world. At last I wouldn't be alone. These were my people, weren't they? I wanted to talk about God, about heaven, about souls, about death, about angels, about the man with the black beard who radiated peace, but I learned all too quickly that Catholic school was the last place I should bring any of this up. We went to Mass every day and we prayed in class, but we weren't supposed to have any of our own thoughts about God. We were supposed to do what we were told, believe what we were told, and not question anything.

The other children sat in class like dutiful lumps of lard and groaned when I raised my hand yet again.

One day, a boy who often teased me arrived in class with a shoe box filled with two garter snakes he had captured. He was showing them off to the other kids.

The principal, also a nun, stormed into the classroom and confiscated the box.

I knew she wasn't going to set them free. "You're going to kill them!" I screamed hysterically. "You can't kill them! It's not their fault he brought them to school!"

"No one is supposed to have snakes in school," she said, annoyed. "Sit down at once, young lady."

I was seething with rage. I wanted to explode. I wanted to leap out of my seat and shake her. But I didn't. I controlled myself somehow. Tapping, counting, twitching. Still, I knew she killed those snakes and I couldn't imagine how anyone could do such a thing. There was nothing holy about a person like that.

Sister Patricia called my mother.

My mother told me that I was so bad that I was going to grow horns on the top of my head. I ran to the bathroom and pulled back my hair to see if it was true. Were they showing yet? How big would they grow? If I had horns, could I charge the kids who teased me at recess? Could I charge the nuns? Could I fight back at last?

All the other kids loved Sister Patricia, but I seemed to bring out her vein of cruelty. I ate too slowly, in her opinion, and one day she grabbed my sandwich out of my hand and shoved the whole thing in my mouth until I felt like I was choking.

If kids chattered, she took a piece of red construction

paper she had cut out and colored to look like a tongue and pinned it onto the child's shirt. The tongues were long and red and looked vaguely obscene dangling from your chest. You were supposed to take them home and have them signed by your mother, but whenever I got them, I threw them away. It disturbed me to think of Sister Patricia, night after night, alone in her room, cutting out grotesque red replicas of human tongues to pin on children. Was that her only joy in life?

"Are heaven and hell real, Sister?" I asked as the years went on. "How come unbaptized babies have to go to Purgatory? What did they do wrong? Is it because of bad things they did in past lives? Because that would make sense. Why doesn't God just forgive them and let them go to heaven and let them have a fresh start? Why does God punish suicides? Aren't they already unhappy? It says that Noah was eight hundred years old, Sister. How can that be? Couldn't he just have been coming back over and over again, one life after another?"

I didn't ask these questions to be provocative, but as I realized how uncomfortable they made the nuns and priests, I began to take a kind of perverse joy in annoying them. Still, my spiritual hunger was real.

I wanted to know about God. I loved going to church. I loved the stained-glass windows, the bells, the smell of the incense, the smoke drifting up towards the vaulted ceiling. I even loved the rhythmic repetition of the prayers. Words said aloud have power as they send their vibrations into the air.

But Mass at my school was endless. The priest was just going through the motions in his self-satisfied way. The kids fidgeted and endured it. The nuns couldn't wait for coffee hour and the plates of pastries. I sat there silently seething.

The service was monotonous and it should have been electric. Jesus may have said that whenever two or three gathered in his name he would be there, but believe me, he wasn't coming to this party. Why would he show up for stale Communion wafers and grape juice? He wanted home-baked bread and wine and joy.

I kept looking around for Him, for the angels, for God. I saw spirits, after all, but I didn't see any in that church. None at all. It was a dead zone.

None of the nuns or priests ever talked to us about mystical experiences. They didn't even teach us how to pray the rosary. We didn't read the Bible. They wanted us to repeat back the words they told us, but not think about what they meant. It was a Catholic-generating factory, that was all.

"Don't wear makeup; make sure your skirts cover your knees; watch out for vanity." Those were the rules the nuns tried to drill into our heads. They were all about proper behavior and how we looked and acted. Although the most important rule was not to question what the nuns said.

Sometimes when I spoke in religion class the nuns just glared at me, sometimes they icily told me that I would have to study theology one day, and a lot of times they kicked me out and made me sit in the hall. But I didn't shut up. I couldn't.

The nuns wanted us to believe that God was a man with a long white beard who lived in the sky and was just waiting to trip you up and catch you. They didn't put it quite like that, but that was the general feeling. They didn't talk a lot about Jesus. It was the sixties and plenty of young men were beginning to walk around with long hair and beards and messages of peace and love, but the nuns hated the hippies. I had a feeling the nuns would hate Jesus if he actually showed up. He'd probably get a red tongue pinned on his chest.

I knew that the nuns didn't have a clue what they were talking about when it came to religion. Their whole understanding of the universe was wrong, and I could tell they were actively bringing harm into the world. I was surrounded by blind, dumb, unthinking faith.

After one Mass, I asked a sister about the bells that were rung to keep away the demons. Like many things, I knew all about this, but I didn't know how I knew it.

"What are you talking about?" she said, irritated.

"The bells have always been rung during church services to frighten away demons. I just wanted to know more about the demons, what they're like." I was thinking of the man in the black hat, but I knew enough, at least, not to bring him up. "Are they really dark and scary? If Lucifer was the angel of light before he fell, couldn't they look like they were angels and fool us?"

"You are a very rude child," Sister Helen said haughtily.

As I got older, I became more and more upset with religion class.

I had no exposure to other cultures or other religions or different belief systems, but in my heart I knew that the priests and the nuns were caught up in a colossal delusion. Why was Eve to blame for all the sin in the world? Was that why the poor Virgin Mary had to keep herself all covered up? Was that why the nuns had to hide away from life and love? Was that the only way to be good and pure?

I knew there was another Mary and that she danced and laughed. She had wildness in her. She took lovers because she reveled in love. She wanted to touch and be touched. I knew nothing about the Wiccan ideas of the Goddess, but I believed that the real Mother of God would know how to live life to the fullest. She wouldn't be controlling and judgmental. She wasn't prissy. She wouldn't be embarrassed about the things that happened *down there*.

I got my period when I was eleven, and I had no idea what was happening. Basically, I thought this was another strange thing that only I was experiencing. My mother sent my sister to the store for pads and told me that I should never speak of this again. If I bled, I was to tell my mother that I had hurt my leg. That would be our code. Reading a *Cosmopolitan* magazine at the library on a Saturday morning was how I finally figured out what was really going on and that all girls got their periods.

Soon after this I began to hear bells in my room. They were beautiful, soft and tinkling. I knew that they were bells being rung in a church somewhere. They were both surprising and peaceful, their sound clear and pure. Other kids were listening to rock music in their rooms and I was transfixed by my bells.

"Do you hear them?" I asked my mother.

"There are no bells in this house," she said adamantly.

But one day I heard her whispering to my sister, "The bells are coming from her room again." My sister nodded furtively and they both shut up when they saw me.

I began waking up before dawn, at five o'clock each morning. No matter the weather or the season, I would go open my window and kneel before it, looking up at the sky. There was one light in the heavens that I found particularly comforting. Maybe it was Venus, the morning star.

I began bringing whatever book I was reading with me to

the window. It might be *The Secret Garden* or *Great Expectations* or one of my beloved Narnia stories. I would get down on my knees, hold the book before me, and begin reading out loud.

I knew someone was listening. I knew someone could see me. I could feel the deep, still pond of memory held in the sky. Was I reading to the spirits of the dead or to the angels? I don't really know, but I could feel the gratitude of my listeners. I was always very careful about the books I chose. They had to be classics. I wasn't going to read Judy Blume to the heavens. I have no memory of anyone ever reading me a book as a child. Not my mother, not my older sister, not my father. But I read to the dead.

Day after day, month after month, year after year, I did this. At eight o'clock my mother would call me down for breakfast before school and I would stand up, stiff from hours of kneeling, and put my book away. My father teased that I was going to wear out my knees. My sister called it my chanting. My mother never once spoke of it. My aunt Mary brought me a music stand so I wouldn't have to hold the book. But I needed to hold the book before me. It was part of the ritual of my "morning prayers."

I suspected I was participating in some ancient tradition from another life that I couldn't abandon. I loved this time of day. It was my time. I didn't have to face my family or the nuns or the other kids. I didn't have to answer to anyone or try to behave normally. The whole neighborhood was sleeping, the world was quiet, and I could be alone with the spirits.

Years later, when I described this event to a friend, he told me about the medieval anchorites. They were women, often healers and mystics and seers, who lived in a small hut or building attached to the church. They were both a part of the religious community and separate from it. They lived alone, but they would open their windows to read the Gospels to the illiterate villagers and to offer counsel and advice.

Whom was I reading to?

I still don't know.

I do know that I began to realize that the bells were welcoming. My mother was aghast at my becoming a woman, but something, or someone, in the spiritual realm was celebrating it.

I felt very connected to Mary Magdalene. I wasn't sure she'd been a prostitute like the nuns said and my mother clearly believed, but I felt that she was an outcast like me.

Ten years later I would read the just-published *Holy Blood, Holy Grail*, one of the books on which *The Da Vinci Code* would be based, but as a young girl in the early 1970s in New Jersey, I already knew that Jesus Christ had been with Mary Magdalene. I just knew it. But I probably shouldn't have brought it up in religion class.

"Couldn't Jesus have had a child?" I asked Sister Perpetua, a giant old nun with hairs growing out of her chin. "With Mary Magdalene?"

There was dead silence in the room. Even the kids stopped breathing. Sister Perpetua looked liked she was about to explode.

"Of course not!" she spat.

I suppose psychologically there was a part of me that wanted my mother to revel in the full-blooded woman she really was, like Mary Magdalene, rather than hide behind the good lady she pretended to be, like the Blessed Mother. When any kind of sex scene happened in a movie, my mother would be aghast. "This is disgusting," she would hiss. Yet as a little girl, I had sat outside her bedroom door each day while she "entertained" Steve. Wouldn't she be happier just being with my father instead of sneaking around behind Daddy's back? Wouldn't the nuns be less ferocious with us if they were allowed to love whomever they wanted?

Wild images from a long-ago time often arose in my mind of myself dancing in the woods in the moonlight with other women. We were naked. We were healers. Needless to say, I didn't share these particular thoughts with the sisters. Even I knew that there were some things you just didn't say out loud or the nuns would have had to erect a stake in front of the Oak Knoll School of the Holy Child and burn me while toasting marshmallows.

When I was twelve years old, I saw the movie *Brother Sun, Sister Moon* about Saint Francis of Assisi. I had always felt close to Saint Francis because of his love of animals. He knew animals had souls; I was sure of it. In the movie I realized that he also had visions, like I did sometimes. As a young man in medieval Italy, he went off to war, ended up in prison, and came back a changed man. In the movie everyone thinks he's retarded because he's so mesmerized by the flowers and in love with the birds. "Your son is touched," people tell his father.

I knew what it was to have people think you were touched.

There's a scene when Francis goes to church and he's horrified by the gold everywhere and the elaborate rings on the priest's hands. Francis starts to feel suffocated. "No, no," he says. "This isn't the way it's supposed to be." He starts pulling off his silks and satins until he's stripped off all of his clothes.

Naked, he heads out into the streets and gives everything away to a beggar.

Tears rolled down my cheeks as I watched that scene. This was the message of Jesus. It wasn't about stuff. It wasn't about the nuns' comfy chairs, endless meals, and fancy televisions in their residence. It wasn't about saying these words or that prayer for protection. It wasn't about eating a lamb at Easter; it was about bringing the lamb inside and recognizing it as a being just as important as you were. It was about kindness. It was about celebrating life.

I had a little money from my aunt Mary, so I went out and bought myself a Saint Francis medallion. I loved Saint Francis. Maybe he would protect me from the nuns.

———

"I'm looking for the psychic," said a very put-together woman who came into my store.

"I'm her," I said. "But I don't do walk-ins."

"It's an emergency."

"It's always an emergency," I noted. "I've already done my two readings for the day."

"But I need you. I need to talk to my husband. Today."

"And how long has he been dead?" I asked.

"Two years."

"And this is an emergency?"

The woman sighed heavily, put out. "Yes."

I don't know why, but something about her intrigued me. "Okay," I decided. "C'mon into my room."

"Do you know how my husband died?" she asked when we sat down. It was her way of testing me.

"He killed himself."

She nodded. "Tell me what his name was."

"Michael," I said. He was already in the room. "He was happy to go, but he stays close to you, doesn't he?"

"I can't get rid of him!" she exclaimed. It was the first real emotion I'd seen her show.

"And you want to get rid of him?"

"Yes! No! I don't really know! I miss him, but I'm ready to move on, too!"

"No," I told her. "He doesn't want you dating."

"I know; that's what's making me crazy."

"He says you're his wife and you're his responsibility."

"Then why did he kill himself?"

"You know he worked for the CIA?"

"Of course."

"Did you know he was a gambler?"

She gasped. She swallowed and nodded. "I thought so, but I was never sure."

"Well, he was," I told her. "And he owed $350,000 . . ."

His wife interrupted me. "That's the exact amount."

"He couldn't think of a way out, so he went into the garage and turned on the car—"

"That's what he did."

"But he didn't want to stop being married to you. He did it because he loved you. He didn't want to destroy your life together."

"I want him close," she whispered. She was crying now. "But I need to see other people again."

But Michael was telling me the whole time that he was willing to go, only his wife wouldn't let him. She kept begging him to stick around, but then she'd be going on dates with other guys, like she couldn't make up her mind. "Is that true?" I asked her.

"Why can't I do both?"

"He'll go or he'll stay. It's up to you. But he says you have to choose."

"But I don't know! I want both."

I felt like I was doing couples therapy with a dead man and his dysfunctional wife.

"It wasn't my fault he killed himself, was it?" the woman asked.

"No. It was the money, the debt, and the fact that if the CIA found out about it, he'd have lost his job and been blacklisted."

She nodded.

"You know, you don't need me to talk to him. You knew all of this before you came in here, didn't you?"

She looked up at me through her tears.

"It's funny," I said. "Now I see your husband and he looks like a boy, like he's twelve years old. He's with another boy. They're both wearing red swimming trunks."

"That's Michael and his brother! His brother died of a brain aneurism when he was fourteen."

"They're together again. That's why your husband is happy. You can let him go. He's happy now. He's a little boy again. It's all right now. Just let him go."

4

All They Can Do Is Bite Ya!

We moved from Staten Island to a haunted house in New Jersey when I was ten. No one admitted it was haunted, of course, but it was. It was the kind of old, dark house that gives you the chills and raises the hair on your arms when you walk into a room. It was filled with all kinds of unsettled spirits.

There are so many different kinds of hauntings. People don't have to have been murdered in a house to fill it with ghosts. They can have been miserably unhappy and their strong vibrations will linger behind. When you buy a house, it's not a bad idea to cleanse the energy, whatever it is, before you move in, although even then, there are spirits that will linger behind, if they choose to, if they need something. I have to kind of wonder if my mother didn't invite the bad spirits to come out of the woodwork in that house. She was very upset because just when we moved out to New Jersey, Steve went down to Florida to live with his parents, and she couldn't see him anymore.

Between her muffled fury and the unhappy ghosts, that house was very frightening. One day soon after we moved in, I knocked on the door to the attic and it knocked back from the inside. It unnerved me and I had to tell someone about it.

"Mommy, Mommy, the door knocked back at me!" I shouted.

"Don't be silly," said my mother dismissively.

I pulled my fears back inside of me where they made me jittery and upset. I was always ready for something terrifying to happen.

That house had one of those screen doors where the bottom part is solid metal and the top half is a screen, and I often saw little dark eyes peering back at me through the mesh. The girl had the hopeless expression of one of those starving Third World kids you're supposed to donate money to. I probably should have let her in. Instead, I told my mother and she told me I was ridiculous. It was just more confirmation that I must be crazy.

On Christmas morning our first year in New Jersey, I woke up excited to open the presents. I remember that I was sitting on the edge of the bed in my mother's room, waiting for her to get ready to go downstairs, when I heard an odd scratching sound, as if something were scrambling across the wooden floor. And there, scuttling towards me, was something like a giant dog-sized spider, a human spider, in a black suit. That makes it sound kind of cute and funny, but it wasn't. It was unnaturally weird and unsettling.

I wasn't frightened of my fever fairies, but this entity was off in a way that they weren't. What was it? I still don't know. Perhaps it was the suit. Perhaps it was its size. Perhaps it was the twisted rage of its face. It was ugly, hideously ugly, and I knew instantaneously that it was some entity of absolute evil. It crawled across the room as I watched, transfixed and terrified; and then with a final shudder it disappeared into the closet. I've often wondered if it wasn't a thought form of my mother's negativity, a being issuing forth from her fury and frustration. It was like that alien monster that bursts out of the astronaut's stomach in the science-fiction horror movie, but I was the only one who saw it. Merry Christmas. Ho, ho, ho.

I overheard my mother admitting to my aunt Mary a few months later that the house was haunted. But my mother wouldn't talk about it with me. What if she had? What if just once she had acknowledged that what I was experiencing as a child might be real? But my mother wouldn't talk about anything.

She did tell Daddy that I needed to go down to Florida for my rheumatism, that the warmer weather would make a huge difference in how I felt. So my mother and I started flying back and forth to Florida . . . and to Steve. My mother was right about one thing. These trips did make me feel better, especially since I finally got to meet my other grandmother.

Steve's mother, my grandmother, was a funny little woman from the Carpathian Mountains in Transylvania. She looked like Björk, that dark little Icelandic singer, only my grandmother was smaller, maybe only four feet tall, when I knew her. She was the shortest woman I have ever met, and I'm very small, too, so it was hard to take her seriously. She loved to laugh. She'd giggle all the time. She was still very beautiful, with a rosy little face and eyes as dark as mine. Her family had been violin makers, and she used to talk a lot about the old country.

When I had headaches, she would place her hands, very soft, very small, on my forehead and spit over my shoulder, muttering something I couldn't understand. Every time, the headache would disappear. She told me that her grandmother had been a Gypsy and read the Tarot. I didn't understand what that meant, and by the time I did, my grandmother was long gone from my life. She told me these things quietly and secretly. They were things you weren't supposed to speak about. Her husband, a Sicilian, had thrashed her with a strap whenever she mentioned them. He was cranky and unpleasant like my mother.

Whenever there was a thunderstorm, my grandmother would run outside. There she was, a little old lady with bare feet, running through the rain and the lightning. She loved to play outside in thunderstorms, and she told me, when she invited me to join her, that nothing in nature could ever hurt me.

When I was with her, I could relax and be myself in a way that I never was anywhere else. She was the same kind of being I was. Instinctively, I knew that and trusted her.

I loved her house, which was filled with old-world charm and gold goblets and blown-glass figurines. That house had no unhappiness in it, only Florida sunshine.

In the mornings, bright and early, Steve and I would walk along the docks and rescue fish that had been left to die on lines cast out overnight. We'd take the hooks out of their mouths and throw them back in the water. Steve understood how to treat animals. He also taught me to swim and snorkel. "Come on over here!" he'd yell. "I think there's a shark! You've got to see it, Suzan!"

My mother would never go in the ocean. She was frightened of deep water and stayed on the beach.

I was swimming along with my snorkel mask on one day when I saw the pale sand disappear into black depths. I was headed out to sea and didn't realize it. I heard flute music under the water and was hypnotized by a vision of cobblestone streets and dilapidated buildings on the ocean floor. I wasn't experiencing myself as drowning, but apparently on the shore my mother and Steve were hysterical when they saw my snorkel disappear under the waves far out from shore.

Steve dove into the water and was swimming frantically out to me, but it was a strange man with dark hair and blue eyes who reached me first and carried me back to the beach. I came to as the lifeguards were pushing down on my chest, giving me CPR. The man with dark hair had disappeared and no one knew who he was when I later asked about him.

I had nearly died, but it wasn't frightening in any way. I was simply curious about the whole experience as it was happening because it was clear to me that it wasn't my time to go. The land I was swimming towards was the past, I knew that, but I had forces keeping me in the present. People treat death like it's some kind of mistake or accident, but it isn't really. It's part of nature, too. Everything dies.

Once, we all took a cross-country road trip to Disneyland—Steve, his mother, my mother, and my poor sister. Steve had traded in the Renault and now had an old beat-up convertible filled with five million cigarette butts and old newspapers. If anyone complained about the car, he'd say, "This? This is a classic!" We kept running out of gas, but Steve didn't care. We stayed in old run-down motels and stopped at every White Castle between Florida and California.

Once, in the desert, we came to a place where everywhere

we looked there were cautionary signs that said: "Beware of Snakes!" But Steve stopped the car and started running out across the white sands, calling to me to join him. "C'mon, Suzan, all they can do is bite ya!" He wasn't scared of anything.

That's what I needed more than anything, growing up: his fearlessness.

My mother couldn't stand Steve's wildness. One afternoon in the flatlands of the prairie, we saw a funnel on the horizon that looked like it had come from *The Wizard of Oz*. I remember my mother screaming at Steve to get in the car because a tornado was coming. Steve just sat at the picnic table at the rest stop, eating hamburger after hamburger, ignoring her. It was almost as if he wanted the tornado to arrive and sweep him up in it.

"What are you doing? What are you *doing*!" My mother was getting increasingly hysterical. The wind was rising.

"I'm not going anywhere now!" he announced.

I loved his courage and his defiance. I wanted to be like him.

My mother and Steve fought incessantly. They were always yelling and screaming at each other in public about some other woman he'd been with. He made my mother wild, and she was both repelled and attracted to him. I think the best part of my mother was the part that kept returning to Steve and bringing us to be with him. He was so completely alive and without fear. Some part of her must have known that and wanted adventure and passion.

When I was twelve, though, my mother discovered that Steve had another daughter in Florida. I would find out much later that he had other children, too, but this was the one my mother found out about. She went wild and then she sank into a terrible depression, and we never went to Florida again. Steve called almost every day after that and she would talk to him, but she would never let me get on the phone. I never saw my Transylvanian grandmother again.

My mother told me I couldn't have anything to do with Steve anymore. She claimed now that he had forced himself on her and that she had gotten pregnant by accident and that he had wanted her to have an abortion.

"Can you imagine? Your father wanted you to be an abortion. You could have been an abortion. An *abortion*."

You don't say that to a child, especially not a ten-year-old. Waves of anger swept through me and I thought I might drown in my own fury. I wanted to scream at her, to hit her, to destroy her, but I couldn't. I just kept it all inside. I'd gotten good at that. Unlike my father, I didn't fight back. I didn't say anything. I just pulled further away from her than I had ever been before.

She tried to make me hate him, but I knew that she was really speaking for herself. She hadn't wanted me to be born. Steve loved me, and nothing could erase that knowledge. But to my mother, I had always been some kind of mistake. She took her fury at Steve, at herself, at everything out on me.

A lot of psychics are bliss ninnies. They don't want to talk about evil. They act like if you don't notice it, it'll go away. The white light is everywhere! But there's evil everywhere, too. It's not just in the murderers and the psychopathic killers and the torturers; it sneaks into everybody's life. Everybody's got a little evil in their daily planner. We're all stepping on spiders and eating our pork chops and wearing sneakers little kids in China have stitched together. I've done readings for hit men, who kill for a living, but I've also had the nicest-seeming people ask me if I could predict when their mother-in-law was going to die, if maybe, just maybe, through my psychic powers I could make it happen a little faster than nature intended. Is the medical researcher who kills dozens of rats each day in the name of science really any different from the serial killer? And what about the mother who tells her daughter she should have been an abortion? That sure felt evil to me.

Steve used to tell me that he didn't believe in God, that if he went into a church he'd be struck dead. Whenever my mother got pious, Steve would upset her by telling her, with a twinkle in his dark eyes, that he prayed to Lucifer. But Steve just said that for shock value. In reality he walked along the docks each morning, his heart wide open to the fish in need of rescue. He loved life and he celebrated it, and I would never forget that, even though it would be a very long time before I would see him again.

———

She was a sweet, gentle-voiced girl, but she was having horrifically violent dreams. That's why she came to me. Every night, she was seeing people bludgeoned, stabbed with kitchen utensils, force-fed, injected, and tortured. Nothing in her life seemed to be connected to these vivid nightmares, and she felt oddly emotionally detached from them. She wondered what was the matter with her. "It's like they're not even my dreams," she said.

They weren't.

She lived in an old building in New York City in what had once been terrible slums, and at night while she was asleep she was tuning in to long-forgotten horrors. She was very sensitive, and she was picking up on hundreds of years of secret terrors that lingered in the whitewashed bricks.

Our dreams aren't just a way of making psychological sense of what's happening in our own lives; they can also be journeys into the past and into the future and into other people's memories and lifetimes.

"When you move, the dreams will stop," I told her.

And they did.

5

The Artful Dodger Steals My Heart

Other than Steve, the only real friend I had growing up was Jack Wild. Except he didn't know it yet.

When I was eight years old, the movie *Oliver!* came out on my birthday, and I'll never forget my first sight of the little English boy playing the Artful Dodger. He had a round face, sparkling brown eyes, and a mop of long dark hair. He was small and agile as he danced along the cobblestone streets. My eyes widened as I watched him. My heart opened.

I felt a deep joy watching him, like nothing I had ever felt before. He was a magical being, a being from between the worlds just like me. I knew it. I wasn't alone after all.

Part of it was how much the movie spoke to me. I related to poor, unloved Oliver, shuttled from the poorhouse to the coffin maker's and finally adopted by a troupe of street urchins. I wanted to be taken in by Fagin's gang. I wanted the Artful Dodger in his tattered top hat to wrap an arm around me and consider me part of the family.

But it was more than that. I felt like I was falling through a time warp or a wormhole as I watched the movie. I was flooded with memories of garret rooms with faded flower wallpaper, damp to the touch. I smelled dark coal smoke. I knew that's what it was. I also knew Jack Wild. I recognized him. We were deeply, profoundly connected in some way I could not begin to understand.

He even affected my mother, who otherwise seemed to be resistant to anything sentimental. I would always drag her to Jack Wild's most recent movies, and it was only during *Flight of the Doves*, a tale about two Irish orphans on the run together, that I ever saw her cry. She was usually bored or distracted in movies, but during this sweet film she was riveted to the screen. It wasn't a very good movie. It was about children and she hated children. Still, I saw tears in her eyes, and for a moment I felt an effortless swell of love for her. She could feel the magic, too, of Jack, of Ireland, of the two children alone together in the wilds. I held on to that moment for years. How bad could she be, really, if she, too, loved Jack?

Many years later, I would meet Jack Wild in person and discover that we had had a strange bond and, strangely, he had one to my mother as well, but as a little girl in New Jersey I didn't know that one day we would be friends. I only knew that without him, my childhood would have been unendurable.

Once, I came home after school with yet another misfit. When I came up the walkway, I saw my mother standing at the front door with her arms crossed, tapping her foot. She was insanely furious.

"I have been waiting for you all afternoon."

She was so weird and neurotic. She was panicked, I think, that I might reveal her adulterous affair to some little girl who would tell her mother. The neighbors might find out. The nuns at my school would condemn my mother. By the time I was home, she had worked herself into a panicked rage about where I might have been and what I might have said. I would do anything to calm her down.

I thought that I was afraid she would burst a blood vessel and die if I stayed away too long, and that was true. But there was also a part of me, completely unacknowledged until I was much older, that actually wanted her to die, I think. I wanted to be an orphan like Oliver. If I were an orphan, then my real family could rescue me and I might know what it was to be part of a family that loved me. I was frightened of how much I wanted that. I never admitted it to myself when I was young. Instead I devoured stories about pitiful orphans and worked my way through every novel Charles Dickens had written. On Saturdays I would either sit in the library, alone and reading, or go to the movies by myself.

After seeing *Oliver!*, I became Jack Wild's most devoted fan. I collected every photo of him that I could find, wrote him fan mail, and got the form letter back with more photos. Jack became the star of a psychedelic sixties kids show called *H.R. Pufnstuf*, and every weekend I was glued to the television watching it. I ordered all the books, the cards, the plates, and the collectibles that featured Jack. I read celebrity magazines avidly for any news of him. After his Oscar nomination, Jack made over thirty films and I went to them again and again, often on the same day. When PBS aired *Our Mutual Friend* by Dickens, it was on every night of the week and I watched Jack Wild in it every night of the week. I was thrilled when

Donovan, the folk musician from England, helped Jack with a music album. Donovan had composed the soundtrack of *Brother Sun, Sister Moon*. Jack's music now reminded me of Saint Francis.

Jack and I were connected to each other. I was sure of it.

One day in 1973, when I was thirteen, my mother took me to a local store to pick up some new clothes. It was called Nice Stuff, as if you might not know this unless they told you so. My mother had a lot of opinions about what I was supposed to wear. When all the kids were in jeans and sneakers, I was still wearing pleated slacks and patent-leather shoes. She insisted on laying out my clothes the night before school and she expected me to wear whatever she put out. If I came downstairs in something else, she'd say, "I don't know those clothes," and I would be expected to go upstairs and change.

This day in Nice Stuff, however, I fell in love with a pair of mod bell-bottomed overalls. They were green. And to be fair to my mother, they were truly hideous. But I loved them, and I insisted on buying them. We actually had a fight about it and I ended up paying for them with my own money.

I put them on as soon as I got home. I was cool. I was hip. I was thirteen, and I was going to fit in at last.

That night, Jack was scheduled to be a guest on a British variety special with singing acts and funny skits. I couldn't wait. I was jumping up and down in the TV room in my overalls.

We were all in the TV room, even my sister, who was living at home and commuting to graduate school to study teaching.

Jack bounded onto the set, his long dark hair waving around his cheerful face. He joked with the host. But I don't remember

a thing Jack said, because all I could see were the green overalls he was wearing. They were just like mine.

My mother's head swiveled around from the television to
me, from me to the television, like she was in *The Exorcist*.

Jack's black hair was shoulder length, just like mine, we
both had the same dark brown eyes, and we were both wearing the same overalls.

"You could be his sister," said Daddy, stunned.

Even my mother couldn't believe it. "My God, Suzan, you
look exactly like him." She turned to my sister to see if she
agreed.

"It's uncanny," said my sister.

The older I got, the more intense my connection to England and Jack Wild became. I'd see a photo of the flag and
feel this rush of almost alarming patriotism. We'd be saying
the Pledge in school and I'd want to shout out, "God save the
Queen!" It was kind of nuts.

I had memories, too, of other lives lived there. Sometimes
I'd awaken at night to the sound of sirens and the high-
pitched keening of what I later found out were doodlebugs,
the bombs dropped on London during the Blitz. I knew that
once, long before, I'd lived in an attic in London and that I'd
been cold and hungry most of the time. How did I know
these were memories of past lives and not just an overactive
imagination?

How do you know your own memories are real? Can you
tell the difference between a memory and a daydream?

What is imagination anyway? A lot of people think you
can create something out of nothing inside your head, and yet
I've come to believe that a lot of imagination stems from being able to tune in to other lives, other lifetimes, and other

dimensions. We're not making things up; we're experiencing things that are real. We're like Harry Potter finding himself inside Voldemort's head.

I started traveling to England in what I called, for myself— because I didn't tell anyone about this—instant dreams. I'd be out shopping with my mother and suddenly I would disappear. I would look like I was there, but I wasn't. I was roaming the streets of London, checking out the miniskirts, the plastic earrings, the Mary Quant makeup on the girls. Sometimes I visited a boy who went to a British public school. I could see all the students in their uniforms walking to classes. When Jack was making a movie, I found I could transport myself to the studio and see him. Years later, he would confirm that all I had seen had actually happened. My instant daydreams were real. I was inside of other people's memories and experiences. When I finally went to London, I knew how to get around effortlessly because I'd been there so often.

A woman I did a reading for years later told me that she had been in therapy for three years when her psychologist finally told her that she had been dreaming about *his* life in ways that had completely unnerved him. Twins who grow up apart meet each other in adulthood wearing the same outfit or discover that they both broke their legs in eighth grade. Writers wake up in the middle of the night with whole novels in their head. Who's to say they haven't been sharing memories and experiences?

We think our skulls are fortresses around our minds, but consciousness is much more free and loose than people realize. I think a lot of writers are capable of finding their way into other people's minds. They're mediums and channelers, too. In the late eighties when I met Marion Zimmer Bradley, the author of *The Mists of Avalon*, a feminist rewrite of the Arthurian legends, I was stunned to find that the author of this epic, visionary book was a complete and total potato. Solid and mannish, she didn't feel like she had any creativity in her at all. No way did she imagine those characters and that reality. She *saw* it; she *channeled* it. But she never did it again, and you know that if you've read any of her other books.

One of the framed pictures in my childhood bedroom was of Dickens sleeping, surrounded by tiny pictures of the hundreds of characters that he had created. He was tuning in. People used to know that artists and poets were channelers, and because of my psychic abilities, I know that they still are. When I saw the movie *Hereafter*, about the psychic George Anderson, I was not surprised to find out that he, too, had an obsession with Dickens and knew about that picture.

Ordinary people dismiss their daydreams and their experiences of déjà vu, whereas more-aware people will arrive in a new town and realize that it's familiar because they've visited it while they are sleeping. Truly crazy people I've tried to do readings for seem to be flooded by other people's perceptions and memories. They literally forget who they are in the cascade of other sensations. There's too much electricity crackling around them for me to see what's going on just for them.

I often worried that I was crazy, but I never lost myself in my adventures. The little old woman inside of me kept me on a short leash and wouldn't let me fly away forever. She told me who I was, what reality was, and let me know that I was only visiting.

But I never traveled anywhere in my instant dreams but

to England. I didn't hop on down to Florida to visit Steve. I didn't drift away to some tropical island paradise. I went to Carnegie Street. I walked along the Thames. I went to Eton.

That little old lady inside of me wanted to go home. And home was in England with Jack Wild.

---

*A man in the middle of a contentious divorce came in to see me,
but I didn't think he and his wife were actually going to split up.*

*"I don't see you in court. I don't see you apart from your wife.
I don't see any more fighting between the two of you."*

*"Really? Really?" The man was soft-spoken and gentle and he
was barely speaking above a whisper. "How can that be? The lawyers are almost done with the agreement."*

*"It's not going to happen," I said. "I see some kind of anguish
around you, but it's not part of you. And I don't see you divorced."*

*"I can't tell you what a relief that is. But how is it going to
happen?"*

*"I don't know, but it is." But I also had to share with him some-
thing strange that was coming through. "In seven years you are
going to have sole custody of your daughter."*

"How can that be if I don't get divorced?"

"I don't know. I really don't. But that's what I see."

*A week later, the man's wife came in to see me. She was visibly
shaken. After our appointment, her husband had told her what I
had said, and she had mocked him. She was getting a divorce and
that was that. It didn't matter what some psychic had said. Their
marriage was over.*

"But it wasn't." She began to cry. "You were right."

*It took her a long time to calm down and tell me what had
happened. Her husband had gone on a routine business trip a few
days after I'd met with him. He'd flown with a friend in a small
airplane and it had crashed. They both had been killed.*

*"I saw that he was happy, though," I told his wife. "I didn't see
pain or tragedy in his cards, just peace."*

"Is he at peace?"

"He is."

I don't know why I hadn't seen him dead, except I feel like there is something so sacred about the moment of death that I'm not supposed to witness it.

I didn't see his wife for seven more years. She returned all those years later to tell me that her daughter had just died of leukemia. "You were right about that, too," she said. "He has sole custody of her now."

6

There Goes the Neighborhood

I got kicked out of Catholic school at the end of tenth grade. My grades were fine, but I had a reputation as a troublemaker. Then I got accused by some of the field hockey–playing girls of "being too close" to another girl, the implication being that we were "unnatural," a Catholic school euphemism for being gay. The girl and I were just acquaintances, we weren't even real friends, but the nuns had wanted to get rid of me for a long time.

My mother was appalled that I'd been expelled. "You've ruined your life. Ruined it. That was such a nice school."

But I didn't care one bit. I wasn't leaving behind any friends. There weren't any teachers I was going to miss. And now I'd actually be able to meet some real teenage boys for a change.

I wasn't used to having them around, though, and I was very shy at the public high school in Summit, New Jersey. I dressed horribly. I couldn't see. My hair hung down over my face. But there was a drama teacher who literally saved my life. He invited me to be in the after-school plays and helped me begin to speak up for myself a little. He was gay, I'm sure of it, and very kind.

I ended up befriending a girl in his class who was even more unpopular than I was.

Maya was a mess of a person, a total pathetic pigpen who smelled like chicken soup and whatever strange Greek dish she'd brought for lunch. We'd sit down at a table in the cafeteria and everyone in the nearby vicinity would scatter. She was also incredibly frustrating to talk to and so annoying that even I wanted to slap her sometimes. I found myself sympathizing with the school bullies for a change, which tells you something. But I didn't. Because Maya had a pen pal in England.

"You've got to go visit her," I urged Maya.

"I don't know," whined Maya. "What if she doesn't like me?"

"Don't you want to visit her? We could stay with her family." I would have gone to England with King Kong himself, who honestly might have been more fun than Maya.

"We?"

"Yeah, I'll come with you. That'll make it less scary, right?"

"Maybe," said Maya hesitantly.

"It will," I said. "It will be great. On our own in England, you and me."

So I got her to write to her pen pal, and we basically invited ourselves over for a monthlong visit right after we graduated from high school.

It was soon after we heard back from her pen pal's mother confirming our plans that the man in the black hat returned. I'd stopped sleeping with my mother when I became a teenager, but I hadn't seen him in years. Now every night he haunted my bedroom again. His hair was long and white, and sometimes fire crackled out of his blank eyes. I dreamed he was on a horse riding towards me, but I had a long spear now and was able to impale him and make him disappear. The next night he was back.

Children came to me, too, in my dreams. One of them had burns down the whole side of her face. Another I saw again and again. He was a little boy with brown eyes. Years later I would discover that he was my son, Gavin. But all I could feel then was that these children wanted me to come to England. It was urgent.

One night not long before Maya and I left, I woke up from a deep sleep to see a thick, smoky coil twining out of my body, like a spider's web, like an etheric umbilical cord. I tried to touch it, but I couldn't.

What the fuck is this? I thought. *Am I dying?*

I looked around my room and I could see my Jack Wild albums on my bureau, my posters on the wall, my Dickens novels in the bookcase. I was in my room. But with that thought came the revelation that I wasn't actually touching the bed. I was experiencing myself hovering above my own body—connected to it but not confined by it. I didn't know anything about astral traveling at that point, and I was terrified.

I know now that this is what happens at death; the etheric body separates from the physical body. It's also what happens when we astral travel. Heading to England was stirring me up spiritually.

I'd never been to a sleepover; I'd never gone to camp; I'd never gone anywhere by myself. My parents couldn't believe I was going on my own to England. But I was. I had to and they let me go. I had a little money from my aunts for gradu-ation and I was going to liberate myself.

I wasn't scared on the airplane. I wasn't scared about flying to a foreign country or being away from my family for the first time in my life. I was delighted. I was thrilled. I was ecstatic, even. But Maya began crying almost as soon as we'd left the ground. She cried like some kind of desperate dormouse, homesick and sad. We took a taxi all the way from Heathrow to her pen pal's family, the Frumptons, in Surrey and eventually pulled up in front of a small thatched cottage surrounded by gardens. I felt like I was in a Disney movie; everything was enchanted. I was sure someone was going to burst into song and then Mary Poppins would appear.

Instead, there were the Frumptons, all lined up in a row and waiting for us when we arrived.

They were, to a one, red haired, rotund, and stern. Alice was Maya's pen pal, and she barely smiled when we got out of the taxi.

Aside from Alice, there were three other little Frumptons and Mrs. Frumpton. There was no Mr. Frumpton.

Immediately after she met me, Mrs. Frumpton gave me a look. Her eyes bored into me. All throughout dinner she stared at me without saying anything.

It was the most repulsive meal I have ever eaten.

Everyone else had fish-and-chips, but because I was a vegetarian, they got me a pineapple fritter. Imagine slices of pineapple deep-fried in fish batter. I tried to eat it, I really did, and to smile, but I'm sure I was making these Elvis-like grimaces instead. I tried to break the fritter apart and drop bits of it into the potted plants behind me. It was the worst thing I've ever eaten in my life. I was sure that was why Mrs. Frumpton was staring at me. I was sure she thought I had terrible manners.

But even with the fritter and this large, pasty woman checking me out, I was still ecstatically happy. I was staying in a thatched cottage in a little old-fashioned village in England, and the French doors of the guest room where Maya and I were sleeping opened up to a garden filled with roses and other flowers.

I barely slept that night, I was so excited.

The next morning when I walked into the kitchen, though, I knew something was up. In a voice that was almost completely without expression, Mrs. Frumpton said to me, "I've told the vicar that you've come."

"Oh, that's nice," I answered, trying to be polite.

"I want you to meet him."

I smiled. "Sure. Why?"

"Because you have the sight."

"The what?"

"The sight. You're a sensitive, aren't you?"

I'd never heard either of these words used this way before. Still, I knew what she was talking about. I knew she meant I was sensitive to the spiritual world. I could see things. But I'd never had a word to describe myself other than *crazy*. I'd never thought of myself as talented or gifted or anything but shameful or possibly insane. I thought of my mother whispering to my sister and giving me furtive looks out of the corner of her eye. Whatever I could do was embarrassing and frightening to her and there was no name for it. It was the skill that must not be named. But this woman wanted to tell the vicar that I was . . . *sensitive*. A rush of unfamiliar pride was flowing through me. "You told the priest that I'm here and he wants to meet me?"

"I work in a hospital cleaning up at night. I see things, too.

You're not the only one, young lady. I can see Death walking down the hall. I always know who's going to die. You do, too. You have the sight."

In her gruff, granite-like way she said it respectfully. Okay, I hadn't been a cheerleader in high school or starred in the musical, but I had the sight. That's what it was. It was a gift. No one in my life up until now had directly acknowledged what I was and what I could do. Not my mother, who'd raised me. Not the priests and nuns, who supposedly knew about the spiritual world. Not even my aunt Mary, who clearly was aware of at least some of my abilities. None of them had been able to explain what was happening to me. They had all left me to feel dirty and ashamed and worried that at any moment someone was going to cart me off to a padded room. But this heavy, plodding English cleaning woman had seen how I was special the moment she had met me and swept away an entire lifetime of worry about what I was. I wanted to wrap my arms around Mrs. Frumpton and give her a grateful hug, but Mrs. Frumpton didn't seem like a hugger. But it didn't matter. It felt like the universe had opened her arms to hold me.

I kept saying the words over and over to myself. "I am a sensitive and I have the sight."

A few moments later, Mrs. Frumpton had me on the phone with the vicar and he was proposing that I go with him to an exorcism.

"No, I don't think so," I said, startled. It was all happening a little too fast. It was one thing to be identified as a sensitive, but another altogether to suddenly have to start performing as one. I couldn't help but think this was all a little insane. I was eighteen years old and I was finally in England. But I wanted to go to London. I wanted to go to the zoo. I wanted to walk on cobblestone streets and dance in clubs. I had not been imagining going to an exorcism, not ever, really, and certainly not within twenty-four hours of arriving in a foreign country. Besides, it felt a little creepy to go in the car with some man I didn't know. I politely explained that I didn't think I could make it. "I have a friend with me," I said.

Maya had just come into the kitchen and was crying again.

But the vicar wouldn't get off the phone. He started telling me about a local housing development that a number of people had told him might be haunted. "I think there are ghosts there and I'd like a second opinion."

I felt an odd mixture of confidence and disorientation. "You want me to go there and tell you what I see?"

"Exactly!" said the vicar. "It would be a marvelous help if you can spare the time."

Our first day in England, Maya and I didn't visit a castle or eat lunch in a pub. Instead, Mrs. Frumpton wrote down the name of the project on a piece of paper and sent us out with directions on how to find it and orders to talk to families about what was going on there. "You need to go there today," she told me, completely ignoring Maya. "It'll be a big help to the vicar if you can confirm if it's haunted or not."

I sighed, because it didn't seem like I had a choice. "Okay, I'll go investigate this."

Maya was really scared now. I'd never talked to her about any of my visions or psychic experiences, and she didn't have a clue what was happening. Besides, I was getting all the attention, and she didn't like that one bit. I have to admit that I was feeling very important and lording it over her. After all, I was a sensitive. She cried some more.

We found ourselves walking from house to house in this development cheerfully called Greyswell Circle. July in England was a Technicolor explosion of flowers, but there were no gardens in front of the flat-roofed low-income buildings. Greyswell Circle was gray. Gray cement, gray asphalt, gray dirt pocked with gray grass, and gray faces. As hot as it was, Maya and I both shivered and zipped up our jackets.

Full of importance about the first real job I'd ever had in my life, I'd knock on the doors of tired-looking council houses and announce, "Hi, I'm Suzan from New Jersey and the vicar at St. Andrew's asked me to come by and talk to you about anything unusual you might have been experiencing. I'm a sensitive and the vicar wants me to talk to you about spirits."

It was amazing the things people told me. I was surprised at how open everyone was. In America, people would have thought I was crazy, but here, they immediately started sharing their stories. And there were so many stories. Birds were found dead on the ground. Dogs wouldn't go outside. Babies were stillborn. Everyone had a sense that Greyswell Circle was a cursed place, filled with bad luck. I could feel it, too.

Just like people and animals have identifiable essences, the land has a soul, too. In Greyswell Circle, the energy was so heavy it was almost dead. There weren't any children outside in the yards or on the sidewalks playing. It was as if the Pied Piper had come and lured them all away.

I didn't really know what I was supposed to be doing. I was making it up as I went along. But I could sense the bad energy of that place.

At one house, a Pakistani woman opened the door and invited me in to meet her son, a boy of seven or eight, who was very ill. His mother told me that he couldn't sleep at night, because no sooner would he shut his eyes than a man with a black hat would arrive.

"Does he have eyes?" I asked.

Shuddering, the boy shook his head. "No."

I knew it was the same man and that this was the reason I was here. I realized that the children who had been visiting me before I came to England were from this piece of land and that they had all died here. But I didn't know why the boy also saw the man in the black hat. I didn't know what to do about it.

When I got back, I called the vicar and told him everything that I had seen and felt. "There used to be a workhouse there a hundred years ago," he told me. "I think there was an epidemic or a fire and the children were all buried in a mass grave."

He didn't know who the man in the black hat was, though. "Maybe he was a cruel landlord," the vicar suggested, "who hurt children." Possibly, but it felt like something more powerful than that. The vicar told me that he would do a ceremony to help the souls of those doomed children move on.

After talking with him, I stopped at a bookstore in the village. There was a whole section on ghosts and hauntings, and I actually found a booklet, which I bought, called *Eyes on Fire*. It was interviews with people all over the south of England who had seen a man in a wide-brimmed black hat. It documented their experiences, but it didn't offer any explanations of who this particular demon really was other than saying that he was a powerful ghost of some sort.

I felt increasingly strange at the Frumptons'. I lost track of time in the bathroom and in my bedroom. Hours would disappear. It was even worse than when I had fallen into the mirrors at home. It didn't feel like I was listening to something from another world. It felt like I was visiting some other realm, although I could never remember what had happened.

One morning I woke up just at dawn, it must have been around five in the morning, my usual wake-up hour, and I got out of bed and opened the French doors to the garden. I heard the softest of music. Petals and blossoms and leaves were softly falling, and something I can only describe as feathers drifted through the air. I felt as though I were looking through gauze in that soft light just before sunrise.

I can't tell you how long I stood there in my nightgown. Three, maybe four hours, although it felt like only moments. And I can't tell you what happened. I will never forget that morning, and yet I can't remember anything consciously about the experience. The hours disappeared. But I do believe in fairies and a dimension where we can commune with the souls of everything that's alive. I knew with certainty that my old life was done, that the taunts and bullying were gone forever. I knew who I was and who I was supposed to be. I was home.

Mrs. Frumpton put milk out for the fairies every night. In those days a lot of the country people still did. When Alice Frumpton, Maya, and I took a bus tour to Glastonbury, I saw the pans of milk left out everywhere for the little people. At Glastonbury they left out bowls of apples for the fairies, too. Maya tried to eat one and was scolded for it.

Mrs. Frumpton had insisted that Maya and I visit Glastonbury. I'd never even heard of the place and didn't know how it was connected to King Arthur and was supposed to be the place where Arthur sleeps with dragons. Supposedly, Joseph of Arimathea, the man who gave his tomb to Jesus and brought Mary Magdalene to France, had founded the first Christian community there. I would learn all about that much later.

Today Glastonbury is very beautiful, with the remains of an ancient church and gardens and a sacred well, but what I found most striking, without then even knowing the history, was the energy I could feel rising out of that earth. People think that God comes from the heavens, but in Glastonbury the divine is in the earth itself. *Something* is under the ground there.

I had never heard about ley lines, the geographical energy alignments that connect sacred places, but I can feel them. And I felt them at Glastonbury. Call them dragons, call them ley lines, there is something happening under the earth there and it is filled with magic and power. If the ground beneath Greyswell Circle had felt cursed, this land felt blessed. I could feel the electrical energy rising up through the soles of my feet and coursing through my body right out of the crown of my head. Everything within me was awakened at Glastonbury. Every light was turned on. I had never felt this kind of pure joy before.

Winding our way up the ancient hill called the Tor to St. Michael's Tower, I had an unexpected vision of Jesus and Mary Magdalene walking there together during their lost years. They had been there. I knew it. It doesn't jibe with anything you'll ever read about them, and there's no way I can prove what I know, but I believe they visited Glastonbury as a couple, before they began teaching. Was King Arthur really buried there? Was Merlin? I don't know, but it's one of the most sacred places I have ever been in my life. It's one of the few places left where you can feel the ancient pagan energy intersecting with Christianity. No wonder so many people of different faiths go there on pilgrimage.

Towards the end of the day, just at sunset, I was walking around the thorn tree, the one that blooms in winter. Joseph of Arimathea is said to have brought it into being when he thrust his staff into the earth. I saw a rusted safety pin in the grass. As I bent over to pick it up, a very nondescript old woman appeared beside me. Her shoulder-length brown hair was flecked with gray. She wore glasses. She took my hand in hers without a word and looked into my eyes. The others had gone ahead into the church.

"Do you know who you are?" She smiled. "You belong here. This is your place."

"Yes." I nodded. "I know."

"This is your land."

I couldn't say anything more. I was overwhelmed with emotion. Her words gave me a surge of unfamiliar power. It would be years before I would read *The Mists of Avalon*, about the pagan priestesses of Glastonbury, but I could feel the Goddess welcoming me home on that trip. I didn't even know what that meant or who she was. At eighteen I had no name for her; all I knew was that she was the energy of the earth beneath my feet and I was hers. For the first time in my life I felt taller than my five feet.

The rest of our visit seemed to be charmed. At least for me. People welcomed me everywhere we went. I got admitted free to places, handed ice-cream cones out of the blue. When Maya, Alice, and I hitchhiked to London, we were picked up by a man who told us he'd happily take us all the way into the city, but first he had to deliver something to Shepperton Studios.

Shepperton was where they filmed *Oliver!*

When we got to the famous studios, I begged to see the old sets, and it turned out they still existed. They were like a ghost town, dilapidated and falling apart, but still there. I walked through the undertaker's shop and Fagin's den. I took a stone from the ground and a cap one of the boys had worn that a nice woman let me have from the costume shop. As we were leaving, I saw Sigourney Weaver walk by. She was there making some top-secret movie about aliens.

I had my first drink in London, a Harvey Wallbanger. I danced at a club, visited Dickens' grave at Westminster Abbey, and walked through the streets knowing exactly where I was and where I would be when I turned the corner.

I was mesmerized by the murky waters of the Thames. I wished I were alone, that if I were I would be able to read something about myself in its currents. I wanted to dredge up my past with a towrope. It was there in that river, the lives I had lived. I felt thrillingly restless.

But when we got back to Surrey, Mrs. Frumpton announced that Maya and I had to leave. At once. The next morning. No question about it.

"There's too much going on. You're getting the spirits riled up," Mrs. Frumpton said.

"But we can't go home now!" cried Maya. "Our tickets home aren't for two more weeks."

"Everyone's complaining about the ghosts," said Mrs. Frumpton, unmoved by a new torrent of tears from Maya. "Hauntings, bangings, it's too much. I can't keep track of the furniture. And little John was run over by a motorbike today. And we know why *that* happened, don't we?" She glared at me, certain it was my fault even though I'd been in London all day. "You've got to go. You've got to leave this house," she insisted. The littlest Frumpton, John, appeared in the doorway, tread marks still visible across his forehead.

I was devastated. I felt like I had been betrayed by the very people who knew who I was. I imagined running out into the street and getting hit by a car and put in the hospital so I wouldn't have to leave.

"And another thing," added Mrs. Frumpton. "The flasher's back."

"What do I have to do with a flasher?" I protested.

"He's a ghost flasher and everyone's seeing him again," said Mrs. Frumpton. "The ghosts are all churned up because of you. You're ruining the neighborhood."

I almost laughed at the thought of a spirit exposing his noncorporeal dangly bits, but I was too upset. What a hell that must be, doing that for eternity. Still, I didn't want to go. I think I'd imagined I'd find a way to stay in England forever. I imagined that I was going to find Jack Wild.

Somehow Maya and I got home. Maya's tears made it easy for me to lie at the airport. I said our mother had died and they put us on a plane back to JFK. Daddy picked us up and drove us home.

After England, the bland suburbs of New Jersey felt intolerable. In so many places in America, especially for some reason in New Jersey, the old energies of the land have been obliterated. The land was stolen, raped, and paved. Everything has become superficial, vapid, and disconnected from the earth. I hated it.

For a week or so after I returned, the kitchen clock began running backwards whenever I was in the room.

"It's showing us the time in England," said Aunt Mary suspiciously.

"Something's wrong with the battery," said my mother, glaring at me.

I didn't have anything to say about it because I was still in shock. How could I be recognized everywhere I went, how could I know that I was home and yet not be allowed to stay? I'd been asked to leave Catholic school and now I'd been asked to leave England. No one wanted me.

My mother was right, after all. I *was* a failure. At no time in my life have I ever felt such hopelessness and despair. I didn't know that my destiny was in America, that I had to be here for reasons it would take so many years before I would ever understand. I thought I belonged in England. I thought I was in exile.

Always in my pocket was the safety pin I had found at Glastonbury.

———

AT&T hired me for their corporate picnic once. I was supposed to sit at a table under a tree while executives and their secretaries wandered over to me for a reading. I was the novelty act.

It's never a good idea for people to think my readings are free. There's a deep meaning behind crossing the Gypsy's palm with silver. A number of the men tried to trick me and pretend that what I was telling them wasn't true. One man, in a very snazzy suit, came over and stared down at me for a long time.

"What are your credentials?" he finally said.

"My what?"

"Your credentials. Who taught you to do what you're doing?"

I nearly laughed out loud. My credentials? Did he mean what school had I been to? Had I gotten good marks in Being a Psychic 101?

"Who licensed you?" he added.

I looked him straight in the eye and answered, "God."

7

Night School for X-Men
(and Misfit Girls)

I got a job at a Baskin-Robbins and was fired almost instantly for scooping too big. Then I started waitressing at the local pizzeria for $1.50 an hour plus tips and sexual harassment. I spilled Cokes on people's laps. I'd clean tables by blowing off the crumbs. The man who owned the pizzeria would grab my buns every time I walked past. I had no friends, no talents, no guidance. I felt hopeless.

I knew I shouldn't be doing this, that I had some kind of mysterious calling in life, something that made me special, but I didn't really know what it was or what to do with it. What kind of job could you get if you had the sight?

Anyway, I couldn't even drive because my eyes were so bad. I walked back and forth two miles each day to this crappy job while truck drivers and perverts honked at me as they roared past.

When I came home from work, if I was at all late, my mother usually would be staring out the window, often bashing her hands against the glass. "Where have you been?" she'd scream hysterically. She'd start banging pots and pans, harder and harder, muttering to herself. She'd ball her hands into fists and start pummeling the walls.

I'd have to restrain her hands so she wouldn't hurt herself.

You didn't have to be a sensitive to know she was nuts. I couldn't breathe in her house. There was always a storm on the horizon; the air was always dark and heavy. I wanted to hide in my room and I felt trapped by both how angry she made me and how sorry I was for her.

She opened all my letters from England. She still put clothes out for me to wear and flew into a temper if I tried to dress myself. If I put on mascara before work, she'd slap me across the face with a towel and scream at me to scrub it off. But when I didn't wear makeup, she'd stare at me and shake her head. "Steve would be so embarrassed if he could see you. Your skin is terrible."

Sometimes I clawed at my face, leaving streaks across my cheeks. I was so upset. Then I did have to wear makeup to cover the marks.

"You think I'm ugly, don't you?" my mother would scream.

"No, Mommy, you are beautiful, so beautiful," I would reassure her. "Calm down, calm down."

Often I'd come home and she'd just be sitting in the dark in the living room, staring at nothing.

"What's wrong?" I'd ask her, concerned.

"What do you mean?"

"You look so sad." I wanted to find a way to talk to her. I wanted to be genuinely close to her.

"What is it? Is it my face? You don't like my face. What?

Do I have to smile for you? Is that it? If you don't like me, don't look at me then."

I never yelled or cursed at her. I never even argued. I was cautious. It was like my higher self, or my guardian angel if I had one, knew that this was not really my life, that this woman was not really my mother. I came from somewhere else. And yet I couldn't abandon her. Where could I go? The one place I'd dreamed of my whole life had rejected me.

My mother would whisper to me that she was sick and going to die soon and that we didn't have much more time together. She told me not to tell my sister or my father. She said I had to keep it a secret.

I dreamed about going back to England and going to school. I'd study literature and history and psychology. But my mother told me there was no money for me to go to college, even though she'd paid for my sister to go. So I read and read and read. Pictures of different times poured through my mind—cathedrals, wars, plagues. Maybe if I'd gone to school, I'd have channeled all of this into writing books or learning about the past or being a novelist. But I didn't. My mother made sure of that.

I still feel angry at her, haunted by her, really. Sometimes even today I find myself wanting to scream at her, "Why didn't you help me go to college? Didn't you know I wanted to be a psychologist? How come you could pay for my sister to get a master's, but you didn't expect anything of me at all? Why?"

"Because I knew you'd fail," is what I imagine her answering.

I often wonder, in my line of work, about free will. How much of our life is determined by the choices that we make? And how much of it is destined to happen? What if I had gone to college? What if I had become a psychologist? Would my psychic powers have blossomed so fully? I don't know. Maybe having such an unhappy mother was the real training I needed for the work that lay ahead of me. When I look back at my own life, I know that so many of the things that happened to me were part of some plan I could barely glimpse, much less understand. We think we are the agents of our own destiny, but there are forces at work in our lives that are so much bigger than we can possibly ever understand.

Out of desperation, for some kind of distraction from home and waitressing, I decided to audition for a musical at the local community theater, a production of *Jesus Christ Superstar*. I got a small part in the chorus and a bigger role as the hidden girlfriend of the music director.

He was my first love.

I thought he looked like James Taylor. He had those soulful eyes and a lovely voice, but he really wasn't very nice to me. Whenever we were out in public, he'd say, "Pretend you don't know me. I don't want other people to see me with you."

When I had first started going around with him, he had taken me to the movies and afterwards we had parked and kissed a bit. I gushed about it in my journal. But the next day when I walked into the house, my mother, who'd read my diary, started hurling English muffins at my head and screaming at me that I was a whore. "You dirty slut!" she yelled at me over and over again.

What was strange was that I felt like one deep down inside. I reacted like she was right, even though I was a just-kissed virgin at that point. Needless to say, my mother's attack on me helped me decide to sleep with the music director. If she was going to call me a slut, why not be one?

He told me I was weird and strange, but he was happy to take my virginity. I used to go visit him at his house where he lived with his parents, sneaking in and out of his bedroom window.

How could I hook up with a guy like that? All I can say was that I was used to having someone be embarrassed by me. My mother had prepared me for someone who would want to keep me hidden.

"I don't know how to love him," sang Mary Magdalene in our play and I felt deeply connected to her, more deeply than ever.

It was an exciting time. The people in Summit were in an uproar over the production, even picketing the theater where we were performing, primarily because of these love songs between Mary Magdalene and Jesus. Was the musical blasphemous or wonderful? After refusing to speak to me about my participation in it, my own parents ended up coming to see it twice, which made me happy. Backstage, all the kids were reading the Bible, and I certainly learned more about the Gospels from that show than I did in ten years of Catholic school.

At the cast party for *Jesus Christ Superstar*, however, I walked in on the music director kissing another girl from the show and was devastated. I was heartbroken and somehow, despite everything, surprised. I think I'd been telling myself that it was because of the play that we had to keep our relationship a secret and that as soon as it was over we could be a real couple.

Apparently not.

He was supposed to give me a ride home, but I left on my own, ready to walk the many miles back to my house. It was late at night, almost dawn, and I was crying as I stumbled along, as sad as I had ever been.

I had nothing—no real job, no boyfriend, no nothing—just a crazy mother waiting for me at home. The only reason I'd probably gotten a part in the play was because the music director wanted to sleep with me. I was just a piece of trash. An invisible piece of trash.

Just then a garbage truck roared up behind me and slowed down.

"You okay?" asked the driver.

I looked up at him with my tearstained face. I shook my head. "My boyfriend just dumped me."

"Then get in the dump truck." He laughed. "I'll give you a ride home."

He dropped me off in front of my house and picked up the garbage at the same time.

I was feeling pretty low on myself.

The next day another boy from the show, Max, called me.

Unlike all the other boys in the cast, Max had not wanted to be an apostle. In fact, he refused the part of Peter when offered it. Instead, Max insisted on being a Roman soldier at the crucifixion. There was something feral and out of control about Max, and all during rehearsals he wouldn't stop staring at me. Soon after he met me, he started insisting that I meet his foster father, the priest at the local Episcopal church. "Bob says I'm a wolf, because I like to howl at the moon," Max told me. "He'll love you."

I wasn't so sure I wanted to meet anyone associated with Max, but when he called after my heartbreak, I was down enough that I was ready for anything. A few days later, I found myself following him to the rectory behind Calvary Church.

An older woman, heavyset and with long hair, was sitting in the kitchen and offered us a cup of chamomile tea when we came in. She introduced herself to me as Susan, Bob's wife. A moment later, Bob himself appeared, long black robes flapping around him, eyes sparkling, as if he were Fagin about to meet a new young pickpocket.

He extended his hand formally. "I'm Father Bob Morris. Max has told me so much about you." He was a small man, balding, with glasses and a soft, high-pitched, almost feminine voice. He peered at me without letting go of my hand. "You're an intuitive, aren't you?"

I was taken aback. "What has Max told you about me?" I could just imagine the kinds of things he'd say.

Father Bob shook his head. "Oh, Max didn't tell me that you were psychic. I can tell just from looking at you."

"You can?"

"It's in your aura. Other people have recognized you before this, haven't they?"

My experiences in England had begun to feel like a half-imagined dream until this moment. Maybe I wasn't crazy. Maybe I wasn't useless. I felt an immediate release of tension inside of me. Everything was going to be okay from now on. This was what was supposed to happen. It was a psychic recognition that I was destined to meet this man, that I had been waiting for him.

Father Bob's face was open and curious. He wanted to hear what I had to say. Almost instantly I trusted him.

I found myself telling him everything about my trip to England. We sat at his kitchen table and he listened to me with genuine warmth and attention. He was the first person I told about my strange experiences as a child. I confided in him about falling into mirrors and reading cards and seeing the man in the black hat. Nothing I said seemed to alarm Father Bob. He asked a few questions from time to time, but mostly he listened and encouraged me to speak. Max eventually left, but Father Bob and I kept talking. Our tea grew cold.

I told him about waking up before my trip to England and seeing that spiral of gray smoke above my abdomen.

"Have you ever seen a dead body?" he asked me, to my surprise.

"My grandmother's," I answered, remembering her wake.

"Did you have the experience, by any chance, of looking at her body and thinking you could still see it breathing?"

"Yes!" In fact, I had.

"It's very common. What you are seeing is the etheric body still attached to the physical corpse. It can take up to three days for it to let go, that's what you see still breathing, and that's why we don't bury people right away. We want to let them make that transition. The etheric body is what you saw emanating from your chakra that night. It's what ghosts are, astral beings disconnected from the physical world."

"Would I have become a ghost if my astral body had left my real one?"

"But it didn't," said Father Bob. "That's why you're here."

Before I knew it, I was going over to his house every Wednesday night to study with him. In addition to Max, Father Bob invited a motley collection of local teenagers—a very religious boy who looked a lot more like Jesus Christ than the kid playing him in the musical, a wild girl with far too many boyfriends, and Keith, a hippie artist and dreamer.

We were like the young X-Men, misfits one and all until we met our Professor Xavier.

We'd all been bullied, and it dawned on me as I got to know these kids that there was no reason for them to be shunned and teased. They weren't normal, that's for sure, but they were smart and funny and talented. A lot of times it's the kid walking down the hall with their head down, the kid who doesn't fit in, who's really the most interesting. For the first time in my life, I began to realize how hard it was for people to be spiritually open.

I see a lot of kids who try to ignore their spiritual selves and end up doing drugs or drinking instead, and they freak out when what they really need to be doing is exploring their souls the way we did with Father Bob. Kids really want spiritual adventures, but they don't know how to have them.

A lot of the exercises we did weren't that dissimilar from games I'd played in my high school theater class, but Father Bob was always explaining to us how it was related to the paranormal. We would massage each other without touching, feeling the energy that surrounds the physical body. We fell backwards into each other's arms in a complete state of trust.

Father Bob taught me how to fall. "Do you ever have dreams at night that you are falling from a great height and then you startle awake?"

"Yes," I said. "Often."

"Don't wake up," he told me. "Dare to keep falling. See what happens. That's what you have to do to develop your sight. Fall and keep falling."

For the first time in my life, I was not only part of a group of kids, I was also popular, I was cool. I started writing folk songs, and Keith would play them on his guitar and we would all sing together. We auditioned for the same community theater plays, and every Wednesday night we would go over to Father Bob's. He called me the Black Opal. He said that if I were a jewel, I would be a black opal, rare and precious. It was the first nickname anyone had ever given me, and it made me feel beautiful and loved.

That's probably what Father Bob really taught me, that there was something wonderful about who, and what, I was. When I think back on those days, I don't remember any special techniques or magic tricks or any particularly esoteric information that Bob taught us. He was an odd little guy without a very strong personal presence, but he really believed in a spiritual world and he wanted to create a safe place for us to explore it together.

Just after I started studying with Father Bob, my old dog, Muffet, who'd spent most of her life in the basement, finally died. I came home one day to find out my mother had put Muffet to sleep and already disposed of the body. I had no idea this was going to happen.

"Did you stay with her while they did it?" I wanted to know.

"We left her there," said my mother as if she were describing a shopping trip. "The vet took care of everything."

Nobody had been with Muffet as she passed. Nobody had kissed her or held her. Nobody had said a prayer as she left this life. I ran out of the house and went to Father Bob's. Some of the other kids were there, and they gathered around me and held me. I cried and cried, and they understood why I was upset. It didn't matter that Muffet was a dog; she needed the same love and respect as any other being.

"You need to remember, though," said Father Bob when I was calmer, "that there isn't really any difference between the living and the dead. Muffet's still there. Let yourself be quiet and commune with her."

Muffet began visiting me regularly in my dreams, and I told Father Bob that he was right, that I could feel her close.

One night, Father Bob invited me up to his library. On the shelves were books about the occult and exorcisms and demonic possession.

"Evil's real," he told me. "No matter what anyone says. There is a dark side to all of this and we have to fight it."

I thought of the creature I had seen crawling across the floor in my mother's room and I knew he was right. Some psychics will tell you that evil doesn't exist, but not me. I believe in demons because I have seen them—in the spiritual world, in the everyday world.

Evil, wherever it comes from, and I'm not sure where it does, is finally an absence of empathy. We can see that in serial killers and warmongers and priests who abuse kids, but sometimes it's harder to recognize that complete lack of compassion in people when it's directed at the natural world. I'm appalled by people who kill animals for sport and who destroy the trees in the forest in the hopes of making one more buck. That's evil to me, pure evil.

But Father Bob didn't explain any of that to me. It's taken a long time for me to understand it. Still, I appreciated his acknowledgment of evil. A lot of people, the white-light lovers, I call them, want to pretend evil doesn't exist, that it all comes from bad thoughts, and if we all just smile more it will disappear. That has always seemed naïve to me. That sort of attitude just allows people to ignore a lot of the real suffering in the world.

At a party one night at Father Bob's, one of the kids came over and told me that there was a woman who wanted to talk to me privately. My eyes had met hers at one point in the evening. She was a heavy woman, very beautiful, with a mane of dark hair.

The girl led me upstairs to Father Bob's study and told me that the lady's name was Anna Rawlis and that she was half-Hawaiian and half-English. I walked into the room and shut the door behind me.

Anna Rawlis was sprawled on an old settee like some ancient giant fertility goddess. She radiated an intense spiritual energy. She didn't say anything for almost a minute and neither did I. Slowly, a wide smile spread across her large face.

"Don't you know who you are?" she said at last.

I knew she didn't want me to give her my name. I shook my head. I felt disoriented, woozy almost.

"I can see a few of your past lives, you know."

I felt chills prickling up my body. My arms were covered in goose bumps.

"Your birthday is December 23, isn't it?"

It was.

"You have a strong connection to England, don't you?"

I nodded.

"You were a little girl once in the Blitz. I don't think you survived. You were killed when you were very young by a bomb. You hear the bombs, don't you?" she asked. "And I can see another life. Have you ever seen the movie *Oliver!?*"

I nearly laughed out loud to relieve the tension. "Yes," I said. "Only about a thousand times."

Anna Rawlis nodded. "Do you remember Nancy?"

"Yes." I already knew what she was going to say next.

"You were like her. You were a prostitute once, in England. I can see that."

Maybe I should have been insulted by what Anna said, but I wasn't. Because I knew it was true. And I knew it wasn't something to be ashamed of.

"Women like us often find ourselves on the fringes of society," said Anna as if she could read what I was thinking. "You've always been a medium, lifetime after lifetime. You've always had the sight. I think you were burned for it many times long ago."

No one had ever spoken to me about reincarnation before, not even Father Bob. But I'd always believed in it. And I knew that everything that Anna Rawlis was telling me was true.

When I'm doing readings, I often see people's past lives. I'm always struck that they're never surprised by what I say. A part of them has always known who they are.

I could remember being in an attic with other girls. I knew I'd walked the streets of Victorian London.

Anna Rawlis called my mother the day after she met me. "You have a very special daughter," I heard her saying on the phone. "She has a gift. She's a treasure."

"Yes, yes," my mother chatted politely. "We'll have to get together someday and talk about it all."

I was eavesdropping. I wanted to meet Anna Rawlis again myself.

"Well, thank you so much," I heard my mother continuing. "We'll be in touch with you. I'll give you a call one day. In the spring, when I've got a little more time."

I wanted my mother to know that there was something special about me, that I wasn't a loser. I wanted Anna Rawlis or Father Bob to explain to her who and what I was. I thought that would change everything. But my mother avoided them both. She never called Anna Rawlis.

My mother was especially resentful of the time I spent with Father Bob. She never asked me about what we did, and even though she often drove me over to the church, she'd mutter in the car the whole time that he wasn't a real priest.

"He's in charge of the church, Mommy," I'd say.

But she'd shake her head darkly. "No. He's not a priest."

Still, she never once got out of the car and came in to actually meet him. I think mostly she was resentful of anyone I cared about. Or maybe she was frightened, too. She was a very frightened person.

"You, you care so much about having friends," she said to me around that time, as if that were a bad thing. She didn't have any friends herself, but at last I did. I felt more and more disconnected from her. I suppose she was right in keeping me from having friends all those years, because as I began to make them, I began to realize just how twisted she was. They gave me the courage to break free from her.

I didn't know how I was going to do it, but I knew that eventually, unlike my sister, I was going to move away from my mother. I was going to have my own life. But I also felt like a fairy-tale character locked in a tower waiting for someone, anyone, to finally rescue me.

About two years after I started meeting with Father Bob, he arranged for us to go on a retreat with another group of kids from the Unitarian church called the Liberal Religious Youth. We were all going to travel up to New Hampshire and stay on an island where there was an old hotel, now owned by the Unitarians and used as a conference center but rumored to be haunted. Bob was going to bring an infrared camera to see if we could catch any spirits on film. What I didn't know, because I can never see anything about my own life, was that not only would I see ghosts, but I would also meet my rescuer and my future husband.

I was getting ready for a reading when an unexpected woman showed up in my shop, eager for advice. She didn't have an appointment. She was in a terrible hurry and didn't have time to come into my room. "I just want to know if I should take this job or not. Surely you can do that without me sitting down."

"Do you know someone called Howard?" I asked.

The woman shook her head.

"All I can see is Howard. He's right beside you. He's not happy at all."

"Howard?" She looked completely lost.

"An old man in a green cardigan? He just died—"

"I don't know what you're talking about. I don't know anyone called Howard. I've never known anyone by that name."

"I'm sorry," I said. "Maybe you should make an appointment and come in when you're not so rushed. All I can see is Howard."

A few minutes later, when my scheduled client showed up, Howard returned. "Do you know a Howard? In a button-down sweater?"

"That's my father!" the woman exclaimed. "Really? Really? He's wearing the green cardigan. He never took it off. We buried him in it."

Howard knew my schedule. He knew this other woman was trying to take his daughter's spot, and he wasn't happy about it. Sometimes I think the dead are more eager for my readings than the living.

8

Men in Tights

David Saxman arrived at Star Island wearing a red velvet cape. He had long wavy blond hair and strode around the old hotel like a medieval Robert Plant. David was only a few years older than the rest of us, and I thought he was completely arrogant—and devastatingly attractive. Even worse, he seemed to be ignoring me. That hadn't happened in a long time. All the other girls were getting his attention and I wasn't.

"Don't worry about it," counseled my friend Keith. "He's bad news. He's got a girlfriend back home and not only is she pretty crazy, but I've heard she might be pregnant."

I wish I could say that put me off. But something about David's eccentricities intrigued me. Like me, he seemed to be from another place, another time, another world. He didn't even try to fit in. Even among the hippies and misfits of the Liberal Religious Youth, he stood out as different. He talked about King Arthur and his knights and the Renaissance as if those days were more real and more familiar than anything that was actually happening around him. He had no interest in contemporary music or television. He was always talking about heraldic symbols and falconry. I couldn't resist it.

"Why are you wearing a cape?" I asked him.

"Is your hair naturally that color?" he parried.

It wasn't, of course. I had started dying my hair blond, much to my mother's chagrin.

I walked away from David, but I felt like I knew him deep down inside. I felt like I could say anything to him. And he was carrying a sword. Just like my father.

That first night, I explored the hotel with Father Bob, looking for ghosts, and David joined us, hoping to catch some photos with his infrared camera.

There was a little boy I named Billy who sat in the lobby in a sailor suit. In some rooms I wouldn't see anything, but would get chills. I also saw a woman in Victorian dress. Father Bob couldn't see the ghosts, but he could feel them. Bob explained that sprits can't hurt us. They are just spirits without their physical bodies. There's no reason to fear them, but they do crave our life force. They sort of charge themselves up on it, and that's why you can get that prickly feeling when they are around. David took photos with the camera, and we caught some strange-looking orbs, but not much else. He also took a photograph of me in a long red velvet dress in the graveyard, and I knew then that he'd been ignoring me on purpose up until that moment.

We ended up saying good night to Father Bob and walking out along the rocks overlooking the sea. David took off his cape and spread it out for us to sleep on, and we held each other and fell asleep listening to the crash of the surf below us. We didn't kiss. We just lay beside each other. We'd done this before together. I knew it.

David felt so familiar to me. I felt like we had been together at the edge of the sea for lifetimes and lifetimes. I felt safe with him in a way it's still hard to describe. That safety has nothing to do with paying the bills or locking the door at night and everything to do with the spiritual realm. I told him about the man in the black hat and David took it in stride. He knew there were strange entities out there, but he didn't make a big deal about them the way some people do. It was just the way the world worked. The extraordinary was perfectly ordinary to David, and that was deeply reassuring to me.

The day we were getting ready to leave, he asked me if I wanted to drive home with him and stop off at a Renaissance festival in Massachusetts called King Richard's Faire.

"I've got a lot of SCA friends working there," he told me, clearly expecting me to be impressed.

"SCA?"

"Society for Creative Anachronism. You don't know about them? We get together to re-create medieval life as accurately as we can. There are groups all over the country. I'm in the House of Burgundy."

"Oh."

"So, do you want to come?"

"Okay, sure," I decided on the spot. I was intrigued that there was actually a whole world of people who chose to live in another era.

When I got in the car, David had changed out of his jeans. In addition to the cape, he was now wearing a floppy hat with a feather, leather shoes, and tights. His outfit made me want to laugh. But again, it reminded me of my father all dressed up as Robin Hood. I had on shorts and an African print shirt. I didn't feel any need for a long skirt or any other medieval garb.

When we were alone in the car, David started flirting with me. He told me a lot about SCA, about how he did metalwork, making crowns, and also swords, out of PVC piping. He went to a fighting class on the weekends. I told him about my experiences with Father Bob, and David seemed relaxed and open to it all.

We'd left just after sunrise, and we arrived only an hour or two after the fair had started. Already the parking lot was full. Mixed in with ordinary families carrying picnic baskets were all manner of people in costume heading into the woods. There were girls in bodices and low-cut shirts with wreaths of flowers in their hair. There were men dressed up as knights with authentic-looking chain-mail armor. A court jester frolicked past us, jingling with bells.

Booths were set up under the trees of a beautiful pine glade. A dunking booth. A sword shop. A puppet theater with a Punch-and-Judy show. A place to buy mead and fried dough. In a natural amphitheater beyond the woods, knights would soon begin jousting on horseback.

David got us in without having to buy tickets; he seemed to know everyone. But we hadn't even begun to head over to the jousting when one of David's friends came over to us, clearly having some kind of freak-out.

"Alice didn't show up and I can't reach her anywhere! We don't have a Gypsy fortune-teller today. What are we going to do? Every day it's something with this crowd. Who am I going to get to do the Tarot?"

To this day I don't know what came over me. Maybe I wanted to draw attention to myself in front of David. Maybe it was just because it was almost fall, and you could feel the crispness in the air. I wasn't usually the kind of person who

spoke up at moments like that. But I did. "I can do readings,"
I heard myself saying. I guess I thought it would be a lark. I
was in a good mood after the drive.

"Really?" David's friend was eyeing me in my shorts and
scruffy shirt.

"Sure," I said. I wasn't pretending confidence. I just knew
I could.

"With Tarot cards and everything?"

"Sure."

"Okay, good then. That's one problem solved. Just make it
sound like you know what you're doing, okay? Make it fun
and a little creepy; keep it vague. I see something wonderful
in your future, but there's danger, too. Got it?"

"Yup," I said as he led me to a small table set up under a
large pine tree. There were two seats across from each other
and a deck of Tarot cards, the Rider deck, on the table.

I had never done a psychic reading before. I had never
talked about prophecy with Father Bob. I had never actively
looked at someone and read their future. I had never held a
deck of Tarot cards. No one taught me how to do it. I had
never read anything about it.

I sat down. David said he was going to get something to
eat and check in with some of his other friends. I told him I
was fine. I wonder if there was something about the environ-
ment, the medieval lute music and troubadour singing drifting through the trees, the women in long skirts, the sense of
market day, that triggered something very old and untapped
within me. It's impossible to know.

An older woman, someone's mother, sat down across from
me and smiled.

I lifted my eyes to look into hers and felt like I'd been

punched in the back of my head and that an opening had been created. Words started pouring out of me. I think my hands were turning over cards, but I wasn't even looking at them.

"I see a dog; it's part bulldog and maybe something else. It's got a head that looks like a rock. Rock Face. Is that his name? No, it's Jock, not Rock."

The woman was white. "How do you know that? You can't know that. That's my dog that died last year."

"He doesn't blame you for getting run over. He says it was his fault, not yours."

"But I forgot to shut the gate!"

"Really, he doesn't blame you. He wants you to know he's absolutely fine."

The woman shook her head and got up hastily from the chair. I saw her muttering to someone else as a man sat down.

Again, words started tumbling out of me. Names. Places. It was like a back door had flung open into another mind, vaster than my own. There was rapid-fire ticker tape there, flying past, and I was grabbing words from it, reading the ones I could see before they disappeared. Some psychics hear things, but I'm a clairvoyant. I see words and images. I look into someone's eyes at first and then gaze over their left shoulder, letting my eyes blur until I can feel the opening. I often wonder, if I got damaged in my head, would it all stop? Would it just shut off?

People have often said to me over the years, "Can you teach me how to do readings?" And I've said I have absolutely no idea how I do it. I don't know what the cards mean. I use them; they facilitate something; they kick something in; they spur new directions sometimes. But it's no system; it's no method. It is only something that I surrender to. I can only repeat what Father Bob told me. I fall, and I don't let myself stop falling.

More and more people were gathering around me.

"Cathy's sick. You need to call her," I told a young man with a beard.

An older woman sat down.

"Your husband says he's never been happier," I heard myself say.

"My husband died last June."

"Oh."

I had no control over what I said, didn't know what it meant until I opened my mouth.

"He's happy, though," I said, certain of it.

The woman snorted. "Good, because he sure wasn't happy with me."

David had returned and was listening to what people were saying. He was looking at me in a new way. He looked proud of me.

"Are you going to be here tomorrow?" asked a teenage girl. "I want you to do a reading for my boyfriend. His best friend died last month."

"I don't think so," I said. "I'm from New Jersey."

As far as I remember, no one paid me anything that day. But David's friend did beg me to stick around for the rest of the season. "You were awesome," he said. "People were saying you were the real thing."

On the way home, I was exhilarated. This wasn't just one or two people recognizing some indefinable spiritual quality of mine, but something I could really do. People had been swarming around me, cheering me on, thanking me. I was good at it.

Really, really good at it. And it didn't even seem to take any effort.

"That was weird," I told David. "How did I do that?"

It was as if I had always been a radio, but at last someone had turned me on and tuned me in to a channel. But I hadn't done it. It had happened to me. It's hard to explain to people how little control I have over all of this. They think I can choose what to broadcast, but I can't. I can't change to light FM if you don't like heavy metal. The music pours through me, and I have no control over it.

David was both accepting of what I'd done and not very interested in it. This strange combination of total belief and complete nonchalance would be the thing about him that would be so reassuring to me throughout our many years together. Never once in over thirty years has he ever asked me for a reading.

"You should come to our SCA events on the weekend," David suggested. "People would love you. Only you'll need a new name. We all have special SCA names."

And that's when I became Seretta, naming myself for an English actress, Seretta Wilson, who had once been in a very risqué movie with Jack Wild. No one probably knew about her but me.

I told my mother and Aunt Mary about what had happened, and Aunt Mary immediately set to work making me a Gypsy costume I could wear to events. My mother was less enthusiastic. I probably shouldn't have told her that David's ex-girlfriend was about to have a baby.

But I started going every weekend to the SCA events with David.

The Society for Creative Anachronism was very weird.

Grown men romped through the fields like buffoons playing with swords. And yet everyone was dead serious about the politics and their titles, the lords and the ladies, the counts and the dukes. You could not tread on their houses or make a mockery of their pretend families. There was almost a lack of joy about all of the festivities; it felt almost like an obsession, a compulsion, as if these people had no other choice than to do what they were doing.

David introduced me to his best friend, Richard, and the three of us became completely captivated by *The Mists of Avalon*. I identified with the main character, Morgan, a seer caught between the disappearing beliefs in the fairy folk and the rising power of Christianity.

Both David and Richard were convinced they had been knights protecting me in ages past. Even more powerful, Richard had seen the man in the black hat. He was sure that in another lifetime he had rescued me from him.

I think a lot of the SCA people might have been seeking out remembered lives, accountants by day and earls on the weekend.

I was accepted as an oracle.

I'd sit under a tree in my outfit on a blanket with my Tarot cards in front of me, and people would come to me from the Realm. That's what they called whatever field we were in that day—the Realm. I charged two dollars for readings, sometimes five. What made me popular, I think, and always has, is that what I tell people isn't vague. It's usually very specific, even when I don't understand it myself.

I remember telling one woman she was going to make a lot less money at her job.

"Never gonna happen," said the Countess, who in her day-to-day life had a government job at the Department of Motor Vehicles.

But the next week she came back and, sure enough, they'd taken away her paid furlough.

I was accepted. I was well liked. I was in demand.

Doing the readings was a thrill at first. I was outdoors and in charge of my own schedule. If I didn't want to do a reading, I didn't. There was something wholesome and fresh about everyone frolicking around the fields in their tights. These people, strange as a lot of them were, had an old-world respect for my abilities. They knew how to treat the oracle. They brought me gifts—a dagger with a snake for a hilt, necklaces they'd made, homemade food—and thought of me as an integral part of their community. They had a context for me and a kind of innocence and openness to the whole experience. They didn't expect me to solve all of their problems like a psychiatrist.

In the modern world, people are so lost and spiritually hungry that they become like vampires with me. "You're not telling me what I want to hear!" they'll scream. They don't know how to get what they need. They feel out of control and they want, somehow, for me to make them feel like they instantly understand everything. "I have a busy schedule," people will say when they call me up. "And I need a reading at once."

But the buffoons and the misfits at the Society for Creative Anachronism would approach me with gentleness and reverence. They gave me the confidence to quit working at the pizzeria. One day in the middle of a busy lunch while everyone was demanding slices, I walked out. I held up my head and thought, *They don't know who I am. I'm the oracle, whatever that means, but it means something.*

My mother was furious. "What are you going to do? Sit around at home?" It was as if she couldn't imagine me doing anything better than working at that sleazy job for the rest of my life. As if that were all I was good for.

But the next day, I walked into an old-fashioned toy store that I had always loved, and they hired me on the spot.

Malcolm Bleeker carved doll furniture and built ornate Victorian dollhouses. He wore a little bow tie and had the muttonchops of a gentleman from another century. In his shop he sold, in addition to the doll furniture, Steiff teddy bears, Madame Alexander dolls, and old-fashioned mechanical toys. He let me deal with the customers, mostly wizened old ladies, spinsters with cats, I'm guessing. Not a lot of actual kids came into the store. But that was fine by Mr. Bleeker and me.

On the weekend there were tournaments and pig roasts and festivals. I saw less and less of Father Bob as he became busy founding Interweave, an interdenominational healing center. Besides, I had a boyfriend now, although I denied to my mother that David and I were a couple. My mother wouldn't even let him in the house.

Instead David and Richard, dressed in armor and tights, would pick me up and we'd go camping far out in the woods. We'd swim in lakes and duel, and it reminded me of the best parts of my childhood. They were my knights, my champions, my brothers-in-arms. Mostly they were like my sweet, dear brothers I had never had. At night I would sleep between them in our tent, and it was all a time of a strange kind of innocence. We didn't get up to any of the usual naughtiness. We walked through graveyards and watched the stars. Everything became a portal to another realm for us. Out in the woods, we could have been living four hundred, six hundred years ago. I wore long skirts, they wore their jerkins and their chain mail, and we were all blissfully happy to have found one another again.

But like most Camelots, it eventually came to an end.

One day, a very wealthy doctor came through the door of the toy shop. Word about me had gotten around to him. He told me that he was throwing an Alexandre Dumas costume ball. Guests were expected to come as musketeers and Milady de Winter, the Count of Monte Cristo, and other characters from the novels. The doctor told me that it would lend an air of authenticity to the evening if he could produce a Gypsy to tell people's fortunes. He offered me a hundred dollars.

From the moment I walked into his enormous house at eight in the evening until I left at one in the morning, I had not one moment without people in front of me. I did five hours straight of readings, one person after another. I didn't know how to speak up for myself, to say this was too much, but it was. No one thought to bring me a drink or a bite to eat. I couldn't even go to the bathroom. No one thought of me as anything but the hired help.

I think this was my first glimpse of how draining doing readings could be. I disappear when I'm doing a reading. I'm gone. People are always coming up to me and saying, "Remember me? You did a reading for me last month." But I don't. Because I wasn't there. I step out of the way to make room for something else, and it takes everything I've got.

A quartet of musicians was playing in the hallway and more and more people crowded around me, lavishly dressed in costumes that must have cost them hundreds and hundreds of dollars. I could feel something shifting that night. This wasn't a weekend game anymore.

"I need help with my job. Should I leave it? Should I quit?"

"Is my husband cheating on me?"

"What's the matter with my daughter? Why does she hate me?"

I had been paid ahead of time and no one had to give me anything. They had no reverence for what I did.

I could hardly stand up when the evening was over. Still, I had a hundred dollars in my hand and I was proud of myself. When I came home, however, my mother was shooting daggers at me. She was furious.

"Is this what you are going to do with your life? Really?"

"I worked all night and now you're yelling at me?"

"What? Is my daughter going to be a fortune-teller?" There was nothing but disdain in her voice. She had reduced me to nothing.

I had found a way of understanding myself and she was ready to take it away from me and turn me into a boardwalk Gypsy. She couldn't let me feel any pride in anything. All the long-suppressed rage in me finally exploded.

"Why do you have to do this to me?" I screamed. "How can you do this to me?"

She shook her head. "You're never home anymore. You've always done what you want to do. You don't care about me at all. I'm just your mother. You just want me to die, don't you? Well, maybe I will. And what will you care? You're just like your father, prancing around the world, without a care for anyone."

"It's not my fault that I look like him. You're the one who made that happen. Why do you have to find fault with everything I do, with everything I am?"

I had to get out of that house. It was a house of madness.

My mother was seething with fury. "You only care about yourself. You don't care anything about other people. They don't exist for you. You will never know how to love. You are not capable of love. There's no love in you anywhere at all. There's something the matter with you."

"I do know how to love! I do!" I was weeping now.

"Those boys, they say they like you, but they don't. David's just using you. No one likes you. No one."

I'd been the belle of the Dumas ball, but now I was just a little girl sobbing on the floor again. She could turn me into nothing and no one. I hadn't won, even though I'd tried to express myself. If I had truly won, I would have lifted my head and walked away from her proudly. I would have claimed my power. I might have hopped on a plane back to England. But I was too helpless, too defeated. I couldn't escape her on my own.

We screamed at each other for hours, and when finally we had nothing left, I called David. "Come and get me," I pleaded. "I've got to get out of this house. I've got to get out of here."

So we got married. David wore his cape.

The Ratalin Pirates, me and David, at the Renaissance Faire

Once people get me on the phone, I've already begun their reading. I can't help it. That's why I don't answer the phone anymore. I just can't. It's why I hide sometimes, too. I get reclusive. I don't want to have to know everything.

A woman stopped into my store the other day, hoping there was a chance I might have a cancellation and I could give her a reading. But there wasn't.

She was a nice middle-aged woman, and she looked very disappointed.

"I've just done three readings in a row," I explained. "I'm shot. But I can probably fit you in next August. Just leave your number with me and I'll see what I can do."

As she was writing down her number for me on a slip of paper, words flew out of my mouth, "Don't go to Florida."

She looked up at me, startled. "What?"

"Don't go to Florida," I repeated.

"But that's what I was coming to ask you about! I just got offered this job down there."

She was a very respectful, patient person, and that's probably why she got what she needed from the spirits. If she'd been bitchy or demanding about not being able to see me, my irritation would have gotten in the way of the message. But she was relaxed and open and got what she needed. In a way, we both did. When I can do a reading for someone like that, I feel like I get their positive energy in return. I don't feel so drained.

————

A woman dropped by my shop in a terrible state. She'd finally found an apartment she could afford, but they wouldn't let her have any pets. "I've always wanted a dog," she told me. "I really need a dog."

"But you have a dog," I told her.

"No," she said. "I don't."

"A little Chihuahua? I can see him right beside you."

"A Chihuahua? Pepe?"

"That's him," I said. "He started jumping up and down when you said his name."

"But Pepe's dead," said the woman, looking taken aback. "He was my dog when I was a little girl."

"But there is no death." The words shot out of my mouth, as they often do. "He's still with you. I think he still wants to be your dog. Why don't you try calling to him when you get home to your apartment? Don't talk to him in your head. Say his name out loud. The dead like to hear the vibrations of their names."

The woman looked at me like I was crazy and quickly left the shop.

A few days later, however, she dropped in again.

"I tried what you said," she admitted, a little embarrassed. "And I think I can kind of feel Pepe near me now."

"He's there," I told her. "He wants you to know that."

A week later she returned and told me that now when she came home she could smell him. Sometimes she even felt him jump up on the bed at night. A few weeks later I saw her in town and she was happier than I had ever seen her.

"Pepe's with me!" she told me. "I don't need a dog anymore. I've got Pepe. Thank you for bringing him back to me."

"You brought him back," I explained. "I didn't have anything to do with it. You loved him and he came back."

9

Getting to Know the Dead

Something that's always been hard for me is that I can't see things about my own life or David's. Almost nothing. I can't do readings for myself or those close to me. I can't help myself to make decisions. Sometimes I get an intuition about something that's about to happen, but then, most people get those. I get no names, no addresses, no guidance from the dead about my own life. I can't get what I give to other people and I often feel lost because of it.

My mother did nothing to hide her embarrassment that I was marrying David, and David's mother actually tried to stop the wedding. She called the monsignor and told him not to marry David and me. She told the priest I was a witch. He wouldn't listen to her, thank goodness, and she did show up at the church for the ceremony, even though she scowled the whole time. I wore a twenty-dollar dress and my sister was my bridesmaid. It was really a fiasco. David's brother refused to even come. He told David, "There is no escape for the wicked." Everyone in his family thought I was some kind of evil entity. They didn't like that I was a psychic. At all.

There was a lot of bad blood, in any case, about David's child from his ex-girlfriend. The poor girl was not up to taking care of the baby. David's family blamed him for not marrying her, but she had gotten pregnant by accident and he had never thought she was up to caring for a child. Nor did he think he was.

David's mother officially adopted the baby, a little boy named Josh, but when David and I moved to Boston soon after our wedding, his mother disappeared with his son. She didn't tell us she was leaving, and she left no forwarding address. We tried all kinds of ways to find her and the baby, but we couldn't. David's brother refused to tell us where she was. She and the boy seemed to have changed their names. This was in the days before the Internet, and David and I didn't have any financial resources for locating her and the child. I had no idea where the baby was, and it was incredibly frustrating.

At the time, I was actually finding kids for people who had disappeared in divorces. A man or a woman would show up and I'd see a map of a state in my head; sometimes I'd even see the names of towns and streets. "Your daughter is in North Carolina, a little town in the west of the state." I've discovered over the years that the children I can locate always want to be found. It's as if they are calling to their lost parents through me. But I've also had parents come in desperate to find their kids and I've seen nothing. If the kids don't want to be found, I get nothing.

I'm not sure if that was true of Josh, David's son, because I didn't get any information of any kind about David. In any case, I couldn't find Josh. Or not right away. David was, understandably, very upset.

It was also a hard way to start our married life together.

I don't know how we survived in Boston. We were ridiculously poor. David was a wedding photographer at Sears and worked as a janitor at a movie theater in the evenings. I was doing readings at the SCA fairs. We fought a lot. I don't think I was an easy wife, and David had been my first real boyfriend. I was so young and so on my own. My mother had practically cut me off and didn't call. If I called, she'd say coldly, "You're married now. You have your own life."

I was enraged and lonely. My mother refused to be in contact with me. David's family had rejected me. I wanted so badly to have in-laws and relatives who loved me. I wanted holiday get-togethers and cozy family reunions, but none of that was going to happen. David and I were adrift, orphaned.

I wanted my mother's approval. I couldn't let go of wanting it. I'd thought she would have at least been happy I got married in the Church.

What bothers me in retrospect is that David and I were such good kids. We didn't drink or do drugs. We didn't even smoke. Everyone around us was getting high on cocaine and hitting the discos and we were prancing through the woods singing show tunes. What was so terrible about us? What was so disappointing?

Was it simply that we weren't conventional? Maybe it's because we didn't really want regular jobs and suits and ties and some kind of nine-to-five respectability. But just because we dressed like fairy-tale characters didn't mean we were Satanists.

We were living in an apartment in an old ramshackle house

just outside of Boston, and at night the stray cats would gather to howl underneath the fire escape. One of them was very thin, with rickety legs, and the other cats were always beating her up, so I adopted her. I brought her inside and fed her. She reminded me of myself. I named her Fiona.

Fiona was a black and white cat with a very unusual face with a black goatee. Every night she slept on my head, and whenever I was home she was in my arms. "You can't take care of a cat," said my mother when I told her about Fiona. But I did. For eighteen years she was a gorgeous, loving, healthy cat. I adored her.

I also began taking better care of myself. All of my OCD symptoms disappeared outside of my mother's house, and I even went out and got my first pair of contact lenses. My mother had always said I couldn't manage them, but for goodness' sakes, they are not that hard to wear. At first I was worried that having 20/20 vision might affect my ability to do readings, but it didn't. Not at all. I was seeing everything. Everything.

The dead were coming through and they were teaching me.

"Who are you looking at?" people would ask me.

"No one you can see," I would often answer.

My real education has always been from the dead. What I really know about the world has come from the other side of the veil. My college, my graduate school, my advanced degrees, my honorary degrees—they all come from the other side. That's what I know about.

But I don't really know how to define myself. "What do you do? Do you talk to the dead? Do you see the future? Are you a past-lives therapist?" I did it all. I saw dead people, I saw visions, I saw the future, and I saw the past. Was I a psychic, a clairvoyant, or a medium? I still don't know. I'm what-

ever you need me to be. I'm an open channel; that's what
I am. Whatever you need to know from the other side, that's
what comes through me.

I was most surprised to find that the dead didn't seem to
be much different from the living. They complained; they
worried about money and lawsuits; they fretted about who
was going to get their sapphire necklace. They wanted to make
sure the tombstone was just right. You'd think that when
you're dead you no longer have to worry about earthly things,
but they did. Nothing changes when people die. They don't
suddenly get enlightened. They don't suddenly turn into angels. I began to realize that you've got to do that work while
you're alive. The things that matter to you in this life don't
magically go away just because you're dead. You've got to figure your stuff out while you're right here.

I've noticed that suicides are always quick to tell me that
they didn't mean to kill themselves. All the time, I hear this.
"It was just a big mistake!" I don't know if they're telling the
truth. Maybe they just want to comfort themselves because
they're embarrassed about what they've done. They come
through and say, "Oh, shit, shit, shit, what did I do?" They regret
it. I've never met a suicide pleased with what they've done. And
here's the crazy thing. All that unhappiness and rage they
thought they were going to get rid of by dying? They're still stuck
with it. The work you've got to do is the work you've got to do.

You've got to figure out what really matters while you are
alive. There are these golden glowing spirits that come through
who've let go of all earthly problems and are just filled with joy.
The thing is, I'm pretty sure this is what they were like when
they were alive. They are able to let go of all their worries and
expectations and return to their best, happiest selves.

Animals are always like this. They don't hold on to any bad feelings. They're not worried about their stuff or their money. They just want to let their human friends know how much they love them. And children, too. I've never met a child who died young in an awful car accident or from leukemia who was in any way regretful about the experience. They are always radiant and more concerned that their parents don't despair but know that their children are all right. They are connected to that basic joy that gets so easily lost when the affairs of the world are thrust upon us—money, mortgages, politics, ambition, status.

David's mother and my mother wanted us to be obsessed with that trivia, with the color of the living room furniture and with what everyone else thought about us. But what I was seeing every day in my readings was that those preoccupations got in the way of living and dying. Unhappy lives lead to unhappy deaths.

I also began to see flashes of what I knew were people's past lives. They'd stream across my eyes like fast-moving scenes in a movie, one after the other. I'd get these glimpses of different historical periods, some of which I recognized and many of which I did not. One guy who came to me was in the army, and the moment he sat down I saw battlefield after battlefield. He'd always been a soldier, life after life; he always would be. I never once saw any famous past lives, though—no Cleopatras or Napoléons. Just glimpses of other times. One woman came to me convinced she was Anastasia, the Russian princess who'd supposedly been killed. She wasn't.

Interestingly, I became obsessed with Jack the Ripper when David and I were living in Boston, and I went to the library to read about him. I had this feeling that maybe I had been connected to him. Probably if I'd been a prostitute in London during the end of the last century I'd have known about him and been frightened of him. But that was just a hunch. My friend Richard was convinced he'd saved me from Jack the Ripper, who, he thought, was really the physical incarnation of the man in the black hat. Perhaps. I couldn't do readings for myself, so I didn't really understand what I was experiencing about my own incarnations. Still, I had this feeling that so many other past experiences were influencing who I was.

In the beginning I was very excited by the responsibility I had. Here I was, only in my twenties, and people came to me to help decide if they should keep their babies or not. Now, I'm basically pro-choice, but it seems like the people who came to me were led by their babies. Those souls wanted to come into the world; that's what I always felt. Maybe babies who didn't want to be born made sure their mothers didn't think about it too much and never went near a psychic. I do know that often aborted babies come back to their mothers to be reborn at a better time. I've often seen this. Or the babies go to other families. They are never angry at their mothers. They have so much more wisdom and understanding and compassion than the angry protestors. The movement between life and death felt very fluid to me, back and forth, back and forth. Nothing's ever final. I wish people knew that life and death and rebirth are so much more complicated than one single lifetime, one single decision.

Sometimes I saw terrible medical problems. One woman who came to me seemed to have this thick braid wrapped around her organs, and when I sent her to the doctor they found twenty-eight tumors inside of her. She always said I saved her life.

All of this made me very full of myself. I was discovering my powers, and it was all very exhilarating. But I didn't have any guidance—not from an individual and not from the culture itself. I was on my own, and I started to lose my humility. I didn't know how I did what I did, but I was doing it and it was impressive.

I don't think that was easy on David. He took care of the practical aspects of our life together, the cooking and the driving. But I felt like my work was more important. I was making more money than he was, and I was dealing with life-and-death issues. For the girl who'd spent years under the stairs, I suddenly was the queen of the hill, the star, the popular kid. The only thing that kept me in check was my mother. She certainly made sure that any confidence I had was short-lived.

Our first Christmas together, David and I drove back to New Jersey. The holidays were about being with family, after all. But when I arrived at my mother's, she stood in the doorway and wouldn't let us in.

"What are you doing here?" she said. "You've got your own family now. You're married."

"It's Christmas." I could already feel my heart starting to break.

My mother shrugged. "I'm not letting you sleep with that man in my house."

"But he's my husband!"

She shut the door in my face.

I was hysterical. I had brought presents for everyone. David and I went to church, and we both cried together through the midnight mass. Our families had completely rejected us.

But when Daddy came down with cancer a year later, David and I moved back to New Jersey to be close to my parents. I'd grown up with them. I needed to be close even if my mother didn't want me to be.

The Bleekers had retired, and they gave me all of the remaining toys from the shop. David and I began selling them at yard sales. It was when we were coming back from one big flea market out in a rural part of New Jersey that we first passed the Church of the Mystic Light.

It was a small, sweet wooden building that looked like an Episcopal church. But the name of the place intrigued us, so we stopped for a peek inside.

The moment we saw the floor was painted with the signs of the zodiac, we were excited. The stained-glass windows showed scenes from all different religions—from Bahaism to Catholicism, Buddhism to Native American spirituality. The church was run by a married couple, Reverend Earle and Susan Hoskins, who were studying the ancient religion of Mithras but brought in speakers each Sunday for presentations on everything from Gnosticism to Tai Chi. It was a very open and inclusive place.

David and I had been looking for a church and we both felt like this was it.

David had been brought up Methodist and we'd been married in the Catholic Church, but neither of us felt much connection to mainstream Christianity. I had this hatred within me of the Popes, all of them, and of the Inquisition. It was more than having had to endure a few mean nuns as a kid; it was something else and I knew it. Sometimes I had visions of myself being burned in front of a huge cathedral, and I was pretty sure the Church had killed me. I used to joke with David that if I died, I didn't want to be cremated, I'd been turned into ash too many times before. I've never understood why people have such a hard time understanding and living the teachings of Jesus, but they do. Especially, it seems to me, most of the Popes.

Susan and Earle were very compelling people. Earle did some kind of computer work during the week and would give sermons on Sundays drawing on themes and ideas from world religions. He was very into Mithras and Gnosticism. We'd all sit in a circle and talk about it together afterwards. It was like Father Bob's, only there were whole families of all ages coming together to investigate spiritual topics. It was the early eighties and the New Age was in full swing. Susan was a beautiful middle-aged woman who also happened to be psychic. Early on, when David and I started going to the church, she held a séance that I attended.

It's surprising, I know, but I always go into these kinds of experiences with a fair amount of skepticism. You'd think, given what I've seen, I'd believe anything. But I don't. Still, I was amazed when Susan's head dropped back during the séance and she began speaking in an Austrian accent. She raised up her head and looked directly at me. "I am Agatha," she said.

My mother's mother.

Unlike my Transylvanian grandmother, Agatha had been a fearful, anxious woman all of her life. I was surprised she'd shown up.

"You must return to the old ways," she said to me.

It was unnerving.

She'd been a very conventional Catholic, but I knew that's not what she was talking about. My grandmother was talking about those visions I'd had of a time before Christianity. After the séance, I confided in a much older cousin of mine who had known my grandmother better than I had. My cousin told me that my mother's mother had been a very different woman than I'd always imagined. Apparently she was able to heal with her hands and knew a great deal about herbal medicine. She was very secretive about it, but she would say protective spells around the house. Her daughters even thought she was witchy. Maybe this was what my aunt Mary had recognized in me. Maybe this was what had frightened my mother.

My mother refused to talk about any of this with me.

It made me so angry that this woman had hidden who and what she was until she was dead, and I resolved at that moment to listen to her and return to the old ways. I wasn't going to be ashamed of what I could do. I wasn't going to hide my talents and isolate myself. My Transylvanian grandmother had been beaten by her husband for her psychic powers. My mother's mother had been afraid of her own power and goodness. But I was going to honor them both by being who and what I really was.

Susan offered classes in the Psychic Arts, which David and I began attending together. I learned about chakras and chi and trance states and hands-on healing and prana energy and the Tarot. The strange thing was, no matter what Susan talked about, I already felt like I knew what it was before she described it. Sometimes when I'm doing readings I'll be given information. "Put salt around your bed and the nightmares will stop." "An amethyst crystal in your pocket will shift your energy." I'm not remembering something I've learned. The information just flows through me. It's there when I need it, but I don't have any access to it when I don't.

Perhaps that's why I didn't feel the need to believe everything I heard. David was completely gung ho about the Church of the Mystic Light, as were a lot of the other people in the congregation. It was a kind and creative place. But something essential was missing, although even now I can't tell you what it was. Maybe it was that everybody wanted so hard to believe in *something*. I never felt like I had to believe in *anything*, and that group-think mentality always unnerved me. Once you start believing in one set of ideas, you stop seeing a whole other reality.

A lot of our SCA friends joined the church, including Richard. Susan wrote a play about King Arthur, and cast Richard in the lead and herself as the Lady of the Lake. I was Guinevere, which delighted Richard and David, who was Galahad. We all took it very seriously and immersed ourselves in the Arthurian legends. And, for a change, I was the star of the play. I was beautiful. I was powerful. I reveled in it all.

Nowhere did I feel this more than in the psychic fairs that Susan held at the church. When I first began participating, all the psychics would sit in a circle around the signs of the zodiac on the floor. There were a lot of big, fat mediums. They were huge women. I think they were so heavy because they needed their weight to keep them close to the earth. Not me, though. I was tiny and lost in the ether.

Quickly it became clear that I was a different kind of psychic from the others—different even from Susan—and I became very popular. I began sitting in the middle of the circle. Lines of people would be waiting to talk to me. The other psychics would be flipping through paperbacks with nothing to do. It was all very intoxicating.

This was bigger than anything I'd ever imagined for myself. There was now a waiting list to come and see me. People were stopping by the church hoping to get a reading from me. Word was getting out about what I could do. I felt powerful. I felt like every time I walked in the room people would turn to look at me, not with disdain or contempt like they had when I was in school, but with awe.

I stopped dressing like a medieval princess and fashioned myself into a sorceress. I wanted to be noticed. Every day I'd check the list of people waiting for readings. Ten people. Twenty people. Thirty people on the waiting list. Everyone wanted to see me. I was a celebrity.

My mother heard about me from someone who'd seen me, and one day she came to the fair to see me in action. The moment she walked into the room, I shriveled inside. She made me feel like a nervous, stuttering child. My confidence evaporated. I was still able to do readings in her presence somehow, but I mistrusted what I said. I fumbled. I apologized for myself.

I think she was shocked to see that I was the star of the show. She couldn't figure out why I was so popular. "It's because I'm real, Mommy," I told her. "I can really do this." But she didn't understand that. She couldn't understand that I was special.

Still, I saw her watching the line of people waiting to talk to me, and I heard her say, "That's my daughter doing the readings."

Yet any pride she had in me was because she was trying to fit in with the people around her. She was just copying the behavior and attitudes of the other people in the room, but she wasn't really interested in understanding what I was doing.

"My daughter reads Tarot cards," she would say, always

rhyming *Tarot* with *carrot* no matter how many times I corrected her. And I didn't read cards anyway. That's not what I did. I was doing something else altogether, and when I tried to explain it to her she just shut down.

I shared the books I was reading on the ancient goddesses and spirituality, but she just tossed them aside. I gave her books on animal spirits, but she never opened them. Any pride she expressed publically was a kind of camouflage she threw off when she was alone with me.

There was a program that listed all of the biographies of the psychics, and at the end of the day my mother told me that she thought it was terrible that I had said I was of Gypsy descent.

"It's so low class," she said, shaking her head.

"But it's true. Steve's mother was from Transylvania, and she said that her grandmother—"

My mother sighed. "You don't want to have anything to do with *those* people. You shouldn't say that."

"What difference does it make?" I said finally. "They're coming to me for readings, aren't they?"

Those were busy years, but when I look back at them, I remember almost nothing with any clarity. David will remind me of a mystery play we did together, or talk about the old Cherokee chief who came to chant with us, and I'll kind of know what he's talking about, but it's really a blur, like a half-forgotten dream. I was doing so many readings, and I didn't have any idea how powerful that was. I simply wasn't there a lot of the time. I was gone so I could be an open channel, so I don't have many memories of those years.

Someone took an instant photo of me during that time, and right where my third eye should be there was a blank hole. I was open all the time. It was like being blackout drunk to do that many readings every day, and I stopped feeling responsible for what I said and did.

I was very young still, only in my twenties, and I didn't realize yet what a danger that kind of arrogance could be.

———

I knew he was a corrections officer the moment he walked into the room and hunkered down in the chair opposite me. And he hadn't even said a word when I knew why he had really come to see me.

"You want to kill your wife, don't you?"

"What the fuck are you talking about?"

"You think you're going to get away with it." He was making my skin crawl.

"I just came here to find out if that bitch is cheating on me. Is she cheating on me? Can you tell me that? That's what I want to know."

"Get out of here," I said, standing up. "Right now. And let me tell you one other thing I know. If you do kill her? You won't get away with it. You'll go to jail. They'll lock you up. And the other prisoners will kill you. Get out of here right now."

I don't know if I saved his wife's life. But I tried.

10

The Sword in the Horse

Erik Jasper showed up at the Church of the Mystic Light to sell crystals. He was tall and thin, with long black hair and a long black beard. He wore lots of silver rings on his fingers and lined his dark eyes to make them look darker. It was as if he'd stepped out of the Russian Court at the turn of the last century. He radiated an intense energy that reminded me of Rasputin. Erik's very presence stirred me up and gave me butterflies. I'd never felt this nervous around a man before. He radiated chaos and danger and power and I found him both attractive and repulsive.

Until that moment, my psychic powers had only brought me into greater light. They had led me to a marriage with a kind man, to the gentle folk of the SCA get-togethers, to toys, to yard sales and flea markets, to a kind of regular life. I had never explored the dark side of what I might be able to see with my abilities.

Erik said he had intuitive powers and started to do readings at our small psychic fairs. I don't think he was a real psychic, but he had a talent for saying things that unnerved people and upset them. He could tap into their emotional vulnerabilities. He could stare at people and freak them out. People often walked away from him crying or furious. Sometimes Erik even yelled at them and called them names when he was doing readings. He got right up in their faces.

I could feel him staring at me while I did my sessions. It disarmed me the way he studied me, as if he knew me in a way that I didn't know myself.

At the end of the day, he would come over to talk to me and tell me about the magician Alistair Crowley and his philosophy of "do what thou wilt." Erik told me that Crowley had been a follower of the Order of the Golden Dawn, a secret society in early twentieth-century England that was interested in spiritualism, reincarnation, and alchemy. He said they took drugs to explore their minds. He grinned and told me about their orgies. For people like us, he seemed to say, there was a different kind of morality.

I wasn't scared of him, but he was titillating. He was so different from my sweet and gentle David, so dark and secretive. Erik felt lecherous and seductive and forbidden. He was a Pandora's box of secrets—and he was inviting me to find out what was inside. The women clustered around him, the way they always do around the bad boys, but he only had eyes for me.

David was an angel, but the sad truth of the matter is that the angels are never as sexy as the devils.

Erik ignited something in me. He made me believe there were whole realms of power I hadn't tapped into that, at last, I was going to discover with him. Those old visions of dancing naked around a fire returned, and I wanted to go on a wild ride through the forest with the horned god of Celtic mythology, Herne. I was sure I had found him at last. He told me I was his goddess and bought me lingerie from Victoria's Secret. He told me that he was the only one who truly understood me spiritually and the only one who could truly love me.

He had a store called The Spear of Destiny and he invited me to visit, to see if I wanted to do readings there. "You could make a lot of money," he told me, winking. "If you went big-time."

He called it a metaphysical shop, as if it was some kind of spiritual destination, but I should have known right away that there was danger there. He'd had it only a few months before we met, but the store looked like it had been there for five hundred years. It was dusty and dirty. When you work with crystals, you have to keep them clean, but Erik let everything—the crystals, the jewelry, the books— become covered in dirt. And I became one of those tarnished things.

Behind that store was a lake, and not once in the three years I was with Erik did I ever walk out the back door to look at it. It was as if I didn't want to see myself reflected in the water. I couldn't be close to nature and close to Erik at the same time. He smoked and everything around him smelled like nicotine.

My mother adored him.

It didn't matter that he was married, had a kid, did LSD all the time, borrowed money from me, and was basically a degenerate. Nope. My mother took one look at him and thought that finally I had done something right by bringing him home. Finally, I had pleased Mommy. But I'm not sure I was pleasing myself. There was a part of me that was truly ashamed of my affair with Erik. I knew he was bad.

My mother would invite Erik over to dinner behind David's back. She flirted with Erik. She'd sweetly tell him, "Be kind to my daughter. Take care of her."

"I love her," he told my mother with a kind of overwhelming intensity.

Meanwhile, I had started doing readings in all my spare time at his store to try to keep it afloat.

The worst kind of people came to that store—criminals, drug dealers, the absolute dregs of New Jersey. One woman was always asking me if the cops were on to her yet. I ended up reading about another client in the police blotter in the newspaper.

But it didn't matter. I was wild for Erik and we couldn't keep our hands off each other. We were always sneaking off to be together—to closets, the car, the store, everywhere but outside in the forest where you were supposed to be with the horned god.

Erik used to tell me we were going to run away together to the ocean. But we never did. We never even went to the beach together. It was just bars and psychic fairs and his dirty shop.

One day David and Richard, like the two knights they believed themselves to be, drove up to The Spear of Destiny and tried to physically pull me out of the store.

"Suzan," said David. "This isn't a good place for you. Let's get out of here."

"I'm going to stay here with Erik," I announced. He had an almost magnetic hold over me.

Erik laughed in their faces and took a drag on his cigarette. "Get outta here. She wants to stay." Still, since Erik was married, I went home to David and to my cat, Fiona, every night. That's probably the only thing that saved me—their patience, their loyalty. I was awful to David and kept telling him that sooner or later Erik was going to leave his wife and we were going to be together. I felt defiant and cruel. Erik said that I was his true wife and nothing else mattered, and I believed him. I blackened my hair and we looked like a match made in hell.

Erik told me that the store was as much mine as his, but the only money it seemed to make all came from my readings. When he needed a couple of thousand dollars at one point to keep it going, I gave him all my savings.

Erik suggested we start going together to the big New York City psychic fairs. What he really wanted to do was make money, a lot of money. He dressed all in black and wore long feather earrings. He wanted me to wear a sequined outfit like I was a circus performer, a high-flying trapeze artist.

These psychic fairs were held in the conference rooms and lobbies of big tourist hotels. We'd arrive early, driving in from New Jersey in Erik's truck, speeding on the empty early-morning highways. I don't even know how I'm alive, the way he drove. Erik was usually selling crystals beside me. I'd sit at a table, just one of ten or twenty psychics in the room, and wait for the customers to start coming in and checking us out. It was like being in a bordello; people were looking me and the other psychics over, trying to decide who was real and who wasn't. "I choose you!" they often said when they sat down.

The women who booked us kept us plied with lemonade throughout the day, to keep our blood sugar up, I suppose.

One after another after another, men and women sat

down in front of me. In order for the people who put on the fairs to make money, I'd have to do almost fifty readings a day. I closed every fair I started and was soon the belle of the ball. I got top billing: Seretta was the most popular psychic in the metropolitan area.

I'd walk out with a few hundred dollars in my pocket and a strange kind of pride. People were devoted to me. They came back to me; they sent their friends to me; they told me that there was no one else like me anywhere.

A lot of the psychics around me said the same things over and over again to different people. But it was never like that for me. I saw dates and names coming at me from the ticker tape inside my head.

"I know you said your dad's name is William, but he keeps telling me to say Charlie is here, Charlie is here."

"Really? Charlie?"

"Yeah, that's what he wants you to know. Charlie, over and out."

"It was my crazy nickname for him, Charlie; that's what he always said when he was tucking me in at night. Charlie, over and out."

Eventually, even the other psychics started coming to get readings at my table.

It's interesting to me that the people who came to these fairs were deadly serious. They weren't there for fun or to just see what it was like. They had desperate questions. They were earnestly trying to figure stuff out. I was often their last resort, their last hope, their *only* hope. I began to get a lot of women with big hair and leopard skin outfits and great nails asking about their boyfriends and husbands.

"Does he still love me?"

"Is Mike messing around with Connie?"

One day, one of these women dragged her husband over to my table. "You gotta talk to Seretta, Jimmy. Seretta knows everything."

This big, surly guy sat down opposite me. He was squirming and looking from side to side.

"Are we alone?" he finally said, talking out of the side of his mouth.

"No," I said. "We're at a psychic fair. We're in a hotel lobby." He nodded.

"Go on, Jimmy, ask her. C'mon!" urged his wife.

He looked around again and pulled a shirt out of a brown paper bag he was carrying. He laid it on the table. I could tell the stains on it were blood. I could see the bullet hole.

He raised his eyebrows at me and nodded. I knew what he was asking, and I could have given him the answer without even seeing the shirt. "Tony did it," I said.

The man slammed his hand down on the table and swore loudly. People stopped talking, looked over at us.

The man was breathing heavily. "How do you know that?" he asked suspiciously.

"I'm a psychic," I said, pointing at the huge sign hanging from the wall of the lobby. "This is a psychic fair."

"Yeah but . . . ," said the man, peering at me.

"I told you she was real," said his wife.

Before long I had all kinds of goombahs lining up for readings. It was like something out of *Goodfellas*. I knew who was going to prison and who wasn't. I touched a lot more bloody shirts. I was the unofficial psychic to the Mob, and I knew a lot of secrets. Even today, I'll get these guys showing up who make me promise ahead of time not to tell anyone what I know.

"How do you know this? How do you know that? How do you know about Uncle Luigi?"

The mobsters were always suspicious of me, worried I might be miked. At the same time, there was something strangely innocent about them. Maybe it was because there was a part of them that was still genuinely religious, but they treated what I did with a certain sacred respect. They'd make the sign of the cross and then ask me about a murder. My mother was anxious that one of them would end up killing me, but I never really worried that they would. They had too much real reverence for my power.

I was actually in a lot more danger from the ordinary people showing up for readings. They drained me. They took everything I had.

The desperation of the people at the psychic fairs was often so absolute, so total, that they didn't even see me as a flesh-and-blood human being. They were frantic for information and seemed incapable of treating the messenger with any honor. I might as well have been one of those machines at the carnival spitting out fortunes, a mechanical psychic in a box. I could have replaced myself with a Magic 8 Ball and no one would have noticed—as long as that Magic 8 Ball knew who Billy was sleeping with, or if Charlie would call again, or if dead Aunt Martha was still there.

One woman was ready to pay me $10,000 to get her dead mother to testify to her husband's whereabouts on the night of a murder.

"You want me to channel your dead mother in court?"

"No," said the woman. "I want you to put my mother on the witness stand."

"But she's dead!"

"Get her ghost there. She's the only one who knows my husband's innocent."

"I can't do that, and if I could, I think you should pay me a lot more than $10,000. You'd have to pay me $20,000 at least."

The woman's eyes were darting back and forth. "I can't come up with that."

I laughed. "No? Well, I can't come up with your dead mother either. I don't reanimate the dead. That's not my thing."

There were women, too (and it was only women), who were convinced that my psychic powers included the ability to mentally destroy people. To be frank, they thought I was some kind of hit psychic. They'd usually driven in from Long Island, I hate to say it, and they frequently wanted me to kill their neighbors or sometimes their mothers-in-law.

"Can you tell when the Martingellis are going to die? Do you see any car accidents?"

"My mother-in-law, her name is Charlene, how's her health?"

"Can you make it quick? Can it happen in March before we have to head down to Florida?"

I would have to explain yet again that I could not make anything happen. I also had to be honest that I never wanted to look at anyone's time of death. It feels too sacred. Sometimes that information arises whether I want it to or not, but I often know that I have chosen not to see that, even if a lot of insurance money might be involved.

I suppose I could have accepted the advance of a couple grand and told these would-be murderers I'd give it a shot. But I didn't, of course. They made me laugh, these women. I've had some bad neighbors, real wackadoodles, but I can't imagine wanting to actually off any of them.

Still, I could have used the money. As hard as I worked, it was the organizers of the fairs who pocketed the big bucks. I'd gotten a job at the FAO Schwartz at the Short Hills Mall. I was still in the toy business, but it was a lot more commercial and impersonal. I'd work all day and then ride the train out to Erik's store to do readings there, and then on the weekends we'd head to the fairs together.

During this time, no conductor ever asked me for a ticket on the commuter rail. I thought it was something to be proud of, that I was gaming the system, part of this newfound power I was discovering with Erik. What I didn't realize was that there are no free rides. I was invisible. Suzan had disappeared. I was under a spell, and gradually I was slipping into another reality.

About that time, Erik and I started going to a local dive, The Feedbag, to do more readings at night. I was becoming so weak I could hardly walk. My blood pressure was ridiculously low at 60/54. I was barely alive. I was totally drained from thirty, forty, and even fifty readings a day.

At The Feedbag, the alcohol flowed freely. The bartender invented a drink called The Seretta with Kahlúa, Baileys Irish Cream, Godiva Liqueur, and Amaretto. It was sweet and chocolaty, like a candy bar, and it kept me going. Sometimes I would pass out during my readings from exhaustion and drinking and yet still continue to talk. My head would actually be down on the table, and I'd be talking. People would bring tape players to record the sessions, and they'd show me later that I'd told them all kinds of things when I thought I was passed out. One night I distantly heard myself repeating the words, "The sword is in the horse; the sword is in the horse." I opened my eyes and saw an older woman in her sixties staring at me, absolutely astonished.

"Oh my God," she whispered.

I rubbed my eyes and tried to lift my head. "I'm sorry I fell asleep. Let me try again." I barely knew where I was.

"You told me the sword was in the horse. That explains everything. Thank you. Thank you. You've helped me so much."

She got up and left, disappearing into the crowd at the bar. To this day I don't know what she was talking about or what the sword in the horse referred to. Was it a statue? A painting? Was it about some long-lost treasure? Who knows? But it was clearly crucial, life-altering information.

Sometimes I fell asleep out of boredom as another girl in love with some boy who would never love her back sat down. I'd pretend I was in a trance.

Erik bought dry ice to put in our drinks so they'd steam mysteriously. Increasingly, I wanted to hide away, but he kept pulling me into the spotlight. We fought terribly.

He said terrible things about David and tried to get me to leave him, even though he was still living with his wife. At home I picked fights with David, hoping he'd leave me, but he wouldn't. He endured it somehow. It was one big psychic soap opera. I was out of my mind. I fought with David. I fought with Erik.

One night Erik and I were screaming at each other in his garage. "I can't go on like this! I can't! It's got to stop!" All the other psychics seemed to be basking in the white light and I was trapped in this crazy darkness.

"I won't let you go!" whispered Erik, holding me.

"Leave me alone!" I begged, pulling away.

"I'll do anything for you!" yelled Erik, and he bashed his hand into a rusty nail sticking out of the wall. Blood poured out of his palm like some kind of sick stigmata. "This is what I'll do for you!"

It all felt twisted and screwed up.

He started showing up at FAO Schwartz and staring at me while I worked. If I went to a birthday party with the girls from the store, he'd crash it. Wherever I went, there he was. He was a dark shadow following me around.

I felt lost and out of control. I stopped wearing my seat belt.

I realized that he wasn't powerful at all, that he was just a kind of freakish clown in black who wanted to drain what he could from me. He didn't know anything special. He didn't have any real power of his own; that's why he wanted mine. He didn't have anything to give me.

I think in the beginning I thought he had some kind of special magic he was going to share with me, but I began to realize that there was nothing magic about him. It was all just costumes and eyeliner. I was the one who was really powerful. That's why he wanted to be with me. He was like a parasite feeding off of my spiritual energy

Once at a ritzy hotel in the city, the Plaza maybe, Erik started attacking David, saying he was a weakling.

"Why are you with that loser?" Erik whined.

"Why are you with your wife? Why don't you leave her?"

"I have a kid!"

"I have a husband!"

"He's a dork!" Erik taunted. "He's an idiot! He's a nerd! He's a loser!"

Something broke inside of me, I think I heard my mother's voice in Erik's, and I ran across the lobby of the hotel, leapt on his back, and began pounding him with my fists as hard as I could. He was screaming at me, trying to shake me off, but I was clinging fiercely to him, hitting him again and again.

A well-dressed woman near the reception desk coughed and I heard her say, "When are the psychics going to arrive?"

"Those are the psychics," said the hotel manager as Erik flipped me off his back onto the floor.

I was out of my mind. I had let myself be dragged into a kind of hell. I lay on the flowered carpet of the hotel floor weeping.

That night, when I staggered home after another day full of readings, I collapsed on the bed, unable to move. Our cat, Fiona, tried to rub herself against me, but I just pushed her away. Quietly, David came over to me and asked if I wanted anything, dinner maybe. I looked up at him, and I don't know what came over me, but I bit him on the throat. Like a vampire.

David was screaming, "You bit me!"

He had the mark on his neck for a month.

I realized that what I wanted from David was his life force, because mine was disappearing.

I walked into The Spear of Destiny the next day and broke off with Erik. I wasn't going to do psychic fairs anymore, I wasn't going to The Feedbag ever again, and I didn't care that Erik still owed me thousands of dollars. He wept. He crawled under a table and sulked, but I had to get away from him.

Years later, I went and found his wife and apologized to her. Erik had long since left her, and I am grateful for her forgiveness.

Erik used to have a slogan painted on the wall in The Spear of Destiny that said: "There Is No Blame." What Erik meant, I knew, was that he didn't want anyone to blame *him* for anything he did. If he wanted sex, drugs, and rock and roll then he could have it. He had no sense of the sanctity of anything. He could hunt animals in the woods if he wanted. He could drive as fast as he wanted. He could sleep with whomever he wanted. No blame. But he didn't have any joy either. No blame, sure. But no joy either.

Erik melted down when I left. "No one else loves me," he cried. He called my mother, told her he needed me. He begged her to convince me to come back to him.

My mother called me up and told me that this proved that I was incapable of real love. She was appalled at how I had treated Erik. There was nothing but disdain in her voice. She hung up the phone when I refused to listen to her.

I decided I wasn't going to call myself Seretta anymore after that.

David and Richard made a special dinner for me to welcome me back, and we opened a bottle of wine and raised a glass to Seretta. She was gone. No one from the psychic fairs would ever be able to find her again. None of the thugs from the store had ever known my real name. Seretta was gone, and Suzan was back.

David had remained true to me through it all and never once did he throw what I had done in my face. No blame. David was the one who understood what it really meant. He was an angel or maybe just a saint.

Eventually, I went to a little art gallery with a yoga studio in a small town in New Jersey and said that I'd like to do psychic readings there occasionally. They said that would be great. I'd have a candle on a table in a pretty room filled with paintings and see as many people as I wanted, mostly nice people coming to look at the pictures or do yoga or meditate.

Somehow Erik found me there.

He roared into the parking lot on his motorcycle one evening and crashed dramatically as he parked. He came into the gallery covered in blood. "Come back," he pleaded. He was crying.

But I was free of him. "You're bleeding on my cards. I don't want you bleeding on my cards anymore."

And that was just about the last time I ever saw him.

Life on the dark side with Erik Jasper

———

"Did you ever have a large white rabbit?" I asked the girl sitting in front of me. I could see this enormous bunny hovering over her head.

"I've had pet rats for years," she said. "They're white."

"I have rats, too!" I smiled. "They make great pets."

"They do," said the girl.

"But this isn't a rat. It's definitely a rabbit. A white rabbit."

The girl shrugged. She had no idea what it was about. Still, I was right about her boyfriend and her job, and the girl continued to come and see me year after year. I would never remember her until she sat down and I saw the giant rabbit. I mean, it was a huge bunny.

"Any idea what the rabbit is about?" I'd ask her.

She'd laugh. "You asked me this last time."

It frustrated me. It really bothers me when things don't click and I might be wrong. It's like an itch I can't scratch. But what was wonderful about this girl was that she didn't think I was wrong; she just thought we hadn't solved the mystery yet. She was very open and receptive. She figured one day the rabbit would explain itself and probably explain her life, too.

I don't see everything, just bits and pieces. And I don't understand everything I see, and sometimes my clients don't either, or at least not at first. Sometimes it can take months and even years for one of my readings to make sense, which is why I have people tape them. Normally, though, a mystery like this would have made me feel insane, but I so enjoyed this girl's openness to the universe, I actually looked forward to my readings with her. She wasn't impatient. We didn't have to figure out everything right away.

"If you ever find out what the bunny is, you have to let me know," I begged her.

"You'll be the first to know," she promised.

11

Hobbits, Beggars, and Angels . . . or Why I Love Going to England

Erik had tried to convince me that he was my soul mate. But he wasn't, and after I broke it off with him, all of my passion became focused on the one who had always claimed it—Jack Wild. I was still bizarrely obsessed with him. If I had been able to find a real psychic for myself, one of the things I would have been curious about was my connection to Jack.

Jack had completely disappeared from the movies. His child-star days and even the years of smaller parts in second-rate films were over. This was in the days before the Internet, and I didn't have any idea what had happened to him. Still, he kept visiting me in dreams, telling me he needed me. "Please, you have to come to me." He said he wasn't doing well. He wanted me to find him, but he didn't tell me how. It's hard to describe how vivid these experiences were, as vivid as if I'd gotten a phone call from an old friend.

I had to go back to England and search for him, and I decided I'd use his connection to the singer Donovan. I knew

Donovan had taught Jack to play the guitar and helped him with his albums. Donovan was still popular enough that I was able to find the address in England for the Donovan Fan Club. There was no Jack Wild Fan Club.

David didn't question my need to go. He was still looking for the Holy Grail with his friend Richard, but those days were over for me. I couldn't reclaim that innocence after Erik. David and Richard tried to give it back to me, but they couldn't. It wasn't the same. I had my own quest to go on.

David was born in 1951, right where the aliens landed near Roswell, and there's a part of him that has always been looking to the sky for his people. But I'm a creature of the earth. I belong here, not necessarily in this time, but of this soil. Neither David nor I really fit in with ordinary life, but we don't fit in different ways. But David understood that, and it was his ability to let me go that kept me loyal to him.

He knew I wasn't going off to party or pick up guys or even to have another affair. I was looking for a lost friend. David understood that. In any case, we didn't have enough money for two tickets, and somebody had to stay home and take care of Fiona.

I flew to London by myself, checked into a hotel, and immediately took the Tube up to Lambeth, an area just north of the city proper. It was a pretty crappy section of town. Laundry was hanging on clotheslines out of apartment windows, and there were lots of teenagers in black leather with spiked-out hair sulking around on stoops. This was the eighties and it was clearly a tough neighborhood, but my hair was bleached blond and parts of it stuck straight up and I also wore long extension braids. I was a lot more confident about how I looked than I'd been as a teenager.

I'm no fan of punk music, but I liked the fashion and its complete disregard for conventionality. It was a big fuck-you to everything stuck-up and reverent and conservative. The punk kids then, the goth kids, the steampunk kids today—I always have a special affection for them and their desire not to fit in. A lot of the punk kids I saw had pet rats, too, and I loved their willingness to embrace the animals no one else loved.

I checked the address to the fan club I'd found in a magazine one more time. It was not a very impressive building. I realized that Donovan wasn't at the top of the charts anymore.

I walked up a long stairway, past a lot of doors painted red—many red doors—and knocked on the red door to the Donovan Fan Club.

Two tiny hobbits answered the door. That's the only way I can describe them. Margaret was plump with auburn hair, and Pat was like a little Beatle with his bowl-cut blonde hair. They were both in their early thirties, just a few years older than me. They were very cute, but startled to find a fan actually at their door. It was clearly their private home.

"I'm not looking for Donovan," was the first thing I told them. "Don't worry. I'm actually trying to find Jack Wild."

Margaret and Pat looked at each other.

"Jack Wild?" said Margaret. "Who's Jack Wild?"

"He was a friend of Donovan's," I explained

They looked at me blankly.

"He was in *Oliver!*, *H.R. Pufnstuf.* He made that album *Everything's Coming Up Roses.*"

At last I saw a glimmer of recognition in their faces. Still they couldn't believe it.

"No one is looking for Jack Wild anymore," said Pat. "No one even remembers him."

"Why don't you come in?" invited Margaret.

Their flat was cozy and filled with old upholstered couches covered in tiny petit point pillows. Little antique tables were covered in more antiques. Margaret and Pat were tiny little people with tiny little things.

I explained to them that I was a psychic and that I felt drawn to find Jack Wild for reasons I couldn't really explain. I think I might have done a reading for each of them right then and there, but I can't remember. I do know that we talked for hours and quickly felt like old friends. Some people you meet and you know you've been friends before. It was like that with Pat and Margaret.

Pat was Donovan's friend and manager in addition to running the fan club, but didn't seem to make much money at it. He was just a simple guy who'd gotten mixed up in the music business. But he was very easygoing, and I think I had a bit of a crush on him from the start. He gave me all of these great bootleg Donovan and Paul McCartney tapes.

With a few phone calls, Margaret tracked down the number of Jack's agent, and I gave him a call from their apartment. It was a sad conversation.

The agent told me that Jack was a raging alcoholic. He wasn't even capable of answering the phone. He was incoherent most of the time. He'd become agoraphobic and drank himself into a stupor every day and never left his apartment. Part of me wasn't surprised. I'd known he needed help. I tried to convince his agent to talk to Jack, to let me see him, but it didn't work. Pat got on the phone to speak with the agent, but it was no use. He kept repeating that Jack was a hopeless case who never went out anymore.

Except to astral travel across the Atlantic Ocean and visit me,

I thought. But somehow I didn't think the agent was going to understand that. It was devastating. Not only was Jack a hopeless, impoverished drunk, but also there was no way I could get to him.

I felt frantic with frustration. In my dreams Jack was not a loser; he was a smart, handsome man begging for my help. Who was the real Jack? When anyone gets devoured by drugs or alcohol, their souls are in hiding on another plane. Addictions are a kind of possession and to recover our true selves, we need help remembering who we really are. David remembered who I was, and because he did, I could come back from Erik. He held on to my core. I wasn't looking for a needy alcoholic. I was looking for the real Jack on the spiritual plane.

Margaret and Pat consoled me, and I tried to accept that somehow Jack had led me to them, that this was, for some reason, exactly where I was supposed to be. I had a home in England at last.

I started flying back and forth all the time. I'd be home for a few months with David, and then I'd know I had to go back. It was like I got the Batman signal and I had to drop everything and go. Usually it was a dream about Jack.

Around this time, the musician Morrissey came out with a song called "Little Man, What Now?" "A star at eighteen / And then—suddenly gone . . ." It was about how fleeting celebrity could be and it was rumored to be about Jack Wild. Pat and Margaret cut out an article for me about the song. It turned out Morrissey couldn't get to Jack Wild either, although in the article it did say that Jack lived somewhere in the vicinity of Richmond.

I started walking around the streets and parks of Richmond hoping that I might run into him. Was I a stalker? I didn't feel like one. I had this knowledge within me that if I could only connect with him, he would be all right . . . and I would be all right. Maybe I was insane, but I never ran into him, as much as I hoped that I would.

David got used to me flying back and forth. He was very preoccupied with his medieval adventures, and there wasn't much romance in our relationship anymore anyway. We were old friends, best friends, two abandoned kids making a home together as best we could. I always felt a certain amount of relief when I came back to him, but I never felt any pressure from him to hang around when I needed to go.

I did a lot of readings when I went to England, which helped pay the airfare. It was a really different experience from being a psychic in New Jersey. I'd go to the pubs and sit in a corner, and people would come over to me very respectfully. The men would doff their hats and place a few coins on the table. The women always said, "Thank you, madam," and, "God bless you," when we were done. I didn't feel like these people were as spiritually empty as the people I met in America. They didn't want my life force. They had an old-world respect for oracles, even if they didn't consciously know it. I knew I had found my people.

Pat and Margaret always used to say to me, "You belong here. You're not like an American." But my husband and my cat and my parents were in America, so I never felt like I could stay.

I went to a lot of Donovan's concerts, got my name on the backstage guest list any number of times, but Donovan himself never wanted to meet me. In fact, he ran away from me when he saw me. I felt like he was afraid of me. I did readings for him at a distance. Pat brought me Donovan's harmonica to see what I could get from it. I knew all of his secrets, said Pat. It didn't make any difference to me one way or another.

Strange things often happened when I visited Pat and Margaret. Once, I was doing a reading for some of their friends in their living room and this old-fashioned rotary phone started ringing incessantly through the session. Pat and Margaret just sat there staring at it.

"Aren't you going to answer it?" I said.

"It's not plugged in," said Margaret, wide-eyed. "It's just for show."

The phone was still ringing as Pat lifted the receiver. There was no dial tone. Another time, a record player that wasn't plugged in began to play.

But Pat and Margaret weren't scared by these kinds of things. Not at all. It was just kind of interesting to them. What was strange to me was that from my very first trip, I experienced unusual hip pain from the moment I landed in Heathrow. Maybe it was just the dampness, but even when it was hot and sunny and beautiful I'd still find myself with this terrible limp that I never had back in America. My hip and knee would go out the moment I walked into the airport terminal. I'd be walking down Portobello Road like I was Richard the Third. Once it was so bad I needed to be pushed in a wheelchair around the London Zoo. The rheumatoid arthritis of my childhood came back when I went to England. It was very strange and I couldn't help but feel it was some echo from a past life.

I think a lot of ailments are connected to past lives—breathing difficulties, sore throats, stomach pains. That asthma might be the memory of smoke inhalation. That knife in your back might really have been a knife in your back. I know a woman who can't stand to wear turtlenecks, and I'm convinced it's because she was beheaded more than once.

You can't prove this, of course, but one thing I've noticed is that when people connect to these past lives, their health problems often disappear. Chronic illnesses often have deep-seated connections to reincarnation. Birthmarks can be echoes of old burns and wounds. A kid I saw with a hole in his heart had been speared as a soldier. Sometimes children are born with deformities because they haven't had enough time to heal in the afterlife. They've come back too quickly or the injury was too upsetting for them to let go of it.

The dead need time to heal. The etheric body needs to be healed as well as the physical body.

I think I came back too fast, and that's why I was like a jaundiced old lady with rheumatism.

Still, my London limp didn't stop me from having fun in England.

On one of my visits, I brought a friend with me who was as eager to prowl the London streets as I was. By the Thames is a replica of the Egyptian Sphinx, and my friend Annette and I decided to spend the night between her paws and watch the sun rise over the river. We were two attractive girls alone at night in a big city. But I felt totally at peace, totally happy. Just as the sun rose, two handsome guys approached us. They said they were artists, squatters, and beggars, and they invited us back to the run-down building where they were hanging out for a cup of tea. And we went. Just like that. With a couple of self-professed beggars. It was probably one of the craziest and most dangerous things I've ever done, but I didn't feel scared at all.

I guess that's the thing about being psychic. I may not be

able to do readings for myself, but I do trust my intuition. And I knew these guys were sweet and harmless. We followed them into this decrepit building. They had pasted their poetry and art all over the walls. They had rigged up a hot plate and they made us tea and gave us crumpets. I felt very settled there. Maybe it's because of my real father, Steve, or my own past lives as a beggar, but I've always been comfortable around the homeless. Evil does scare me, but it's usually not inside of people like this. It's not even really inside the mafiosi or the thugs in the bars. No. Where I see real evil is in the witch burners. The righteous do-gooders. The Rick Santorums. Those are the people who scare me. And the people who hurt animals, the rich boys who fly to Africa to bag a cheetah or cut the tail off an elephant. Their lack of respect for the life around them I find disgusting. The most evil things are always at war with nature.

But as Annette and I were sitting there with our squatter-artists, I began to have a prickling, eerie feeling. It didn't feel like I was in danger exactly, but that danger was or had been nearby.

"Did anything ever happen in this building?" I asked the boys sitting on the floor across from us, sipping their tea.

"Oh yeah," answered Mark. "This is White Chapel, after all. Jack the Ripper is supposed to have killed his first victim right around here, probably in this building."

I explained to our new friends that I was a psychic and I could feel that energy. They didn't seem to be freaked out. "That's cool," they said. So many people I met in England were almost blasé about the fact that I was psychic. They were connected to spirits, to hauntings, they lived in a country that was thousands and thousands of years old, and they still had a connection to those old energies. Graves are everywhere in England, and everyone knows it.

When the beggars found out I was psychic, they wanted to know if I'd ever been to Stonehenge, which I hadn't. We ended up going to Glastonbury first and getting to Stonehenge after it had closed. There was a full moon in the sky.

Stonehenge is inside of this compound now and you can't get very close to it, but I felt this almost primal urge to touch the stones. "Get me as close as you can," I said to Mark and Tony. I'm very small, and together they picked me up and held me over their heads like I was flying, so I could see over the wall. And then they began running as fast as they could so I could see the stones up close. Guards were shining flashlights at us and yelling at us, but I didn't care. The moon was full and I was at Stonehenge and I was flying.

Every visit to England felt this charmed, but I couldn't make a decision to live there. Annette came home from our trip together, quit her job, moved back, married a bloke, and settled in Nottingham. But I was torn and confused about where I was supposed to be.

I brought various friends over with me to help me get clear about it all. One time, I brought my sister, and we did all the touristy things together and finally found ourselves at Canterbury Cathedral. It's so massive and beautiful, and maybe it was the medieval setting or something, but I saw a man in front of the entrance steps offering Tarot readings and I was sure he was the real thing. He had long dark hair and a long dark beard, and I was sure in an instant that this was the guy who could explain where I'd been and where I was supposed to be now.

I waited in line patiently while my sister took the tour through the cathedral to see the stained glass.

Finally, I sat down opposite him, respectfully passed him a five-pound note, took a breath, and asked him to tell me what he saw. He had very mystical eyes and stared at me intently for a long time before he spoke. He spread out a Tarot pack before me and told me to choose five cards and lay each one down on the table faceup. I relaxed, I let my mind grow still, and I pulled out a card. And then another. And then another. Honestly, I don't remember what the cards were, because the next thing I know the psychic was consulting a Tarot interpretation book on his lap.

"That's not how you do it!" I screamed.

"What do you mean? Of course it is."

"No, it's not. Anyone can read a book. I can read my own book. If you're a real psychic, you should be able to look at me and just know things."

"Like what?"

I was furious and I could feel that trapdoor in the back of my head opening wide. "Like the fact that your father was too strict and used to spank you all the time and then when he left when you were eight years old you thought it was your fault. His name is Allan, isn't it? And he died a few years ago. You've never been to his grave, but he wants you to go. Bring lilac when you go. Those were his favorite flowers."

"How did you do that?" He was pale and stricken, collapsed in his chair.

"Do what?"

"Know those things about me. Who told you?"

"I just got off the tour bus. No one told me. I saw it. I'm a psychic. That's what psychics do."

He leaned close to me, a look of amazement on his face. "Can you teach me to do what you do?"

"No," I said, which was true, but I was too enraged and disappointed to just walk away. "Look, I came to you because you looked like you knew what you were doing," I said in one last desperate attempt to get some truth out of him.

"I don't know what I'm doing," he said hopelessly. "Please teach me how to be real."

I stood up and walked away, but the line of people behind me waiting to see him followed me into the cathedral, begging me to do readings for them. I ended up getting back on the bus way before everybody else just to escape them. No matter where I went, people wanted me to look into their lives, but I couldn't find anyone to tell me about my own. "You're going to be married three times." "Someone will propose to you, but you should stay in your own house and just visit him on the weekends." I said that stuff all day long. Should I move to London or stay in New Jersey? I didn't know.

"How's whatsisname?" Pat would ask me about David when I came to London, challenging me to leave him.

One of the worst things that I've ever done as a psychic was tell Pat during a reading that he was going to leave Margaret. I saw it. It was true. But I shouldn't have said it. And when he did finally leave her, I felt totally responsible. It broke up our friendship, needless to say.

But just before everything fell to pieces, I did one last channeling session at their flat. It was in October of 1987, but it was an unseasonably warm night. They invited over a lot of friends, and I sat in a red velvet chair with everyone arrayed around me and just let loose with whatever I saw about anyone there. Usually it was a very relaxed kind of atmosphere with people drinking beer, but that night I could feel something in the air, although I didn't know what it was.

People have often asked me if I have a spirit guide or an angel who tells me these things, but it's not like that. It's more that I connect with the spirits that people bring into the room. Or at least that's what I'd always thought.

But that night I shut my eyes for a moment and heard a sound like oars splashing in water, of feathers ruffling the air, and when I opened my eyes, there, standing in front of me, was a seraphim—an angel. She was slender and very, very tall and wore simple blue robes. She was staring into my eyes, and her wings were spread around her. Her wings were covered not in feathers, but in open, all-seeing eyes.

I was not afraid, but my blood was cold in my veins, and there was that moment, there's always that moment, when I questioned my sanity.

There was nothing shimmery or vague about her. She was a real being, a being of enormous presence, completely filling that tiny room. I call her a she, but there was something androgynous about her, and she was more than seven feet tall. I could tell no one else in the room could see her. I hadn't been calling on angels, I hadn't been calling on anything, but there she was.

The room was cold. I could see people shivering. Inexplicably, Margaret began to cry.

I knew we were all protected in the angel's presence and yet, simultaneously, I felt the smallness of human beings and everything we've ever done. Beneath the vast sky, even Stonehenge is small. We are all little men about to disappear, and there are beings so much bigger and more powerful around us than we can possibly imagine. We are too small to even see the spirits that are everywhere around us. How can a gnat comprehend what it is seeing when it looks at us? How can it read our expressions or our gestures, understand our motivations, or even know what we are?

She was showing herself to me in a way that I could see, but I knew she was so much bigger than this in reality.

I can dismiss a lot of things that have happened to me, but not this. In those tiny rooms in Lambeth I saw an angel, and I was never really the same ever again.

She stared at me for a long time without saying anything before she disappeared, but when she did, I remember looking out the window and seeing the sky turning red, absolutely crimson, and a strange wind beginning to blow. She might have been there for a second or an hour. I never knew.

I realized that I was crying and everyone was staring at me.

Life would never be the same again. That knowledge surged through me. It was exhilarating. I wanted to run out in the streets like some doomsday madman proclaiming, "The angel has come! The angel is here!"

But I could barely form words, I was so overcome. "Did you see that?" I whispered.

"Look at that red sky!" said Pat.

"The wind's really picking up!" announced Margaret.

"I've got to get home," said one of the guests.

All they could talk about was the storm that was brewing. I could tell they'd all been unnerved, but they attributed it to the weather. They wanted to leave. Angels are overwhelming even when you don't see them.

There were reports on the news of a rare hurricane about to strike London. I had a friend, Gloria, who was back at our hotel, and Pat thought I should probably get back to her, that the storm was about to get a lot worse. But what I wanted more than anything at that moment was to be outside.

I felt a wildness within me as I stepped onto the street and the winds began to howl. I ran through the rain feeling elated and empowered. I had seen an angel, and it didn't matter if the world was about to end because I knew there really wasn't any such thing as an ending. There's no death, only constant wild and wonderful change, and I felt absolutely like part of it that night.

The sidewalks were covered in leaves and fallen branches. Glass was starting to break, and the sky was even redder than before. I felt completely like part of the crazy energy of the storm. I reached my hotel and ran inside and begged Gloria to come outside and revel in it with me. She thought I was nuts, and I probably was, a certified lunatic, ready for Bedlam.

She locked the hotel room door and ordered me to stay inside. I went to the window and watched the swirl of the rain and felt exuberant and mad. Windows were shattering. Trees were crashing down. Sirens were blaring. At last, somehow, I settled down and went to sleep, but sometime in the night, during the storm, I awoke and there, standing at the end of my bed, was the man in the black hat.

It had been years since I had seen him, and I had forgotten how completely terrifying he was.

His eyes were neither blank nor on fire, as they had been when I was a child. Now they were red, as bright red and glowing as the sky. I felt a gust of dead air. Like a scared child, I pulled my blankets over my head, shut my eyes, and hoped he'd disappear by the time I woke up again.

I thought he was connected to the end of the world, to death and destruction, in ways that I couldn't understand. I felt like he might signal Armageddon. That's what he made me feel like. Crazy. The sky was red, his eyes were red, and sirens were blaring, and the flashing lights of ambulances were casting a red glow into the night. It felt biblical. Something was happening in the spiritual realm that I'd glimpsed but didn't understand

All the spirits had come out to play.

I didn't know that less than a mile away from my hotel room, Jack Wild was drinking a bottle of vodka when the only tree in his yard crashed onto his roof. For the first time in his life, he got on his knees and started to pray. He prayed that God would help him stop drinking.

When I opened my eyes in the morning, the man in the black hat was gone.

Trees fell, cars were crushed, and people died that night. It was a major national disaster, the worst storm to hit London in hundreds of years. David heard about it on the news and panicked. I was calmer than I had been the night before and I felt near me, again, the presence of my angel, even though now I could not see her.

When I got back to New Jersey a few days later, I started to do group channeling like I had done in London. Now every time I sat down with a group of people, I would feel my angel behind me. I never saw her again, but I knew she was there guiding me. She spoke through me, and she spoke much more politely and properly than I ever did.

I would shut my eyes with everyone sitting in a circle around me and then my head would turn in the direction of the person she wanted me to talk to, although she rarely spoke about personal issues. The angel had things to say about what was coming. She was prophetic. Years later I would realize that she had predicted the first Iraq war and the attack on the

Twin Towers, but she spoke more than anything about what was happening to the Earth.

If human beings cannot learn at last to respect nature, the world will get rid of us. It could happen at any moment. She didn't say how, but she wanted people to know how the Earth had been violated, drilled, abused, and raped, and that the Earth herself was a living, breathing being that could fight back. And would.

This wasn't news to me.

And honestly, I don't think it's news to most people. We just don't want to admit it. We don't want to know it. We don't know what to do about it.

One night a number of months after I had returned from England, my angel whispered in my ear that I was going to have a baby boy in 1992. She also told me that I needed to get to the Catskills, that in the Catskills I would be safe from what was coming.

I knew then that I had a ridiculous angel. Not only did I not want to be a mother, but it would totally cramp my style, and the only thing I knew about the Catskills was that it was a kind of run-down old resort area filled with big hotels and has-been comedians. All I could think of was *Dirty Dancing*. Why would I want to go there? Needless to say, I didn't take either of these two messages very seriously, which I suppose is the way a lot of people treat my readings. "What is she, nuts?"

In the beginning I often felt overwhelmed by the presence of my angel, but as time passed I began to doubt that she was real. I began to try to explain her. Maybe she was just my higher consciousness or something. I worried that I'd made it all up, that I really was crazy, that of course the one time I'd get a psychic reading of my own it would turn out to be a figment of my imagination. But that's the thing—the moment I stopped believing in her, she disappeared. I stopped clapping my hands and Tinker Bell died. Not that I think angels die, but she left. She never came back. I'm no different from anybody else, really. I have a hard time believing this stuff, too. I really do.

But, of course, everything the angel told me turned out to be true.

———

A lovely woman from Eastern Europe came to me because the house she'd just moved into was "unrested." She was sure it had an unsettled spirit. Every night when she was trying to fall asleep, she heard footsteps in the upstairs hallway running back and forth.

I saw a little boy, lost and unhappy, as she was speaking.

"Buy a teddy bear for him," I told her, "and put it in the room at the end of a hallway. That will help him feel less upset and give him a place to go."

She came back to me a few weeks later to tell me that the teddy bear had done the trick. But now she felt attached to this boy. Sometimes she went into the bedroom and bounced a child's ball for him. She brought him little presents. She even set up an altar for him, whoever he was.

She wasn't sure he was even in her house anymore, and neither was I, but she had come to love him and she felt like that love would take care of him wherever he was.

Ghosts don't have to be frightening. They usually just need our help. This child just needed to be acknowledged. We can help them. They can help us.

Even now, so many years later, the woman includes him in her prayers.

12

Walking an Anaconda Is Easier than Thanksgiving with My Mother

I didn't want to have children. I didn't really like babies. I'd never babysat, never changed a diaper. I don't even think I'd ever had a baby in any of my past lives. My mother always used to say, "I hope you never get pregnant. You'd be a terrible mother." I was really good about using birth control because of that. But I did yearn for some kind of family experience, probably left over from watching *The Waltons* when I was little.

My Daddy had passed away from cancer while I was with Erik, and my mother was increasingly needy. She became extremely helpless, and my sister took care of the bills and details of my mother's life. She couldn't drive. She didn't know how to write a check. She didn't really know how to do anything. She didn't read. She didn't visit with friends. She didn't have any friends. My sister tried to move out at one point, and my mother threw a fit and screamed that it was just because she wanted to have sex. My sister stayed. My mother made it impossible for my sister to have her own life.

My mother's one experience of being alive had been her affair with my father, but she denied its importance and pretended it had never happened because it didn't jibe with some pious idea she had of herself. If Steve's name came up, she would say that he had forced himself on her. I guess he forced her to make bacon and eggs for his breakfast for ten years, too, and I guess he forced her to fly to Florida and drive cross-country and go to the movies on the weekends. Sometimes she'd glare at me and shake her head and say that I looked just like him. It upset her. She was so ashamed of it, of me, but really it was the one thing she'd ever done that might have given her a little joy.

Steve would still reach out to her from time to time, I think. He would send her opera tapes and these movies that he'd copied onto videotape—beautiful classic movies—and she'd be like, "I don't want to look at these. I don't want any of this." And she'd pile them up in the corner, but she wouldn't throw them away. She'd sit in the room with the television on, not really watching it. She was miserable.

I asked her for his number from time to time, but she would explode and say that he had been a terrible father to me. "He didn't support you. He didn't take care of you. What did he ever do for you?"

Her rage was so upsetting that I almost never brought it up. More than anything, I still wanted her approval.

One Thanksgiving I arrived for dinner with David and I was wearing a new shade of lipstick—Chanel Vamp. It was dark red, almost black, and very elegant. Everyone was wearing it in the eighties. I felt fashionable and beautiful.

"Oh my God. You look like one of *those* people," said my mother the moment she opened the door.

For a moment I just stood there, speechless, winded. "I am one of those people!" I ended up yelling at her.

In my readings, I saw plenty of women who had wonderful relationships with their mothers: "My mother and I are really close. I can tell her anything."

"Oh, yeah, I was addicted to crack for a while, but my mom really stood by me."

"When my boyfriend broke up with me, my mom took me in."

Dead or alive, these mothers all seemed to be nicer than my mother.

The thing I've realized from my readings is that you've got to figure out your shit right here, right now; that's the only real way you can change your karma, whatever it is. We've all got our troubles, in this life, our past lives, and everyone else in our life does, too, and it's all interconnected.

It was around this time that I was struck by a vision of my mother huddled and alone in the corner of a large stone room filled with people. It might have been a hundred years ago or more. Her hair was shorn, she was wearing rags, and she was crying. It was some kind of lunatic asylum, I knew that at once, and she had no one. No friends, no family, no one.

Whether she knew it or not, and I don't think she did, my mother was carrying the memory of that life inside of her. No wonder she was panicked about being crazy; no wonder she was panicked about being left alone. I didn't tell her that I'd seen this, but knowing it sometimes helped me to deal with her.

The one thing we did enjoy doing together was going to thrift shops and rummage sales. My mother had a lot of style, and I liked listening to her talk about good-quality fabrics and the cut of a coat. She was always looking for a bargain, and she could find them, too. I admired that about her.

I just liked touching the objects. I could feel their energy and their stories. I'd touch an old jewel or a glass or a picture frame and connect to the people who had cared about it. I could feel their lingering essences. People don't realize it, but even the most inconsequential thing—an old thimble, a hairbrush, a sweater—every object that once was touched has a story to tell.

In the early 1990s, David and I moved to The Hills, a condo complex in Bedminster, New Jersey. My mother cosigned the mortgage for us in spite of her feelings about our marriage. We got approved for an apartment and taken immediately off the waiting list because I had done readings for so many people on the condo board. It was *the* place to live, with tennis courts and a swimming pool. But it had been built on an old Revolutionary War battlefield. On the one hand, it was a very normal, conservative kind of community. On the other, there was all this weird, powerful underlying energy that I really liked.

I didn't have any formal place to do readings, so I started doing them out of our home. David was working at the mall, at the Nature Place, and he'd come home from work and find five or six ladies sitting in our living room, like it was a bus stop. They'd all be lined up on the couch waiting to come into the kitchen with me for a reading. It was very intrusive into our daily life, I'm sure. But I felt like everyone who called deserved a reading, and it seemed like everyone was calling. I didn't advertise; it was all word of mouth. And I wasn't choosy about who came like I am now. No. I had accepted my calling. Doing readings was my job, and I had to do it no matter what. If people needed me, they needed me.

That was it. I had whole families coming to see me, one right after another.

People tend to come to me for years. Marriages, divorces, babies—I've seen it all before it happens and then it happens. Sometimes my own life seems strangely uneventful when compared with everything I'm seeing.

This one family was obsessed with me. They owned a chain of pizzerias and wanted to consult about every person they fired and hired. Once, in the middle of the night, they were ringing and ringing the doorbell to my condo. Their house had just been robbed! They hadn't even called the police yet. They'd come straight to me. The whole family had arrived, and the mother and father and their sons were all carrying their front door, taken off its hinges, put in the car, and lugged up to my apartment.

"They walked right through the front door!" they told me, pointing at the door. "Who did that?"

I was in pajamas, bleary-eyed, but I touched the door. "You know them," I said. "Three teenagers, they live down the street from you."

"Ha!" shouted the father. "I know who those wise guys are. You can go back to bed now, Suzan. We've got this under control."

I hungered for acceptance and approval. I was waiting for it. I suppose even if I couldn't help my mother, I could help everyone else. That's why I didn't say no to anyone. I was trying to heal everybody else in the hopes that one day maybe she'd walk into the room and I'd be able to do for her what I did for my clients. I think that's true of a lot of healers and therapists—they're people with a lot of pain inside. In any case, it was true of me.

I was happiest when David and I were working at the Renaissance Faire out in Sterling Forest, New York, where people had a harder time finding me. I didn't have to pretend to be normal there like I did at the pool at the condo.

David and I built ourselves a ship and went by the names The Ratlan Pirates. We dressed like pirates and sold crystals and flea market items, and I did readings. But I refused to have a booth on Mystics Way where all the other psychics and Tarot readers hung out. I wanted to be away from them. One of the people running the fair said, "No one will be able to find you." But I told him, "The people who are supposed to find me always do."

The truth is, I was embarrassed to be seen with the other psychics. I had kind of a big head, I suppose, though I don't know why. After all the readings I'd done, I still wasn't even sure if *I* was for real.

I used to dye my hair bright pink and wear a leather bikini with boots and a pirate hat. In the morning I loved to visit the owners of this enormous orange and white Burmese python. The python was huge, way too big to be a pet, but in the morning I'd take it out for a walk on a leash in the fields. It would slither from side to side with its head up. It was an absolutely gigantic snake, maybe twenty feet long, and I'd always get a little worried if one of the fair's midgets walked by. But it would mostly be quiet in the early morning with the dew still on the grass, the quiet sounds of people getting up and making coffee, the rustling of the snake.

One morning, the sun was barely up and there was a low-lying layer of mist over the fields while the snake and I shared our walk. I found myself throwing up beside a bush. The next morning the same thing happened. One of the knights in the jousting show who happened to be walking by asked me if I was pregnant.

"Can't be," I said. "I've been on the pill forever. I never miss a day."

"Whatever. I'm just saying," he added noncommittally, adjusting his helmet.

The next morning I threw up again, and I remembered at last what the angel had said to me. I went back to the pirate ship and took a pregnancy test. It was positive.

———

Two teenage girls came for an appointment that I was sure was going to be a breeze. Prom dates, high school gossip, maybe college plans.

But the moment they sat down in my reading room, I saw a girl between them. Her swollen eye was bashed in, her cheekbone was broken, and her neck was covered in bruises. She'd clearly been murdered.

"Who's Janet?" I asked.

The girls started screaming, "Oh my God, oh my God, oh my God!"

The night of the prom Janet had been found strangled in the dirt.

"But Janet says it's not the newspaper guy who did it. Not the black man they put in jail. I can see white hands on her throat."

The girls were screaming again.

"Steven killed her. She needs you to know that."

Now the girls were clutching each other, crying and shaking.

It turned out that a deliveryman who was kind of slow and disabled had been coerced into a confession and locked up. But Steven, a boy they all went to school with, had disappeared a month after the murder. He'd been stalking Janet.

The girls were hysterical, calling their mothers and their friends on their cell phones. But what could they do? A psychic's testimony wasn't evidence enough to reopen a murder case.

13

It Was Her Time, Whatever That Means

I didn't feel like I had ever known this spirit. I knew my baby was an old soul, but not one I had ever known until now. This was our first time together, I was sure of it, and I was really scared. A part of me was worried that my time with Erik had opened me up to some kind of evil that might hurt the baby. After all, I'd seen terrible things in my readings—babies born with deformities, stillbirths, children who died young. I knew there was darkness in the world, and I was scared.

Most of all I was scared that I wasn't up to being a good mother. I wasn't a normal woman, and my own mother certainly didn't think I could take care of anything despite the fact that my cat, Fiona, was still thriving. I told my mother I was pregnant on the Feast Day of Saint Francis, October 3.

"I've never wanted to be a grandmother. You knew that, didn't you?"

It was as if my pregnancy was some way of punishing her. My sister wrote to me that I should think about not having the baby. But I've never knowingly killed any being in my life. I save spiders. I don't swat mosquitoes. I was supposed to have this baby, and despite what my mother and sister had said, I was determined to celebrate my pregnancy.

I stopped taking the cold medication I was on at once. I stopped taking aspirin. I stopped drinking even a sip of wine. I ate well, better than I'd ever eaten in my whole life. I'm ashamed to admit that I even ate cheeseburgers. For the one and only time in my life, I craved meat, although I ate fast-food burgers so, like everyone else in the world, I could pretend they didn't come from animals. But they did, of some sort. Whatever those creatures were, I still ask their forgiveness.

But the biggest thing I changed when I got pregnant was that I stopped doing readings. I didn't want other people's entities coming too close to my baby. We needed quiet to get to know each other.

I've always been a little frightened of children, maybe because I was so bullied when I was little. But I also know they're not innocents. They arrive here with all of their own karma and then it gets mixed up with ours. It's not so much that babies are born with sin like the nuns used to say, but more that we arrive here with all kinds of past-life experiences and relationships, triumphs and tragedies having brought us to this moment. Everyone's got such a mix of good and bad karma behind them. You look into a baby's eyes and you know they've seen things, known things. I saw children like the thrift shop items I loved to touch—they have stories behind them and ahead of them. They aren't tarnished yet by the events of this life, but they are rarely ever brand-new.

At one point in the pregnancy, a man visited me at night. He was wearing a black cape, and he spoke with a British accent. He said his name was Michael. I don't know if it was Saint Michael—he certainly didn't seem like an angel—or just Michael. His energy was serpentine and he moved like a snake. I felt emanating from him the same dragon energy I had felt at Glastonbury and thought almost at once of St. Michael's Tower, at the top of the hill I had long ago visited.

His presence was comforting. A few days later I discovered that pregnant women often felt compelled to climb the Tor just before they gave birth. I couldn't get to Saint Michael, so he came to me. He reassured me that everything was going to be absolutely okay.

Right before I went into labor, I dreamed that a black bear visited me. I could feel the heat of his enormous body. He reached out his paw and took my hand and his claws were sharp. For a long time the bear and I held hands in my dream, if it was a dream. The bear told me that I was going to have a son and he would be big and strong.

I was in labor for thirty-three hours. Eventually I had to have an emergency Caesarian because both the baby and I were experiencing heart failure. When the doctor put the newborn in my arms, he was as blue as Krishna and absolutely huge. He was nine and one-half pounds, twenty-two inches long, and the first baby I ever held.

I named him Gavin, for the character Jack Wild played in *The Pied Piper* and for Gawain, the knight who served King Arthur, Arturo . . . "the Bear."

My mother was there when I gave birth, fighting with David over my prone, stapled body.

"She needs more pillows. She shouldn't be lying like that."

"She's fine," said David.

"She is not," said my mother, pushing him away.

Here I was, barely able to move after my surgery, and they were screaming at each other, actually shoving each other, about to fall into some Three Stooges routine with pratfalls and eye poking. But in the midst of my hysteria, I knew that David was protecting me from my mother, like he always did, as ridiculous as it could sometimes look. He wouldn't let her bully me. Finally, after they nearly came to blows, he got her to leave so we could have a moment of peace with our new baby. But after all that, my mother almost never visited her new grandchild.

I was on my own. Months would go by without me seeing her, which was fine by me. David's mother had long ago disowned us, so we didn't have any kind of guidance, but David helped out a lot; he was very paternal and would get up at night to feed and rock Gavin.

I just seemed to know what to do. Gavin made me laugh. I looked in his eyes and knew he was one of the oldest souls I'd ever met, so wise, so sweet, so gentle. I knew he was there to teach me, and that if I listened to him he would show me how to be a good mother. He guided me into motherhood. I had a big, fat, fair baby who looked like Henry the Eighth. He giggled and he laughed, and he was happy and as easy as can be. And I had a husband who loved getting up in the night and changing diapers. We would all snuggle together on the bed, including the cat. I thought as a family we could take on the world. It was a very special time. It wasn't hard, it wasn't scary, and you forget the pain.

When Gavin was one and a half, David and I took him to Glastonbury. We'd had him christened in a Catholic church soon after he was born, but I blessed his forehead with water from the Chalice Well and I knew that was his true baptism.

We climbed the Tor to St. Michael's Tower and we prayed to the God and the Goddess for health and happiness for our child. When we came back down to the ruins of the church, Gavin toddled over to King Arthur's grave, or at least where he's said to be buried in the Abbey, and sat down and started picking flowers and stuck them in his overall pockets until they were overflowing with blossoms. As we were coming home on the bus, a young man said, "That's the oldest child I've ever seen." It reminded me of my own first trip to Glastonbury. "He's been here before. He's from here," said the man.

Eventually I started to feel comfortable about doing readings again. Gavin was a very easygoing baby. When I would do readings in the kitchen, he would be there quietly playing, accepting the presence of a stranger, or he might fall asleep. All my loyal clients came back. The family who owned the pizza chain wanted me to help them with their investments. I always wonder how people coming to my little apartment could ask me about stocks and lottery numbers and horse races. Obviously, if I had that kind of knowledge, I wouldn't be a kitchen-table psychic. My gift is sacred; it doesn't seem to help people get rich.

One night when Gavin was barely two, he crept out of bed and pointed at a picture in a book of a man dressed in an army uniform who reminded me of Napoléon. Gavin announced, "That's my grandpa. I lived in a castle with him. He died on a horse in the war."

I also noticed that Gavin was terrified of train whistles and any kind of locomotive. Unlike other little boys, he hated toy trains, although he was happy enough with trucks and cars. If he heard a train, he would start screaming. I don't think it was just the noise, because other loud or high-pitched noises didn't bother him. I asked him what scared him and he said, "All of those people on the train, all of those people, all dead." My intuition was that he was having memories of the Holocaust, and as he got older I was not surprised that he would instantly turn off any movie or TV show that mentioned it.

I know most people would dismiss this as imagination, but I think if you believe in reincarnation you see lots of signs of it when kids are young. They still remember things from their past lives. They let you know all kinds of stuff if you listen.

David and I were still going to the Renaissance Faire, and it was like a great big playground for Gavin. He loved to play with toys of knights and dragons and unicorns. He wore a cape and had a little plastic sword that he carried around, and there were plenty of older girls there to help me watch out for him. It was a magical time. But as Gavin got older, it began to feel like a long way to drive from our condo, and it was harder and harder to keep an eye on him at the fairgrounds.

Then, out of the blue, I started to get all these calls from policemen to help them find missing children. Gavin came into my life—and all of a sudden there were all these cops wanting me to find lost kids. It was unnerving. There were a slew of them in the midnineties. That was when they first started to put kids' photos on milk cartons and do AMBER alerts. I'd be at the fair at our pirate ship and a cop would show up and say, "I hear you do missing kids." What they would do was consult me and a few other psychics and compare information, and if any of it matched they'd follow up on it. On the one hand, it seemed like a sensible way to handle this kind of thing; on the other hand, if you were consulting a psychic in the first place, why bother being scientific about it? What I mean is, I knew a lot of people who said they were psychics and really weren't.

The terrible thing was, all of the kids the police asked me to find were already dead by the time they came to me. Every single one. Nobody was ever alive. I'd know where the bodies were a lot of times. But every time I got a missing person? Dead. It was unnerving, especially as a young mother. It got to the point where I dreaded getting a call from the police.

Gavin was running all over the place, and it started to scare me because of what I was seeing. I got paranoid. I became one of those mothers who put their kids in a harness. Nowadays Gavin accuses me of walking him like a dog on a leash when he was a child, but we were in a huge public space with all kinds of strangers milling around and the police asking me to help them find some kid who'd been killed.

That was when we stopped going to the Renaissance Faire.

Meanwhile, back at the condo, I had mothers showing up who wanted to know if their kids were possessed. Something about becoming a mother had shifted my energy, and I was getting requests for different kinds of work.

Apparently, in the nineties there were a lot of possessed children. Or at least a lot of kids who were misbehaving. A few of them might have been demonic, honestly. They were certainly creepy kids. But I wasn't an exorcist. I did have some vials of water from Glastonbury, though, and I would give them to these mothers. I reasoned that if the mothers calmed down, maybe the kids would, too.

When Gavin was around four, I really felt, despite everything, that we should take him to church to learn about spiritual things. We joined this really beautiful Episcopal congregation. We'd get all dressed up and try to look like a normal family, and Gavin would go to Sunday school.

His best friend was this lovely little girl, Caroline. I remember on Valentine's Day she arrived at church dressed in red velvet with bows in her hair. She was so pretty. Gavin just adored her, and he loved going to Sunday school because of her.

The weekend after Valentine's Day, though, her family wasn't at church and Gavin was disappointed. After I'd dropped Gavin off in the schoolroom, I asked if anyone knew where they were.

"Didn't you hear?" said an older woman who was making coffee.

"No, no," I said, instantly concerned. I could hear the tragedy in her voice. "What happened?"

"Car accident." The woman shook her head sadly. There were tears in her eyes.

Caroline's aunt had wanted to take her to the Crayola crayon factory in Easton, Pennsylvania. It had been snowing the day before, and the roads were slick. The car skidded into a tree and Caroline was killed instantly.

I took it very hard. I couldn't stay at the church. David and I gathered up Gavin and went home. I didn't even know how to tell him yet about his friend; he was still so little. I couldn't stop crying. I couldn't do readings for days. I was utterly distraught. Caroline's death had touched on something very deep in me. Why? Why had this beautiful little girl had to die?

My mother called and I tried to explain to her what I was feeling. I was a mother with a child. Life was so precarious and death could be so seemingly arbitrary.

I knew from my past readings that children were never

alone or lost on the other side. Often I saw them with grand-
parents and pets and even long-ago ancestors. The children
never wanted people to grieve for them. They were never unhappy. But those were other people's children, children I
hadn't known when they were alive. Caroline was different. I
couldn't accept her death.

My mother was annoyed with me, "It's not like it was your
child, Suzan."

"Mommy, it's a child. Every child is someone's child."

I couldn't look at Gavin's crayons. I had to put them away.
Caroline had never made it to the Crayola Factory. I couldn't
look at all those bright colors for days.

I made an appointment with the priest at our church to
talk to him about how upset I was. For the first time in my
life, I was desperate for spiritual guidance. He showed me
into his sunny office.

"Father, why? Why did this happen?"

He looked at me without any doubt, any concern, any
confusion, and said simply, "Because it was her time."

"What?"

"She's in a better place," he added confidently. I think he
glanced at his watch. He seemed completely unaffected by
what had happened. He had this theology that explained
everything, and that kept him from feeling anything at all.
"What better place?" I wanted to scream. "What's better than
being with her mother and her family? That's all the dead ever
want. I know that. What do you know?" But I didn't say any
of that out loud.

It was her time. That's all he could say. Pat phrases. Clichés. Meaningless words. I don't know what I was expecting,
but what I wanted was for him to put what had happened

into some kind of spiritual context for me. *Why* was it her time? What did that even mean?

I left that church and we never went back.

But then, almost a year later, I got a phone call for a reading. It was a new client, and I gave her directions to my condo, and we set up an appointment for the following afternoon. When the bell rang, I opened the door, and standing there was a very thin, dark-haired woman, very pretty. It was Caroline's mother.

The expression on her face was as surprised as my own. "I didn't know it was you. I'd heard that there was a local woman who could contact the dead, but I didn't know it was you." We both started to cry.

After we had hugged each other and calmed down, I led her into my kitchen. Gavin was playing on the floor with his knights. He looked up at her and smiled. I'm not sure if he remembered her.

I didn't even need to take out the cards. The moment we sat down I could see Caroline beside her. "It was my time," said Caroline.

The priest had been right, only he hadn't known what he was saying. I wasn't sure I understood what Caroline was saying either.

"I'm coming back, though," she told me happily. "I *am* back."

"You're pregnant, aren't you?" I asked Caroline's mother.

"No. I don't know. Maybe." She was startled by this information.

"You're pregnant," I told her. "With a girl. It's Caroline. She's already come back."

Caroline's mother began weeping uncontrollably. "That's

all I want," she said, "but why? Why? Why did she have to leave me?"

She told me then what had happened the day before Caroline died. It had been snowing, softly, heavily, and she had been unable to find her little girl anywhere in the house and became panicked. But then, through a window, she had glimpsed Caroline outside in the backyard in the snow. She wasn't making snow angels or snowmen. She was sitting absolutely still with her back against a large tree, her eyes halfway shut and the snow swirling all around her. "She was like a little Buddha out in the snow," said her mother. "She didn't look like a little girl. I called to her. 'Caroline, what are you doing out there?' But she didn't answer me. She could hear me, I could tell, but she just sat there. The snow was covering her, making her disappear."

"She knew she was going to go," I said softly.

"Yes," said her mother. "She was so peaceful, but already so far away."

"But she's not far away anymore," I said. I could see Caroline touching her mother's arm.

"I knew she was back. I could feel her come back," said her mother. "But I thought I must be crazy, that I was just wishing for it so, so hard. But I could feel her close again."

"She's back."

That afternoon Caroline's mother called me. She was pregnant, and eight months later she gave birth to a baby girl.

I still don't know why Caroline had to leave in the first place. Was she sacrificing herself for something? For what? Was she needed elsewhere? Where was she going? I have so many questions these days about life and death, reincarnation and heaven. Why was I even born? What am I supposed to be doing with my life?

For all the women who show up wanting to know if their boyfriends are cheating on them and the men who come hoping for some fast track to wealth and power, there are people who come to me like Caroline's mother, and I feel like together we touch something vast and mysterious and important. That's when I'm glad I do what I do, as hard as it sometimes is.

———

A couple came in who had recently lost their dog. I could see him at once. His big golden head was resting in the woman's lap.

"Yes!" exclaimed the man. "He was a golden retriever."

"Tell my mommy that my kidneys failed," the dog told me. "But I don't know what kidneys are."

The woman began to cry. "He did die of kidney failure. Poor thing. Is there another spirit there to watch over him? To hold him when he gets scared? He was such a big baby."

"He doesn't need anyone else but you," I told them. "He wants you to know that where he is now there are no thunderstorms and there is no night and he is never alone." The words shot out of me and I knew they were true.

14

Burn Me, Drown Me, Kill Me . . .
I Just Keep Coming Back

I was hearing the whistling sound a bomb makes before it explodes more and more often now. I've always had flashes of different times. I think everyone does, but they dismiss the intuitions as a vivid imagination or channel them into some enthusiasm for learning everything about a particular period in time. We all have interests and fears connected to who we once were. But I was becoming overwhelmed by memories of the Blitz in London during World War II, and I didn't really know why.

Every time I would shut my eyes, I'd see bombed-out buildings or the murky underground rooms of an air-raid shelter. Songs from the forties were stuck in my head. I kept hearing Vera Lynn crooning "A Nightingale Sang in Berkeley Square." "When two lovers meet in Mayfair, so the legends tell / Songbirds sing. Winter turns to spring." These visions were becoming ever present and increasingly upsetting. I wanted to let go of them so I could be in my life with Gavin and just be his mom.

I mentioned all this to a client one day, and she suggested I consult with her sister, who was a hypnotist. She helped people process karmic information about reincarnation, but she wasn't all new-agey about it, said my client. She was a real psychologist who did hypnosis on the side. "She's not a flake."

I immediately made an appointment with her, and David drove me to her office the following week.

She was a very ordinary, settled woman with a traditional-looking office—magazines in the waiting room, a potted plant or two. She explained to me that she mostly used hypnosis to help people quit smoking and lose weight. She was more clinical than spiritual. Still, she said she'd helped people "go back" a number of times to conquer phobias. She told me that fears about flying or snakes or spiders were often connected to past-life traumas.

I explained to her that I wasn't a particularly fearful person, but that I felt like there was something I needed to know from my last life so that I could let go and be fully who I was supposed to be in this life. She understood what I was talking about without too much more explanation.

I lay on a couch in her room. It was very comfortable. The lights were dim. Drapes covered the windows. She counted backwards and told me to listen to the numbers and let myself drift into a relaxed state. I let go and began to fall the way I do in readings. My eyes were shut. Apparently, I am very easy to hypnotize.

"What do you see?" she asked softly. "Look down at your feet. What kind of ground are you walking on?"

But there was no ground. There was the piled wood of a pyre and there was smoke. Flames licked at my bare feet.

"You are looking at the moment of your death," she told me.

I was burning.

There was no experience of physical pain, but I knew I was seeing the moment when my spirit had separated from my body. It wasn't frightening. There's no reason to be scared of that moment. *We've all done it before. We're all going to do it again. Here we go again*, that was the thought in my head.

There were people standing around and staring at me. My hair was bound and long. There were mountains nearby.

I wonder if this is why I can never strike a match or light a candle. I'm not afraid of fire itself; it's just that first moment a flame bursts into being that unnerves me. Maybe that's what I'm remembering; maybe that's why I don't ever have candles or incense in my house. I just can't do it, but I do love staring into the flames. Once the fire is roaring, it's not frightening anymore; it's exhilarating.

"What else do you see?" asked the hypnotist.

I was somewhere else now, and I was being burned again. There was another pyre beneath my feet. I could smell smoke. I saw a huge cathedral like Notre Dame and the stone steps leading up to it. There was something I wanted to say, that I had been trying to say, but they had burned me before I could speak. I was in France. I hated France. I would never go back to France. I'd go to London.

I'm not sure how the therapist got me there, but next I saw myself, a chubby little girl hiding in a house. I felt a longing for the mother and the father of that life. That mother had cradled me in her arms when I was a little girl. We had sung together. I saw a room with faded rose wallpaper that I knew from my dreams. It was a poor house, but it was filled with flowers and love. That mother had loved me the way I loved Gavin, with all her heart, with joy, with celebration. I don't think she ever knew I was a psychic, I died when I was so young in the Blitz, but it didn't matter. She had loved me.

I was peeking out through the window and I could see soldiers marching by, and I could hear the steady rhythm of their footsteps. I knew my older brother was a soldier. He had gone off to war in a green woolen uniform. The texture of that uniform was very real to me. I knew he'd been killed. I saw men with headlamps looking through the rubble for bodies. I was running down a street and heard the bomb going off. I was killed in the Blitz. I felt the fire. Always fire. And more fire.

I could smell something acrid—a mixture of gasoline and burning rubber. I was dying slowly. I was burned and crushed beneath the rubber. But again there was no pain, only a consciousness that I was going somewhere else, to a place where the angels were.

Why did that little girl have to die in the bombs in London during World War II? It seems so unjust, so unfair, so wrong.

But what I saw was that the brief, loved life of that child was a gift to me.

We take love with us from lifetime to lifetime, and I had that mother's love inside of me. I hadn't known until now how much her love had sustained me during the sufferings of this lifetime. That short life had been a little recess from the challenges of my so-called gift. When I was born in this life, I was again an old woman, the weary, well-worn psychic who had seen and known too much, but there had been a family, a mother, a father, and a brother who had loved one another. In five short years I'd experienced lifetimes of love. I wanted us to be together again. I wanted my brother again. He was waiting for me on the other side. He had already died.

I called out a name as I was dying. "Jack! Jack! Jack!" I must have called the name out loud in the room.

"Jack?" whispered the therapist. "Who is Jack?"

"Jack, Jack, Jack," I repeated. "It was the name of my brother who had died in battle during World War II. I've got to get to him. I've got to find him."

"He's gone," she said. "That time is gone."

"No, he's not gone. I've got to find him. He came back. He came back to find me. Jack. It's Jack."

"Jack who? Can you remember anything else?"

"Jack . . ." I could feel a name emerging from deep within me. "His name this time is Jack Wild."

I knew this with an instantaneous conviction. The older brother I had lost during the war and longed to see again was really Jack Wild. He had been reborn as Jack Wild. That was why I'd always wanted to find him again. I had to find him in this life. I knew it at that moment. He was my brother. He really was. We had been brother and sister in our last lives, we had both died during the war, we had both been reborn during the fifties, and we had some even greater, inexplicable connection in this life. But what was it?

"We're going to go further back," the therapist told me.

Usually in these sessions you go from one life to another in a straight line, but my lives were all out of sync for some reason. I suppose time is always very fluid for me—the past, the future, the present, it's all happening at the same moment for me.

I was in a cave with bars across it. The walls were soft yellow limestone, wet to the touch. With my finger I was scratching my name into the wall. Estella. The cave was so small that

I could barely stand up in it. I could hear waves crashing at the shore, smell the salt in the air. Maybe I was in Cornwall, maybe Brittany. It was somewhere wild like that. I saw my father coming to the other side of the grate. It was he who had locked me in. He would bring people to me for readings, but only people he chose. There were things I knew that no one else should know. There was no mother in that life, she had died, and I was alone with this terrible man.

He wore a wide-brimmed black hat.

I was about to scream, but I saw his eyes and they were not the vacant eyes of the man who terrified me. Only the hat was the same, as if this man was a strange echo of the figure that had haunted my childhood. This man was a Puritan, a witch burner. His name was Axelrod. Somewhere nearby were my rescuers, David and Richard. My perpetual guardians, one lifetime to another.

I saw more fires, more burnings. Again and again I was destroyed for what I was. Murdered. Raped. Beheaded. Burned. I saw myself kneeling before a block and trying to position my head properly in the indentation. I wanted to do it right this time. This time. I had so much practice at dying. I was frightened that it wouldn't happen fast. There was a rage in me, too, against the Pope. I knew he was one of my enemies.

I'll tell you right now, I can't remember it ever being easy for me. If some people see me as an oracle, there are others who have always wanted to kill me for what I am.

But Gavin wasn't in any of these old memories. Nowhere. I'd never been a mother before. There is something new about the life I am living this time. A mother at last.

I was very, very far back now. For a moment I saw white

columns. Egypt? Greece? Somewhere older than that? At last all I could see in a blue sky was a blue heron flying overhead.

I looked up at the heron flying away, and I knew what I was thinking at that moment. *I'm flying away, flying away . . . and then I'm coming back.*

I was sobbing.

So many people imagine that when they look at their past lives it'll be an ego boost, and they'll know for sure that they were Cleopatra or Anne Boleyn or King Arthur. They think if they can claim some celebrity in a past life, it'll justify their being a loser right now. But it doesn't work that way. You shouldn't live less of a life this time around because of who you used to be. Sure, we can all make up stuff about who we used to be. There's no way to prove any of this. Not really, anyway. But if we are ready to pull back the flaps of time and really see what's there behind us, we can begin to understand a little more about who we are right now and what we have to do. Every life makes us who we are, but we also get to a point where we get beyond what we were.

I look at those memories with some detachment. Yeah, I was there, but I'm here now—and that's what I have to think about.

Why was I born in America? It seemed like the first time I've ever been on this side of the Atlantic. Was it an accident? Are there ever accidents with these kinds of things? Gavin certainly wasn't an accident. He came despite everything. He was meant to be.

What I do know is that I have never been anything else other than a psychic. I saw that very clearly during my regression. This is what I have been and will always be. It's the only thing I can do. I have no other skills. None. Never have. But no matter how often I was silenced or executed or imprisoned, I just kept coming back doing the same thing. Put me in a cage, burn me, it doesn't matter. I'm not going anywhere. None of us are.

The therapist brought me back to this lifetime. She explained that she always stopped just at the point of death, because she didn't want me to experience any pain. I almost wanted to laugh. I had been at the moment of death in every lifetime and there wasn't any pain.

What I hadn't seen, though, was that place immediately after death that the Tibetans call the *bardo* realm. Why don't I have any memories of it, even though I've certainly been there plenty of times? Does anybody? Does anyone ever remember deciding to come back? Or can we only do that in near-death experiences? Maybe if we remembered that heaven, we'd all want to be dead and we wouldn't incarnate again.

Why do I choose to keep coming back? I guess I don't want to miss anything. Persecution, torment, poverty, immolation—who wants to miss it?

She was one of the happiest women who ever came to me for a reading, but she should have been the saddest.

I saw at once that she was surrounded by angels, and one of the angels was very young, just a little boy.

"That would be my son," she said.

"He drowned in a pool when he was only four," I said.

"That's right. But I know he's close. I feel him close. Thanks for confirming that. I always knew it was true. But still . . ."

She was completely serene. The drowning had happened a number of years before. Still, I thought she would be disturbed, even devastated, when she talked about it. But she wasn't. She was totally at peace.

I couldn't help but imagine what a mess I would be if it had been my son.

I am filled with wonder at the faith of some people. And it amazes me that someone like me, with such wavering faith, can help to strengthen theirs.

15

Has-Beens on Parade

Now I really had to find Jack. I was having more and more dreams about him. Increasingly it felt like he was communicating directly with me. He came one night wearing a tweed jacket, telling me he had to meet me. It was real, but also deeply strange. The dreams became more insistent, and I was obsessed with meeting him. I was beginning to sense that he didn't have much time left in this realm.

Here I was, married with a family, and I felt the same pull I had as a child to find this person. Was I just an obsessed fan, like the client who was convinced she was supposed to marry a movie star? It didn't feel that way to me, but it probably didn't feel that way to her either. The past-life therapy had confirmed that once upon a time Jack and I had been brother and sister, but what was our connection *now*? What kind of power could an aging has-been child actor exert over me? Was he part of my soul group in some way? I felt like I should have outgrown this fascination as an adult, and instead each day I was consumed by this nagging feeling that somehow I had to find him.

When Gavin was about four, a girl I used to know from the Renaissance Faire came to me for a reading about her work. I hadn't seen Nancy in a couple of years, and after the reading, she started catching me up on her love life. She was spending a lot of time at the home of her boyfriend, who was into computers, and she started explaining his work to me. This was 1996 and not everyone had a computer yet (David and I certainly didn't), and people weren't on the Internet all the time. She told me that her boyfriend consulted with this teenager who was a total whiz kid when it came to electronics. She was telling me we should drive up to her boyfriend's place, which was about an hour away, and talk to this kid about what kind of computer to buy.

"Everyone in town goes to this kid," she went on. "He's the master, and he's only fifteen years old."

All of a sudden I felt chills prickling up my arms. "What's his name?" I asked. I had an intuition about something. This kid mattered in some way.

"Josh."

Now I was really suspicious. "Who does he live with?"

"His grandmother. Way up in the woods, kind of hidden away from everyone. She's a strange duck. She doesn't let Josh go to school very much. She keeps him home a lot, kind of a homeschooler, but he really is a whiz. I'm telling you. He'll get you and David completely set up."

I was cold all over now. My mouth was dry. Josh was the name of the son David's mother had disappeared with fifteen years ago.

"Do you know what his last name is?" I asked Nancy.

"Wilson, I think."

It was David's mother's maiden name. We had found David's long-lost son at last. Or the spirits had found him. Someone had found him and brought him back to us. No question about it. Nancy called me back after she'd talked to her boyfriend and Josh. Josh didn't know his father, and his mother had abandoned him with his grandmother. It was David's son, all right.

At first David's mother resisted our attempts to get together, but eventually we wore her down, now that we knew where to find her, and David was reunited with his son at last. It was awkward, particularly for Josh, but slowly we found our way back into a relationship with him. We went to their house. Josh came to ours. I tried to forgive David's mother, because it was clearly better for him to be reunited with her, even if he was still furious about her betrayal. When she died a few years later of pancreatic cancer, it meant a lot to David to be with her.

If Nancy hadn't come to me for a reading out of the blue. If David and I hadn't met her at the Renaissance Faire. If. If. If. Is life filled with synchronicities and coincidences, or are some things destined to happen? What if the girl hadn't started talking about computers to me and mentioned this boy? What if?

One day, out of nowhere, when Gavin was about six, I flipped on the television and one of those entertainment shows was on (I didn't even have to change the channel), and they were talking about Jack Wild. Where was he now? asked the host. What had happened to him? I almost laughed out loud. That's what I wanted to know. The universe was on my side and answering my questions. The moment had come;

the stars had aligned. I sat down on the couch to watch the show.

First there was the retrospective of his career. Academy Award–nominated teen actor. Star of a hit sixties TV show. Gradual obscurity and alcoholism. I knew all this, but what I didn't know was that at last he'd finally gotten sober with the help of evangelical Christianity.

The show had some pictures of him today, and he looked terrible, ravaged by alcohol and cigarettes, his boyish good looks vanished. Still, his brown eyes, dark and soulful, were just as I remembered, and when I looked at him the desire to find him was too overwhelming to resist.

I asked David to find out what Jack was up to, and he began searching the Internet, using the computer Josh had recently given us. "He's going to be in California next month," David told me after just a few minutes. "Some kind of Hollywood autograph show."

"Really? Next month?"

"That's what it says. At the Beverly Garland Hotel." He read from the screen: "'Meet the stars up close and personal in one thrill-filled extravaganza! Guaranteed over one hundred and twenty celebrities in one room, including former child stars, Western heroes, sitcom favorites, pop heartthrobs, talk show hosts . . . even Academy Award nominees like Jack Wild, the star of *Oliver!*'"

"I'm going," I announced.

"Of course you are," said David supportively. I didn't have any secrets from David. It wasn't like I was heading out to California to seduce my childhood heartthrob. I had to meet this guy at long last. For some unknown reason. It was a psychic thing. I'd felt it almost my whole life. David understood that, even if the rest of my family thought I was completely nuts. That's the thing about David; he may not consult me, but he understands the spiritual life and its whims.

"Are you really going to waste money on this?" said my mother when she heard about my plans.

"I am," I said. I'd already bought my plane ticket and made a reservation at the hotel. I was going to stay at the same place the conference was being held.

I was trembling with excitement when the cab let me off in front of the Beverly Garland Hotel. I'd left winter in New Jersey far behind. The sun was out; there were palm trees and a pool and a fountain out front splashing water. I headed inside to check in. The conference started the next day, but I wanted time to settle myself and figure out what I was going to wear before I met Jack Wild at last.

A small, rumpled man was checking in ahead of me. He had dropped something out of his wallet and had stooped to pick it up. He had on a leather vest over a T-shirt and was wearing the same ankle-high Doc Martens with the fake crocodile skin that I was also wearing. They're unusual shoes, so I noticed them right away. Then, all of a sudden, this light went off in my head and I realized that it must be Jack in front of me checking in at the very same moment I was. I felt a connection to him that was beyond anything I had ever felt with anyone in my entire life. There was electricity, but also a deep inner sense of calm. I'd never felt anything like this in any reading I'd ever done. It was psychic energy, only much more powerful. This was a reunion. I knew it.

I tapped him on the shoulder. "Hi, Jack."

He whirled around and looked at me. He was scraggly and unshaven. He was no taller than I was.

He dropped something else, picked it up, and smiled at me, clearly a little surprised. "Oh," he said. "It's you." It was as if he'd been waiting for me, expecting me.

It was a surreal moment, outside of time. He wasn't surprised to find a stranger tapping him on his shoulder. He was looking at me as though he recognized me and had been looking forward to seeing me. He knew who I was. I knew who he was.

I didn't feel any of that nervousness you'd expect to experience meeting someone famous. I didn't even really think of him as Jack Wild the movie star. No, instead I was flooded with visions of that loving family in London, singing together, the faded roses of the wallpaper. The longing and the love were overwhelming. This was my family. This was my brother. This was my soul mate. I would never in a million years have imagined saying what I said next, but the words just tumbled out.

"Can I have a hug?" I asked.

Jack expressed neither alarm nor even surprise. Without any other words of introduction or explanation, he just opened his arms and welcomed me into an embrace.

Everything fell away. Names. Faces. Places. Time.

I was home.

What I experienced next was an almost instantaneous replay of my past-life regression. A barrage of lifetimes swept before my eyes. The rubble of the Blitz. A Victorian garret. A cave. An army of blue-painted Picts. In every lifetime there was Jack. We were holding each other in the lobby of the Beverly Garland Hotel and I saw lifetime after lifetime flashing before me. It was like falling down a wormhole. I saw myself sitting alone as a little girl in a movie theater watching him. I saw him in his house, his father yelling at him, his brother yelling at him. I could hardly breathe. We couldn't let go of each other.

Finally, he pulled away and took my hand. I looked down at our intertwined fingers. His hand was the same size as mine, with the same slender fingers and narrow nails. A delicate hand. "Our hands look alike," I said, amazed.

I knew I'd known this person for centuries, and that my connection with Jack was older than any I had ever known. We had found each other again. I noticed he had a huge silver cross dangling from around his neck.

Whoa, I thought, for the first time a little taken aback. *This is a major holiness situation.* This symbol of conventional religion was the only thing that worried me about him. Maybe he wouldn't like that I was a psychic.

"So," he said at last. "Do you want to go and have coffee?"

We hadn't known each other for five minutes and already we had the easy familiarity of old friends.

Still, I could barely breathe. "Let me just put my stuff in my room," I said. "I'll be right back."

The moment I walked away from Jack, I felt bubbly with hysteria. This was so strange. It was too weird. It was insane. It wasn't happening, only it was. I had thought I'd meet him in some big function room and ask for his autograph. Maybe I'd get a photo of the two of us together. Maybe I'd have the courage to tell him some of my intuitions about our connection. I had no idea that we'd fall into each other's arms and he would seem to feel as powerfully about me as I did about him.

Quickly I checked in, raced up to my room in the elevator, and once the door was shut freaked out a little more. Okay, I admit it, I had a full-blown panic attack. I was hyperventilating.

I couldn't sit still. Was this real? Was this crazy? It felt like the weirdest thing that had ever happened in my admittedly very weird life. I'd never felt a soul connection like this. Never. With anybody.

I decided I needed to fix my hair. I forgot to mention that I change my hair color a lot. It's one of the things I do when I need to calm down, and I'd brought some dyes with me. I don't know why I decided at that moment that it needed to be orange, but I did. I also decided I needed to cut it. But I only had manicure scissors in my bag. Still, I began clipping away. Halfway through my hatchet job I realized I looked very strange and decided I could only fix it with real scissors. I decided to run down to the lobby and see if they had any at the front desk. They did, and I dashed back to the elevator. But when the door opened, Jack was standing there astounded. My long brown hair was gone. It was now orange and spiked. And I was holding a giant pair of cutting shears in my hands like a weapon.

"You're a sad girl, aren't you?" He laughed with his Cockney accent. "C'mon, let's go for a drive."

Jack had a rental, a little Toyota that he steered like a madman, puffing on one cigarette after another as we zoomed around Rodeo Drive. He could barely see—because he was diabetic, he told me, from all the booze. He was blaring the Bee Gees from the cassette player. They'd done the sound track for a long-ago film he'd been in with Mark Lester. I'd loved it; it was a movie about British schoolboys.

"I have this memory of you filming it," I told him.

"How's that?"

"I know stuff about your life."

"Everyone does with celebrities."

"No," I explained. "It's different. I know things no one else knows. It was terrible how you heard about your mother's passing. You shouldn't have heard that way."

"What do you mean?" he asked sharply.

"You were in London in a play and you were just about to go onstage when someone appeared in the wings and told you. Right?"

"Yeah . . ." he said hesitantly, "That's what happened."

"I'm a psychic," I explained. "And all my life I've been seeing your life." I described the ramshackle building where he'd studied improvisation as a young teenager. I told him about his brother's jealousies, about his father's cruelties. I told him things no one could have known about the sets he'd been on, about how frightened he had been of the dog in *Oliver!*, about how he used to visit Houdini's house to look for ghosts when he was living in Hollywood for his TV show.

"Who are you?" he asked. He lit another cigarette and I pulled it out of his mouth.

"Don't kill yourself," I said.

He laughed and grabbed another. "I've almost died three times," he told me. "And the last time I saw the white light and Jesus waiting for me, the whole thing. But I kept coming back. I've wondered why. One day I woke up and said out loud, 'Dear God, please, if I'm meant to survive, make me stop drinking.' I've never taken a drink since."

"If you smoke, I'm going to smoke, too," I decided. I hated cigarettes, but I wanted to get his attention. I could tell he was killing himself, and I could see he was going to be dead soon. I knew it the way I knew these kinds of things.

But I didn't tell him that. And I didn't offer to read his cards, even though I'd brought them for just that purpose. I knew what they'd say. They'd say that he didn't have long to live.

We talked and talked that night as we drove up and down the avenues.

I don't think he was entirely human. Some people aren't. I'm not, that's for sure. Some of us are part fairy and Jack certainly was. He was one of the oldest souls I've ever met, but old souls don't always prosper in the modern world.

When he'd been the star of *H.R. Pufnstuf*, they'd had a big puppet in it that wore what looked like a marijuana leaf on its head. But Jack hadn't known that at the time. He told me he'd never really been into drugs, only booze. He told me even if he hadn't been a child star he'd still have been an alcoholic. "It's the way I'm made," he said.

We discovered that many times we'd been just a few blocks from each other. Once he'd stayed a few minutes from my house in New Jersey, and we had been within walking distance of each other during that strange hurricane in London. He, too, remembered how strangely red the sky had been that night. He told me about the tree crashing down in his yard and how he prayed.

He told me a lot of stories about his movies. He'd had a bit part in Kevin Costner's film *Prince of Thieves* a few years back and had hated it. "They got Robin Hood all wrong," he said, lighting another cigarette.

With his nicotine-stained fingers, his black hair and brown eyes, he reminded me at that moment of my real father. "My father knew all about Robin Hood," I said, and went on to explain how he used to dress up and frolic through Sherwood Forest.

"I'd like to meet that bloke," Jack said when I was done. "Sounds like my sort."

We ended up back at the hotel and sat in front of the fire for a long time. He asked about Gavin, and I showed him the picture of him I always carried.

Jack took it from me and was visibly startled. "What? Did we have a kid together? He looks just like me!"

I hadn't noticed it before, but it was true. The same brown eyes, the same hair, the same expression on his face, even. I couldn't fathom what the cosmic joke might be. He showed me a photo of his dog, but he didn't mention the girlfriend I knew he had.

"Who are you anyway?" asked Jack just before we parted at the elevators.

"I'm your little sister," I joked, remembering my past-life session. I hadn't told him yet about those memories.

Jack nodded. "That feels right," he said to me. "Okay, good night, little sis."

The next morning we had breakfast together, and Jack asked if I could help him out during the show. His assistant had come down with the flu and couldn't show up.

"What do I have to do?" I asked.

"You know, help me collect the money for autographs, that kind of thing."

"Sure," I said. "I'd love to."

The show, which was in the ballroom of the hotel, was really a collection of losers. All the has-beens and might-have-beens and one-hit wonders were sitting in front of tables heaped high with glossy photographs they were hoping to autograph and sell. It was a pretty pathetic group, and I'm including Jack among them. Cory Feldman, Gary Busey, James Darren, the guy who played the Incredible Hulk, Linda Blair. Jack was glad his table wasn't near hers, because he said *The Exorcist* had freaked him out for weeks. I went over to her and said, "Hi," though. I knew she was a big animal rights activist. There were a lot of minor *Star Trek* actors and a midget who'd been one of the original Lollipop Guild Munchkins in *The Wizard of Oz*. He was about a hundred years old and still going strong.

The thing is, we're all has-beens and might-have-been and could-have-beens. We've all been someone else, so many times.

While Jack and I were getting set up, this man who'd been a star in the sixties when he was a kid came over to talk to Jack. He was feeling overly sentimental and already weeping about the abuse he'd suffered on the set when he was little. He was sobbing about how he'd been drugged and beaten. He wanted to compare notes with Jack, but Jack just sort of laughed. "Yeah, but look, mate," he said to the guy. "Look at where you are now! Isn't it great?" Jack winked at me. There were clearly losers even among this group of losers.

By now a lot of people were filling up the banquet room, mostly middle-aged woman but men, too, and even some people in their twenties. Jack was surprisingly popular. There were a lot of *Oliver!* fans and people who had grown up watching *H.R. Pufnstuf*. The only problem was that Jack had forgotten to bring enough glossies to sell. Luckily, I'd brought a lot of old movie stills and lobby posters for him to sign, and I gave these to him, which seemed fair since he was buying all my meals. The books he'd written hadn't turned up either, but somehow I managed to get on the phone and track them down for him and get them delivered. But I didn't ask for one myself. Jack was surrounded by these weird fans and I really didn't want to seem like one of them. I wasn't one of them. I was something else.

"And what movie did you star in?" asked a woman.

"Oh, I'm nobody," I answered.

"That's not true!" said Jack. "She's somebody all right. She's my little sis!" He winked at me again.

Jack was terrible about his diabetes. He was eating candy and drinking soda. I kept having to remind him to take his insulin. He reminded me of my father, who was also diabetic and careless about his treatment. Jack even reused his needles, just like my dad. He really was a fucking mess, but there was also something wonderful and real about him, too.

Gary Busey, who'd once played Buddy Holly, stopped by Jack's table and said, "I really loved you in *Oliver!*"

"That guy is so full of shit," said Jack to me when Busey had left.

Women wanted to pose with Jack and have their pictures taken with him. A B-list blonde came over and flirted with him for a while. "What happened to your hair?" she asked me.

"She looks great," said Jack. "Don't talk to her like that."

"That's not lamb anymore," said Jack after the faded starlet had left. "That's mutton."

We both laughed. He was really very sweet to me. Throughout that whole day we talked and joked together. I've never found it so easy to talk to someone.

That night he was going out with Billy Hayes, who'd played Witchiepoo on *H.R. Pufnstuf.* She and Jack were still friends, and she felt very motherly towards him. She wanted to buy him some new clothes because after the show he was headed up to the Hard Rock Cafe in Seattle, where the coat he'd worn as the Artful Dodger in *Oliver!* was going on display.

"Do you want to come?" he asked me.

But I needed to rest after the day, so we arranged to meet later on by the fire.

I called my sister from the hotel room and told her that I wasn't coming home. "I'm staying with Jack."

"This is crazy," she said. "What about Gavin?"

"I'll come get Gavin," I said. "I have to be with Jack. I have to."

Then I fell asleep.

Now, usually, I am a very light sleeper. But that night the fairies made sure I wouldn't wake up. Later Jack would tell me that he had pounded on my door for over an hour and searched the hotel for me. But I was dead to the world. I slept for fourteen hours without waking once. Thank goodness, too, because the next morning I woke up and I knew something with that same certainty I have when I am in my reading room, and if I hadn't realized it, I might have made a terrible, terrible mistake with Jack.

What I remembered as soon as I opened my eyes after that fairy sleep was that my father's merchant marine ship used to dock in the port of Manchester in the 1950s. Manchester was where Jack was born in 1952.

I got dressed and went down to breakfast. Jack was already sitting at a table, and I joined him.

"Tell me about your mother," I said after he'd told me about trying to find me all night.

"She was blond," he said, "Very pretty when she was young. Her name was Vera. Her birthday was December 9."

"December 9?"

"Yeah, that's right. Why?"

"That's my mother's birthday, too."

"Is it?"

"It is. Isn't that strange? And you had a much older sibling, like me. And you didn't feel close to your father, like me. We have so much in common."

"That's true," said Jack.

"Hold up your hand," I said. "Look at our hands."

"They're the same. We could be brother and sister."

I took a deep breath. "Jack," I said slowly. "I think we are."

"Yeah, you're my little sis," he joked.

I shook my head. "My father was in the merchant marines and he spent a lot of time in England in the fifties. He had a lot of girlfriends. And your mother and my mother..." I didn't know how to explain it. "Could your mother have, you know, had an affair?"

I could see Jack trying to take this in. I didn't say anything. He didn't have to believe it for me to know that it was true. But sitting there opposite him in that hotel restaurant I knew he was my half brother, a brother in another life and a brother in this one. "That's why Gavin looks like you," I said.

"Little sis," he said, considering the name in a new light. "Well, maybe."

That day, in between the fans and the autographs, I told him about my past-life experiences, and he, too, it turned out, had memories of dying in World War II. He began to open up to me, too, about the voices he heard in his head. "I'd say I was crazy," he said. "But I've always known not to mention them to anyone."

I felt very protective of him. Motherly? No, sisterly. There was also the knowledge that if our lives had happened in different ways, he would have been my lover. He was my soul mate. It's just that in this life he was my brother again. I was sure of it.

Everyone who comes to me wants to find their soul mate. They imagine it happens in every lifetime. But it doesn't. We're always missing each other. Sometimes we're wildly different ages; sometimes we're the wrong gender; sometimes we only see each other for a moment or two at a subway station. I met my soul mate in California and we spent four days together. Knowing who he was in this lifetime and that ours was an ancient soul connection was enough. I knew he wasn't going to last much longer, but I had seen him in this life, at least.

Our last day together we walked around Universal Studios. Later on I used a Sharpie marker to give him a star on Hollywood Boulevard. He drove me to the airport in his Toyota.

"You are going to visit me, aren't you?" he asked. "You'll come to England?"

I nodded, but I knew I wouldn't, as strange as that must sound. I didn't need to anymore. I knew who he was at long last. These four days with him had been almost as much as I could bear in this lifetime. By the time I went to England again, I knew that he would be dead.

We were both crying as I said good-bye. "I just want to tell you that I love you, I have always loved you, and I always will."

On the plane home I tried to write him a card, but each pen I used would dry up. I went through pen after pen. It was like one of those frustrating nightmares where you can't do something no matter how hard you try. I finally got my note written and sent it to him, but that was the last time I ever contacted him. I clearly wasn't supposed to anymore.

He e-mailed me over the next year from time to time, but eventually he was too sick to stay in touch, and I never responded. It wasn't that I feared disappointment exactly, but I needed our relationship to stay a fairy tale and not get mixed up with husbands and wives, illness and death. We were deeply connected spiritually, and I'd had that confirmed at last.

"You are much loved, and you will be much missed." I said that to him at the airport. Later I would find out it was what he had etched on his tombstone when he died.

I think he really was the wild Jack, Jack in the Green, Jack be nimble, Jack be quick, a nature sprite, the child who never grows up. The mischievous spirit of youth. And none of us can bear to say good-bye to that.

I continued meeting him in my dreams, however, as if in the world of the unconscious our souls could meet as they really were.

At home there was Gavin, and in him I saw Jack as I had loved him as a little girl, the way he'd been before alcoholism and life's other struggles. He was the boy I really loved, my own little boy.

I was different when I got back from California. I had been yearning to understand something my whole life and now I had. I had been going back and forth to England for twenty years and now I didn't need to anymore. I could settle down where I was. Maybe now, for the first time in my life, I could be normal.

Reunited after lifetimes with Jack Wild

Debra was looking for a man. She was a big, blond woman with lots of hair, giant boobs, and long, glorious eyelashes. She was a knockout. She was also very warm and friendly. One day she showed up with a photograph of this man she'd just met.

"He's the one!" she gushed. She was deliriously happy.

But when I looked at the man's picture, alarm bells started ringing. Sirens, warning bells, flashing lights were all on high alert. Something was the matter. Only I didn't know what.

I shook my head. "I don't trust him," I told her.

"Honey, honey, you've got to meet this man. He bought me a diamond ring. He's taking me to Hawaii with my daughter, who adores him as much as I do. Even my priest loves him. He's going to marry us next month. I'm in heaven!"

Sometimes I get such specific information—names, dates, events. Maybe if I'd been able to tell her something about him, she would have listened to me.

But she didn't. She married him.

They'd only been married for a few months when the police showed up at their door. He was a bigamist. He had two other families, each of which he'd abandoned. He'd changed his name each time he left and started over.

I felt terrible. I wish I could have seen it, but I couldn't.

"It's not your fault," said Debra. "That man fooled us all—me, the priest, you. What a scam artist!"

Still, I worried that my affection for her had interfered with her reading. I'd let her enthusiasm get in the way of what I could see.

16

The Prom King Takes Me
to the Ball

A neighbor stopped me in the parking lot about a week after I got back from California. "Something's different about you," she said.

"Probably my hair," I said. It was still orange and spiked.

"Your hair's always changing colors," she said. "It's something else. You're a different person. I can't explain it, but I can see it."

But it wasn't that I was happy.

Destiny had thrown me a curveball. Yes, I'd found my soul mate, but he was my brother, not my lover. All of my life until this moment, there had been a part of me connected to Jack, waiting for him, reserved for him, but not anymore. I was alone in a completely new way when I came back from California. I looked at my life as if for the first time.

David was still hanging out with his friends from the Society for Creative Anachronism. He was still wearing his medieval garb, and his buddies would come over and talk about

Star Trek and *Star Wars* and *Lord of the Rings*. Never reality. It was all so boring. I had outgrown it, and it left David and me with nothing to talk about. Where once I had thought it was charming, now it infuriated me. David was a dreamer, and until I met Jack I had been a dreamer, too, dreaming of lost loves and lost lives. But now I wanted something real and electric—in this life.

I started craving romance, real romance. I didn't want to be Guinevere or a High Sorceress. I just wanted to be a normal woman. I wanted to try life without costumes.

David and I had been together since I was a teenager, and our life together had become dreary. I usually slept in the top bunk in Gavin's room. David and I never had any money. I dreamed of living in a real house instead of a condo. I hated having to be on Food Stamps all the time. I was talking to dead people on a daily basis, but I was struggling to buy the groceries. Worst of all, David and I never did anything together. David was still working at the Nature Company, I did readings all day long, and at night we watched television. And that was it. We never went out. I felt old.

Gavin was seven and he was a constant joy to me, but now he was in school for much of the day, and I was alone. As he got older, too, I found myself wanting more security for us as a family. Now he was meeting ordinary kids, and I didn't want him to feel like he lived with the Addams family. I wanted him to be able to fit into the world the way I never had. David couldn't talk to me about any of this. He couldn't even carry on much of a conversation about ordinary life, much less toss a Frisbee with Gavin or teach him to ride a bike. David was too much of a child himself to be a real father, or so I thought at the time in my frustration and desperation.

I just felt so lonely when I came back from California, more lonely than I had ever been.

One night after a long day of readings, of advising people on who to be with, on what to do next, on why this or that had happened in their lives, I ran out into the woods near our apartment complex in a state of complete despair. I lay down on the ground among the fallen branches and the roots and the dry leaves. I wanted to disappear. I shouted up at the stars, "If there are aliens out there, this is the time. Come and get me. Take me back. If you exist, please, come get me!" I felt trapped, like there was no way on earth that I could escape.

I'm not justifying or excusing what I did next, only explaining it. If I could go back and change one thing about my life, this would be the mistake I would not make. But we don't get to do that. And maybe I had to make that mistake, even if it did hurt Gavin beyond measure. I don't know. Whatever speaks through me to other people almost never offers me any guidance about my own life.

When I got back from California, a lot of messages had piled up on the answering machine from people who wanted readings. I called them all back and penciled in their appointments on my calendar. There were my regulars and the newcomers; there were always new people seeking me out. Like I've said before, I never turned anyone down for a reading in those days. If they needed me, that was what I was supposed to do. I had to offer my gift to them.

But there was one phone call I didn't answer.

A man who identified himself only as Bob had left me three messages. He was a real estate lawyer who worked for our condo complex, he explained. A lot of people had recommended me to him. He needed a reading as soon as possible. It was urgent.

From the moment I heard his voice on the phone, I knew he was going to turn my life upside down. I had no idea what he looked like or what his situation was, but I knew in my deepest being that he was a can of worms I didn't want to open.

What I liked most about the sound of his voice was how normal it sounded, like a grown-up on television. It didn't conjure up past lives or magical enchantments. It was a deep, mature, ordinary voice, the voice of a regular guy.

He kept calling. But I didn't answer the phone, and I didn't dare return his messages. Still, he was persistent. Weeks went by.

"Hi, it's Bob again," he'd say. "Perhaps you're away, but I really need a reading as soon as possible. I've got a big decision I've got to make. It's kind of a desperate situation. Other people are involved."

Finally, I just couldn't put him off anymore, and I called him back with an opening for the next week. "I've been really busy," I explained. At least that much was true.

The day of his appointment, I was scared to death and I didn't know why. I found myself peeking through the front window to catch a glimpse of him before he arrived, like an overanxious teenager waiting for a date. Each car that drove past made my heart flutter. I think there was a part of me that already had a crush on him, or at least his voice.

Right on time, an expensive sports car pulled up in front of our building. Out of it stepped the handsomest man I had ever seen, with the classic good looks of a taller Tom Cruise. He was wearing a dark, elegant Italian suit. He was well-groomed, without any authentically medieval facial hair like the men I usually hung out with. The medieval lifestyle does not emphasize hygiene, and after fifteen years it and David were getting a little old and a little ripe.

When the doorbell rang, I started trembling.

This was not the kind of person who usually came to me for a reading.

Guys like this don't need my help. They have all the answers. They have it all figured out. They have money in their wallets, plenty of girls; they're moving up the ladder. They don't need a psychic to tell them what to do. They know what to do.

I opened the door.

Later on, Bob would tell me that I wasn't what he was expecting either. He was imagining the old Gypsy fortune-teller, a kerchief tied under her chin, bangles on her arm, the usual warts on the nose. Instead, I was a young mother in her thirties. I was blond. My hair had grown in since the California manicure scissors massacre, and I'd dyed it to a more natural shade.

He had a kind of effortless confidence as he chatted with me on the way to my kitchen. I was struck by the smell of his cologne, the cut of his suit. They were both expensive and carefully chosen. He had so many decisions to make, he told me, about women and money.

When we sat down at the table in my kitchen, he showed me two photographs—one of his ex-wife and one of his fiancée. "I'm feeling really confused," he said. "I don't know what I'm doing with the ladies anymore. Was I right to leave my wife? Should I get married again? My girlfriend's pressuring me. I just don't know. What do your cards say?"

The cards didn't say anything, but a voice in my head, clear and ringing, announced, *None of these women are the right girl for you. I am the girl for you.*

Why couldn't I be with a man like this? I'd offer him the spiritual guidance he so clearly needed, and he would give me the comfort and security I craved. Maybe the spirits were finally giving me something easy and fun, a simple normal life. My husband was a bit of a kook, and here was this great guy right in front of me. That was why he had been so persistent about coming for a reading. Some force had driven him to me. He didn't even understand it. But what could I say?

"These are not the girls for you," I said, looking at the photos as if I were examining them but really trying to collect myself. "Your wife, she has a horrible energy."

He laughed bitterly. "You're telling me!"

I swallowed, looking at the picture of his fiancée. "And this woman, well, this woman, she's not the girl for you either."

The voice in my head was shouting now, *I am the girl for you. I am!*

No way was I going to say this. I was married. I didn't know him at all. I had just met him. I used all of my willpower to keep the words inside of me. It was the first and only time I have ever lied during a session. I'd never made up a reading before, but this time I did. I had to say something. I couldn't say what I was really seeing, which was us, together, surrounded by sunshine, a pretty house, a white picket fence.

I was fumbling with my words. I was giggling, flirting, and then catching myself.

"Go to New Orleans! Today. This week. Soon," I announced desperately.

"What?" Bob looked completely confused. He had a silk pocket handkerchief. Who did that anymore? It was so dapper but appealing. He wiped his brow with it. It smelled of cologne.

"Yup. New Orleans," I repeated. "There you will meet the girl for you." It was a total lie, but at least it would ensure that he would be far away. It was ridiculous, but I wanted to get rid of him and never see him again.

If I had told him to go to Pluto, I think he would have gone, though. He was a very open, trusting soul beneath the polished exterior.

I felt terrible, terrible for having lied and terrible for having sent him away.

After I shut the door behind him, I collapsed on the couch. Why couldn't I be with a guy like this? Not only was he handsome, but he also was clearly rich.

What would it be like to have money? I wanted to make a beautiful home for Gavin; I wanted to take him on vacations; I wanted him to have a father who didn't get dressed up like an Arthurian knight, but would throw a ball with him in the backyard like a regular dad. Our apartment had never seemed so drab and messy. David's stuff was everywhere.

My mother was always criticizing David. "Why couldn't you have found yourself a nice lawyer?" she said to me time and again. I laughed ruefully. I just had.

With any luck, though, I'd never see him again.

But a few weeks later Bob dropped by. He was back from New Orleans.

"The whole city is full of drunks and people pissing in the

streets. I didn't meet a single girl I felt any attraction to at all. Why did you send me there? You sure it was New Orleans?"

"I guess it wasn't in the cards." I shrugged. "But you're going to meet your soul mate someday. I'm sure of it." I was trying to figure out another way to get rid of him, but my mind was a blank.

"Okay." He smiled, leaning back in his chair. "But in the meantime, why don't you come out and have lunch with me?"

And that was that. I surrendered to fate. I'm not a big drinker, but I had a couple of glasses of Sambuca with him at an Italian restaurant and I couldn't stop flirting. It was so easy between us. He had such vitality. He worked out and had a great body. I knew he'd been the popular boy in high school. The jock. The prom king. I hadn't even been to my prom. But here he was, pouring me another glass of Sambuca and telling me how pretty I was. He talked about his work and his love of country music and how he played in a band on the weekends. He told me about his family and why he'd moved back in with his parents since his divorce and how much he loved them. He told me he loved to travel. He just seemed so—normal.

I found myself pretending that I loved country music and that I wanted to go hear him play. I'd never lied like this. It was so upsetting.

I kept thinking about all the women I'd done readings for over the years who had been married and then met the guy they really were supposed to be with. If they could reach for what they wanted, why couldn't I? No voice ever came through telling me they were bad women. Everyone got divorced these days, right?

I found myself telling Bob all about my father. Something

about this handsome man reminded me of him, made me miss him more than I had in years. "But he's kind of insane," I told Bob. "He used to live under the Verrazano Bridge and hoard newspapers. He used to dress up as Robin Hood. I haven't had any contact with him since I was seventeen. "

"Why don't you find him? You loved him, right?"

"More than anything," I said. "He's down in Florida, I think. Fort Lauderdale maybe. I don't have an address or even a phone number for him."

"I can help you find him. You've got to find your father, Suzie."

That's what Bob started calling me right from the very first. Not Sue. Not Suzan. But Suzie. It made me feel like a teenager headed to a sock hop. Psychic Suzie. Malibu Barbie. I should have known from the get-go that anyone who called me Suzie didn't have a clue who I really was.

He wanted to see me again, so I invited him to a group reading I was doing at the Westfield Yoga Center later that week. I figured there would be a lot of people there. That would make it safer for me.

That night, I put on a very pretty floral dress. I didn't dress like a psychic, but like a woman about to go on a date. I couldn't stop thinking about the fact that Bob would be there.

My mother also showed up that night, and I introduced her to Bob when he arrived. "That man would make a great catch for your sister!" she whispered to me before sitting down. "He's so good-looking." Then she explained to the person sitting next to her that she was the mother of the fortune-teller, but her other daughter was a schoolteacher.

I hated it when my mother called me a fortune-teller. She said the word with a certain pride, but it seemed to demean what I did. I'd rather be called a sensitive, or an intuitive, or a plain old psychic. I don't know how many times over the years I'd told her this. Being called a fortune-teller made me feel like a little girl dressed up for the school carnival.

I took a seat in the circle. The first thing I saw when the lights were dim was a woman holding a baby. "Does anyone know a baby called Anne? I think she died when she was very young, but she's with her mother again."

I looked around the room. There was the usual mixture of older women in long skirts and a few men with long hair. And then there was Bob, looking out of place in his business suit. There were tears on his cheeks. I told myself that he was soft and sensitive because he believed. It's amazing how we can turn people into who we want them to be in our imaginations. I wasn't paying any attention to the amount of effort he put into his personal appearance or how naïve he was about the spiritual world.

"You know a baby called Anne?" I said, happy that I'd seen something about his life.

He nodded. "My mother's sister Anne died in infancy. You're real, aren't you? You're the real thing!"

"I'm also getting a message from someone's uncle Pete," I said.

"I have an uncle Pete!" exclaimed Bob.

But before I could find out what Uncle Pete's message might be, I heard a brusque voice call out from the first floor, "I have to go speak to someone up there. Let me past. I have to speak to Seretta."

It was a real person, not a spirit.

I could hear the owners of the yoga studio talking to a man, a certain amount of arguing, and then heavy treads on the stairs leading up to the room where we were.

A moment later, Erik Jasper burst through the door.

I barely recognized him. It had been years since I'd last seen him.

His long black hair was shorn off into a crew cut. His eyeliner was gone. His tights were gone. His cape was gone. He was dressed like a police officer, and he had a gun in his holster.

"You're a cop?" They were the first words out of my mouth.

How could he be a cop? This was a guy the cops kept an eye on. It was like a reanimated dead body appearing right in front of me. And that repulsive. Was this the man who had so intoxicated me years before? Was this who he had really been? Was this his true self? This swollen, overweight, doughnut-eating cop with a buzz cut? This was scarier than any black magic he'd ever said he could do.

I wanted to vomit. I wanted to hide. I wanted to evaporate into the ether with the spirits. Most of all, I didn't want Bob to know that I had ever been involved with this grotesque monster of a man.

Why had he shown up at the very moment my life was taking a turn for the normal?

Everyone turned to stare at him. He was a huge guy with a booming voice . . . and a gun.

My mother instantly jumped up. "Erik! It's Erik! Hello, Erik! We've missed you so much!" She was glowing. She was thrilled to see him again.

Bob was sitting there, completely baffled. I felt like I was falling into pieces, with fragments of my past and my future lying all about me. Could the world really be this small? What did this mean? Why at this very moment had the darkest, strangest person from my past appeared?

I grabbed Erik and pulled him into the hallway, explaining to my group that I'd be back in a few minutes. I tried to catch my breath while Erik told me that he was remarried, with kids, and that he'd become a cop. A police officer! I was so lucky I'd left him.

I told myself that the torch was being passed, that I was moving on from this. *Phew!* I was thinking. *Now I can be a real girl; I am done with the craziness. Done. Done. Done.* "Erik, you've got to go. I don't have time for this—"

"But Seretta—"

"I'm Suzie now."

"Suzie?" Erik bellowed with laugher. "Suzie! Suzan, maybe. Seretta, you will never be a Suzie."

"We'll see," I said. "I've got to go. I'm in the middle of a big reading."

Erik pulled me, reluctantly, into a hug, and I felt no trace at all of my former attraction to him. Not one little sizzle. It's amazing how your desire for a person can disappear. I took one last look at him as he lumbered his huge body down the stairs. A cop. That's what he'd become? Well, maybe he just wanted to be normal, too.

"Suzie, Suzie, who was that?" asked Bob when I came back. "Is everything okay?"

"Everything's fine," I said. But Erik's appearance had unsettled me. It felt like some kind of warning, only I didn't know what the universe was trying to tell me.

Three months after Bob started coming to me for readings and taking me out for lunch, he took me to the fireworks in Summit, New Jersey, on the Fourth of July. It was the town I'd grown up in without any friends. Bob had brought a picnic blanket, and we spread it out in Memorial Field right near the crypt where I used to hide. I'd come back to my old haunts, and beside me was a movie star of a man who was treating me like a princess.

An orchestra was playing "The Prayer" with Andrea Bocelli singing. The stars were beginning to come out, and in a moment the fireworks would begin. Bob went down on his knees in front of me.

"Suzan Ellzer, I love you so much," he said.

He called me by my childhood name, and I felt the complete redemption of all the suffering I had ever experienced.

"If only I had known you when you were a teenager," said Bob. "Think of all the time we could have had together."

Bob had been raised in the next town over, but I knew that if he had known me in high school, he would never have fallen in love with me. He would have passed me in the halls without seeing me. But I didn't feel like such a freak now with Bob on his knees in front of me. I didn't have to be weird anymore.

That was the night I knew I'd fallen in love.

Still, I felt at that moment like my mother—married to one man and beginning a relationship with another. But I wasn't going to give Gavin two daddies, one secret and one public. I wasn't going to sneak around. I wouldn't make him sit outside a locked bedroom door and keep watch for the return of his father.

I thought at the time that the important thing was not to lie—to myself, to David, to Gavin. I would be honest and responsible, and that would make everything all right. But you can still make mistakes without acting like your parents.

Bob had invited me to take a vacation to Florida with him. "We can travel together; we can buy a house together; you won't have to do readings anymore. I can take care of us.

And we can go find your father. Let's go find your father, Suzie. You've got to find your dad."

I finally told David that I had met somebody else and that I was in love with him. "I don't want to sneak around behind your back. I don't want to make Gavin lie for me like I had to lie when I was a kid."

But what I said undid David. He smashed his hand through the wall in the laundry room, then cried for a long time, and then retreated into himself. He didn't fight to keep me this time, like he had done when I'd become involved with Erik. His friend Richard raged at him for giving up without a fight, but David was finally too defeated. He became even more lost in his medieval world and took to clanking around the condo complex wearing chain mail at night.

I packed a week's worth of outfits into a pink suitcase that looked like it belonged to a little-girl princess. I made sure to include a formal dress, all flounces and sparkles, like a teenager would wear to a prom. I actually packed a rhinestone tiara. Bob had told me to bring something fancy.

I really believed that I was making the best choice not only for myself but also for Gavin. Gavin and I would get to be normal now. We could be tourists at the Renaissance Faire instead of the carnies themselves. I ignored the little voice inside my head that was saying, *This isn't really you. This can't be you. This isn't your life.*

At the door, David had one last thing to say to me. "Nobody else can tolerate you, you know. You're too weird."

"David, I'm going to have a normal life. This is a normal guy."

But of course that's not what happened. My adventure into normal life was anything but normal.

———

I saw this woman the other day for a reading, and her life was a blank. When I looked at her, I saw absolutely nothing—no past lives, no spirits hovering close, no stories, no secrets, no lost loves, nobody waiting for her around the corner. She had two cats and that was it. This is going to be absolute hell, I thought to myself.

She sat across from me in the little room where I do readings and we stared at each other. Nothing. There was nothing in her life. I felt like saying to her, "Go, you have got to go." But how do you say that without hurting a person's feelings?

She'd never been married, never even had a boyfriend. She'd been stuck at the same job she hated for twenty years. She was never going to leave it. And yet she comes to me, hoping I'm going to tell her something that will change all that. But what could I possibly do for this woman? I can't make a life when there's nothing there. That's not what I do. I don't make things happen. All I can do is see what's there.

My eyes were glazing over. I felt like I was in a coma. I was just about to tell her, "I can't do this. I'm not even going to charge you," when I saw the violin.

"You play the violin, don't you?"

"I used to. How do you know?"

"Well, I see a violin in your house. It wants to be played. In fact, it's screaming to be played."

"I volunteer at the orchestra sometimes."

"Good," I said. Something else was becoming clear to me. "Oh, and your cat? The striped one? He's got something growing on his liver."

"*Aren't you a ray of sunshine?*" she said, clearly rattled. "*I wouldn't want to have your job.*"

Sometimes I don't want to have my job either.

Readings aren't always good for people. Too much information can be unnerving; it can even make some people crazy.

This elegant, polished woman paid me a visit one day. All of her accessories matched, her hair was expertly styled, and it looked like she had a monogrammed handkerchief in her purse. She was very put together.

During our reading, I saw her surrounded by stray dogs, and I was struck by the insight that she had the heart of an animal rescuer. I told her so, and at the time she seemed both surprised and delighted by the information. After she left, I imagined her going to one of the local pounds and adopting a mutt and walking him around her neighborhood in a little jacket.

Months later, however, I was at the grocery store when I heard someone calling out to me. I looked around and saw a big pickup truck, the back of which was stacked with animal crates, each one filled with three or four howling, peeing, miserable dogs. There must have been sixty dogs all crammed together. Emerging from the truck was the woman, barely recognizable. Her hair wasn't brushed; she was wearing an unwashed shirt. She looked terrible.

But she was delighted to see me. "I'm doing what you wanted me to do!" she exclaimed.

I was horrified. She wasn't fostering stray dogs; she was hoarding them. It was eye-boggling insanity. I didn't know what to do.

"What have you done?" I asked in horror.

"You've changed my life," she said. "I've never been so happy. Come, come pick out a dog for yourself. You have to!"

I looked at all those poor dogs. I wanted to get them all away from her, but all I could do was rescue one pathetically thin dachshund.

When I took her to the vet, she had pneumonia and parasites. I wanted the vet's advice about the other dogs, but he already knew about them. It had been in the news. They'd found the woman's house packed floor to ceiling with muzzled dogs in crates. She'd been adopting them from kill shelters all over the state. In the end, she was jailed for animal cruelty.

Was I responsible for what happened? I have no idea, but sometimes good readings go bad.

17

Just by Accident (Ha!)

I knew my father had a real estate office in Fort Lauderdale, and Bob managed to find out the address. "Steve Citta and Associates," said a small sign near the front door. There were large storefront windows, but they had both been painted black.

"You ready, Suzie?" asked Bob in the car.

I nodded and took a breath. I was jittery with fear and excitement. I hadn't told my mother anything. Bob had become fascinated with my father from the stories I'd told him. He felt it was really important that I reconnect with Steve, and maybe it was time. When I had been with David there hadn't been room in my life for another costume-wearing wild man, but maybe, now that I was an ordinary girl, there was. Even more than that, when I was with Bob I found myself missing my father more than I had in years and talking about him all the time.

"He's just kind of crazy," I warned Bob. "Who knows what we'll see?"

I decided to go into the real estate office by myself, but I wasn't sure if I was going to reveal who I was right away. As I approached the door, I heard this boisterous Gypsy music blasting from inside. I knocked, but no one answered. I wasn't sure if anyone could hear me over the music. But I turned the handle, and the door was open. So I stepped inside.

It didn't look like a real estate office. Old suits, shiny from wear, were hanging on the walls; boxes piled high were strewn around the room. There weren't any glossy photos of apartments or houses to buy. There weren't any computers. There was no secretary. The walls were yellow with nicotine. There was a cot in one corner covered in rumpled sheets and blankets. The office smelled like the stale butts of a thousand, maybe a million, cigarettes. Nobody in their right mind was going to come here to try to buy a house.

Two young men, clearly gay, their arms linked, were dancing and gyrating to the music. Behind a desk covered in papers was my father, clapping along and smiling. All three men turned to look at me when I came into the room.

I hadn't seen my father since I was seventeen, and now I was in my late thirties. I was tan and blond, not a little black-haired waif anymore.

"Is this a real estate office?" I asked tentatively. My mouth was so dry.

"Yes, it is." Steve was much older but still handsome. A well-worn George Clooney. He was wearing glasses and had another pair on his head. A third pair was dangling around his neck on a chain. His shirt had pockets on either side, and out of each pocket poked a dozen Bic pens. Above the desk was a large Victorian painting of two knights jousting.

"My name is Suzan Wild and I'm from New York and I'm looking for a place for the winter. . . ."

While I was speaking, Steve had taken off the glasses he was wearing and positioned the pair that had been around his neck on his nose. "Sue? Is that you? How did you get here? How did you find me?" He came around from behind the desk and wrapped me up in his arms. It had been over twenty years since I'd seen him, and he recognized me instantaneously. Tears were already pouring down his cheeks. I don't think I cried. I was in too much of a state of shock.

I can't pretend that the filthiness of the place didn't upset me. Clearly, he not only worked in this room, but also lived there. His clothing was covered in cigarette holes, as if he'd burned himself accidentally a hundred times and hadn't even realized it. He smelled rank, of old cigarettes, of sweat, of unwashed clothes. There were used diabetic needles littering the floor.

My feelings weren't simple. I knew many things at once. I knew that he was hopeless, and that I couldn't fix him, much less clean him up. He would die soon; that was clear from the cigarettes and the needles. He was such a mess, such a madman, and I was trying to make a go of having a normal life. No wonder I had never gotten in touch with him, even after I stopped living with my mother. What would Bob think of all of this?

But Steve was gazing at me with such an expression of love that it overcame all of these other feelings. He might be a lunatic, but he was my father.

"Sue. Sue. You don't know much I've missed you."

One of the dancing men clicked off the tape recorder.

"Boys, we'll dance tomorrow," said my father, still holding

me. "But I need some time with my daughter. I haven't seen my daughter in a long time. A long time."

The reality of it began to hit me, and I started to tear up. He was filled with such sweetness. He was dabbing his eyes with this old tissue. Everything about him was rumpled. When I was a little girl, I wouldn't have noticed any of that, I would just have seen the dancing men and his joy. Children can see a person's true spirit so much more easily than grown-ups can.

We were both crying now as the men left the office. Through the door I waved at Bob to come in.

"I have a son," I told Steve.

"I heard," he said. "From your mother once. Merlin, isn't he? I keep up. I keep up."

"Gavin," I said.

Steve laughed. "Remember this?" From behind his desk he pulled out a plastic stage sword. It was the one he'd used when he taught me how to duel.

Bob came in a few minutes later, a bottle of wine in his hand.

"What a beautiful man!" exclaimed Steve. He took the wine, opened up the back part of his toilet, and stuck it in. "Don't have a fridge, but it'll stay cool back there."

Bob looked at me, laughing, and I knew he was thinking, *You were right.*

We ended up going out to dinner at a seafood buffet where Steve not only helped himself to platefuls of fried shrimp, but also casually borrowed food from my plate and Bob's plate and the other diners' plates as well. Somehow Steve managed to make the whole thing dreadfully amusing and charming.

"Thank you, m'dear, for this bread stick." And the person whose table Steve had taken it from would smile at him as if they were honored that he'd done so.

I told Steve about my life, my trips to England, and becoming a psychic. He didn't seem either particularly impressed or skeptical. He didn't make a big deal out of it. He nodded as if it was the most natural thing in the world. "My grandmother was a fortune-teller in the Carpathian Mountains and so was my mother. It makes sense." But he didn't ask me for a reading, and I wouldn't have given him one. While he ate, he lit cigarette after cigarette.

I felt with my father as I had with Jack. Steve didn't have much time left. That was the only thing there was left to know.

"Are you going to eat that?" my father asked a woman, pointing at the baked potato on her plate. He flashed her a smile as she let him have it.

"Thank you so much," said my father. "This is my daughter, by the way. I'm so proud of her."

"I met Jack Wild," I told my father.

"The English actor? The one in *Oliver!* you had such a crush on?"

"That's right, him. We had a very unusual meeting."

"Oh, did you?" My father chuckled again. He had finished the baked potato and was peering around the dining room of the restaurant.

"Maybe we should order some dessert?" suggested Bob. He was smiling in amazement at my father.

"Did you ever have a girlfriend when you were in England in the fifties?" I asked Steve.

He raised his eyebrows and made a low chortle. "A girlfriend? I had *lots* of girlfriends when I was in England."

"Named Vera?"

My father looked at me sharply. "Vera? Yes, for a while. Blond woman like your mother. Married, too."

I nodded. I had thought so. "Did she have a child?" I asked.

My father shrugged. "I didn't stay in touch with her. I suppose she could have."

While we were talking that night, I asked my father what day his birthday was. I wanted to be sure to note it. I was stunned to discover that it was July 27, the same exact day as Bob's. There are 365 days in a year and what are the chances these two men in my life would have the same birthday? Not that they were anything alike, not at all, unless I looked at the enormity of their egos. Both were men who liked to command attention. But it felt like more than astrology. It felt like destiny.

The next time I came down to Florida, I brought my father a photograph of me and Jack. Steve put it on his desk next to the one of me as a little girl and the one of his other daughter. It would be the only photo he would take with him to the hospital a few months later. On this trip I also brought Gavin to meet his grandfather.

Gavin walked into Steve's office and within a few minutes had whispered to me, "Grandpapa is ape shit."

He really was.

Bob took us all to Animal Kingdom, and Steve was outrageous.

It turned out that because of his diabetes, Steve was often incontinent, but he refused to wear adult diapers. He only brought one pair of pants and was constantly flapping them out the balcony of the fancy hotel where we were staying to try to dry them. He swore like the sailor he'd been. He was wildly politically incorrect. He was racist, rolling his eyes whenever a black person passed us. He was a pig, making lewd comments and gestures whenever he saw a pretty girl. He was kind of like a possessed Archie Bunker, only movie-star handsome still—despite everything, despite the urine stains—and exuding this impossible, reckless, irresistible magnetism.

When I'd met Jack, he'd reminded me of my father, but now my father made me think of Jack. They were so alike, only my father was so much older and more decrepit.

Poor Gavin shared a room with him that first night because we had no idea how awful Steve could be. He started calling out and swearing in his sleep and groaning, "Jesus Christ! Jesus Christ! Oh my God! Jesus fucking Christ!" He wailed; he moaned; he thrashed in the bed.

Gavin knocked on our door. "Mother," he said. "I think Grandpapa needs an exorcism."

Bob and I got up and went over to the other room. Steve had opened the window and was screaming out into the night.

"Steve, why don't you just get back into bed," said Bob calmly. "Say your prayers and head to sleep."

"Say my prayers?" bellowed Steve. "You think I pray to God? I don't. I pray to Lucifer! That's my only god. Lucifer!"

But Gavin had been going through Steve's things. "Then why do you have a card, Grandpa, saying you're a Catholic and that if anything happens to you to call a priest?"

Steve looked at him, wild-eyed, but didn't say anything. Finally, Bob and I got him to settle down and go to sleep.

The next morning at Animal Kingdom, though, he was in fine form again. We went to the Monkey House. One of the

exhibits was a display of all the artwork that these two goril-
las had painted, with real paintbrushes and everything. The
paintings were selling for thousands of dollars to raise money
for the zoo.

"So what do you think of the paintings, Steve?" asked
Bob. "Shall we get one?"

"I could paint these with my balls," bellowed Steve. "My
balls are better artists."

Everyone was staring at us. Bob, Gavin, and I quickly
hurried Steve out of the room. But Bob wasn't embarrassed
by Steve; he thought he was a riot.

Steve lit up a cigarette as soon as we were outside.

"Please don't smoke around the animals, sir," said a guard.

"Fuck the animals!" exclaimed Steve.

Bob couldn't stop laughing, and the love I felt for him was
growing stronger by the minute. His acceptance of my father
was his acceptance of me. He let me love my father for who he
was, despite everything, and I was overflowing with gratitude—
for my son, for my father, and for this man who had made it
possible for us all to be together.

I wanted so much to create this brand-new family, but
Gavin refused to cooperate. Bob and I bought a house on a
lake in New Jersey; we got pet cockatoos; we traveled back
and forth to Florida. But Gavin wanted to be with his real
father. He wanted his dad, not Disney World. You can't force
love. It took me a long time to understand that.

Bob insisted on taking my father on a cruise at one point.
"He'll love it," Bob explained to me. "You will, too. It's so
relaxing, and there's nothing to do but eat and sleep and
hang out."

He insisted on buying my father a whole wardrobe, and he

also, somehow, managed to talk my father into wearing adult diapers at last. Going through security, however, to get on board the ship, my father managed to set off all the alarms. Bells were ringing and clanking. Guards were rushing over. "I'm sorry, Mr. Citta, we're going to have to take you out of the line."

They frisked him, patting down his arms and legs. They sent him through the screener again, and again all the alarms went off.

"Do you have any guns or weapons on you, sir?" asked security.

My father shook his head. They had him take off his belt and his shoes. They frisked him again. He went through the gate again, and again the alarm was blaring.

At this point a lot of people were staring at us. Bob was looking at me and shaking his head. "Leave it to your father!"

My father was making all of these faces at us like he couldn't figure out what was the matter.

"Sir, do you have any metal on your person that we might have missed?" asked a guard.

My father thought for a moment and then finally nodded. He knelt down, rolled down his sock, and pulled out a six-inch hunting knife. "Could this be doing it?" he said.

Eventually Steve's diabetes got so bad he had to have his leg amputated. He was in this awful VA hospital, but he eventually escaped in his wheelchair and ended up hiding out behind the hospital. One morning he tried to cross a thruway and ended up getting bumped by a car and toppled out of his chair. He was alive but badly bruised. Bob and I flew down to be with him and he was as irascible as ever, Robin Hood imprisoned in the Sheriff of Nottingham's castle.

Steve kept trying to show Bob his bloody stump.

"There are many things in life that I want to see, but not that," laughed Bob. He was so gentle with Steve, spooning him his food while we visited with him.

I told my mother what had happened, and all she wanted to know was what had happened to the leg.

"I'm sure they threw it away in some special container or something."

"That seems like a waste," she said.

"What?" She'd resolutely had no opinion up until now about my new relationship with Steve.

"The leftover leg. You could mount it, put it above the fireplace or something."

I thought she was joking, but my mother never joked. She was always trying to say the proper thing, and this was clearly in no way proper. It was bizarre. I realized that my mother, too, was deteriorating. It was the first sign we had that she was becoming demented.

A week or so after we got back to New Jersey, I woke up one morning and knew we had to get right back to Florida. It was as powerful a psychic intuition as I have ever had. Bob got us tickets at once. We had to fly into Miami, though, then drive to Fort Lauderdale, and when we got there we couldn't find Steve anywhere. He had checked out of the hospital and his office was closed. Nobody had any idea where he'd gone. Nobody had seen him for days.

We drove all over Fort Lauderdale with nothing to go on. We called my half sister who was estranged from Steve. We talked to the doctors and nurses. At last, defeated, we got in the car and decided to drive back to Miami.

We were on the highway out of the city when we saw a man in a wheelchair by the side of the road. This is the God's honest truth. It was Steve. If we hadn't been driving to Miami, we never would have seen him.

Bob pulled the car onto the shoulder and slammed on the brakes. Cars were whizzing past. Steve looked up at us, smiling.

"What are you doing here?" I yelled as I hugged him.

"I was praying that you would come. I was praying and praying. And look at that, you found me, just by accident."

He was filthy.

Did we find him because I was a psychic or was it simply because I loved him? I think Bob and I found him because we both loved him so much. I think love finally is the most powerful psychic power of all.

Steve was begging us to take him to the Olive Garden. He was ravenous. But he was such a mess, smelling of cigarettes, urine, and feces.

"I'm sorry, Steve, but we can't take you to a restaurant like this."

"I'm dying to go to the Olive Garden," he insisted. "I love their shrimp."

We had no place to bathe him, but we bought him some fresh clothes and got take-out shrimp that we all ate in the car. We didn't have any idea what to do with him or where he should go. He wanted to go to the homeless shelter where he'd been earlier, so finally that's where we took him, though later I wished we hadn't.

"How did you know where to find me?" he kept asking.

"I don't know. We just found you. We all need to check into a hotel."

But Steve insisted on having us take him to the homeless shelter first. He felt more comfortable there, he said.

"We're going to get a house, though, where you can live with us," said Bob.

"Are you sure you won't come to the hotel with us?" I asked again.

But he wouldn't. We arranged to meet him at the Winn-Dixie next to the shelter the following morning.

All that night at our hotel I dreamed about him.

The next morning we went to the Winn-Dixie and waited and waited. He never showed up and finally we went to the shelter.

An older man who was sweeping started shaking his head. "Didn't anybody tell you? Didn't you get a call?"

An hour after we'd dropped him off, Steve had died of a heart attack.

If we hadn't found him, I would never have seen him again. But Bob thought maybe the shrimp we'd given Steve had killed him.

"No," I said. "He loved those shrimp. We just gave him one last great meal."

"I think I've been in your life to make sure you were able to be here with him at the end," said Bob.

I never knew what happened to Steve's body. His daughter in Florida didn't want to be in touch with me. Growing up with him had been harder than finding him at the end, I guess. But my father was gone again. There was no funeral, no final resting place to visit and pay my respects. Bob and I went to the McDonald's Steve loved the most, and I wrote "Rest in Peace Robin Hood" with a permanent marker on the concrete of an outdoor table. Years later when I visited, it was still there. That's the only memorial I was able to give him.

"You know your father was mentally ill," said my mother when I told her he was dead.

But was he really? Or did he just not fit into our crazy culture? My mother could pass in polite society, dress properly, and say the right things, at least when she was out in public. But she was, I think, much more deranged than my father. Steve's problems were right out in the open. My mother's were expertly hidden inside her heart. It's hard in our world today to sort out who's really crazy and who isn't.

Soon after he died, my father began visiting me in dreams. He is always young and always dressed as Robin Hood. He stays close, and I can tell he's happy. For a crazy man who didn't believe in anything, it sure seems like he didn't have any trouble finding heaven.

A woman had me come over to her house for a reading, and when I arrived, there was a giant boa constrictor on the dining room table. The woman served me dinner, and the snake was coiling around the plates the whole time we were eating. She asked me to do a reading for the snake.

"The snake?"

"Please?" she asked. "I want to know what he has to say to me."

I put my ear up to him, but he was just a big, black void of nothing. Now, I've done readings for lots of animals. Guppies have come through and forgiven their owners for messing up the acidity of their tanks. Guppies! It turns out even feeder fish are capable of forgiveness and affection. But this boa? That snake was really dull. I don't think he was very smart or very interesting either.

"I'm sorry," I told the woman. "Talking doesn't seem to be his thing."

18

Cruise Ship Suzie

Bob and I were constantly going on cruises. Bob worked all the time when he was at home; he'd set up an office in our bedroom, and he'd be on the phone yelling and swearing, going at high speed. But then we'd take off on a cruise every month or so, and then he'd turn on the television in our stateroom and relax. We became preferred members with free drinks and special services.

I loved getting dressed up in pretty clothes and having our portrait taken every night. There were cheesy Broadway shows to go to, and then we'd get off the boat and walk through the streets of Bermuda or Jamaica and the locals would call out, "Is that Tom Cruise?" because Bob, in his movie-star dark glasses, was that handsome.

Bob liked me blond, so blond it was. I stopped dying my hair any other color, except for one Halloween when I gave it a modest streak of red that amazed Bob's country music friends. They thought it was wild. They had no idea what wild really was.

What I liked best about the cruise ships was sleeping on the decks at night under the stars, the water all around me, still and vast. I wanted to be out in the elements, especially when we were in the Bermuda Triangle. It was one night up on deck by myself that I realized that I was still waiting for something to arrive, to happen, to transform me inside, to take me away again like I had begged for that night in the woods when I had run out of my apartment in despair. I had changed the outward appearance of my life, but it was just another game of dress-up, like when I'd been a pirate wench reading the Tarot at the Renaissance Faire.

One year at Christmas we were at sea and started hearing reports about the tsunami that had hit Indonesia. I was glued to the television, devastated by the death and the tragedy. Bob was standing in front of the mirror, getting dressed in his tux for dinner. "C'mon, Suzie, let's turn that off," he said. "We're on a cruise. We don't need to let all that negativity in right now. Let's go enjoy ourselves."

I was dumbfounded. How could you forget that something like that was going on? How could you think about anything else?

Bob sighed, looking at me. "I just want to enjoy this cruise. I want to sleep and I want to eat."

Eating was really the main activity on those cruise ships. Sometimes I imagined we were cattle being plumped up before the slaughter. I felt like they were feeding us so they could eat us. It became more and more grotesque to me—the chocolate fountains, the unlimited buffets, the huge quantities of shrimp and meat and pastries.

When we stopped at ports, I'd always make sure to stuff my pockets with hot dogs and hamburgers to feed to the stray dogs I'd inevitably see roaming in packs through the side streets of these Mexican and Caribbean towns. The lawyer in Bob was frantic that I was going to get caught and in some kind of trouble.

"They're gonna lock me up for taking hot dogs? I'll just say I was hungry. They've got food everywhere on this boat. I'm not going to go to jail for feeding strays." This was the real part of me that hadn't become someone else.

Bob was uncomfortable off the boat. Once, we were in the jungle in Bermuda, and we heard this strange clacking noise. We looked down to find giant land crabs scuttling across our feet. Bob nearly climbed a tree.

"They're going to bite us!" he cried.

"No, they're not," I knew. There's very little in nature that you need to be frightened of. Honestly, those buffets of fried food were a lot more dangerous. But Bob didn't like being off the beaten track—and, well, that was usually where I was most comfortable. Off the beaten track was where I was from.

At first I'd been very touched when I discovered that Bob said his prayers every night before going to sleep. He'd been raised Catholic but had never gone to church much; still, he was a believer. But I came to understand that religion for him was, just as it is for a lot of people, as much about fear as faith. He wanted to be protected from evil and demons and calamity.

He worried about work and money. He worried about his good looks and how long they would last. He worried that somebody would break into our house while we were away. He was a typical American—working too hard, worrying too much, buying too much, eating too much, and never, ever thinking about what was really happening in the world.

No one in front of those buffets of meat was thinking about the blood-splattered slaughterhouses where those pigs and sheep and lambs and cows had died. Those women covered in diamonds weren't thinking about the people slaving in the mines. No one was really thinking about anything on those boats. They just wanted the best of everything . . . without realizing that it could only come from the worst of everything.

I've wondered why Bob fell in love with me, and I think it had a lot to do with my fearlessness. He was a worrier, and all of a sudden he had his very own traveling psychic. He liked asking me what I thought was going to happen next. "Should we go to Mexico?" "Do you think we should buy this house?" "Should we do this?" "Should we do that?" He must have thought he had the inside track at last.

The only person close to me who's never wanted a reading is David. He didn't even ask my advice. I used to say to him, "People pay for my advice, so maybe you should listen to me sometime!" but it didn't make any difference. He was always worrying about things that were never going to happen.

"But it could happen," he'd say.

"No," I'd answer. "It's not going to. It can't."

"But it might."

He never believed me, and in some ways I began to realize it had been kind of a relief.

Bob often talked about his wealth, how much he made, how much he was going to make. On our first cruise together he tried to explain to me what commodities were.

"What do you think, Suzie? Should I buy this stock or that one? Or both?"

I didn't have a clue. I had no idea what he should do with his money. I felt like he thought I was some kind of psychic cash cow, but I never get information about that kind of stuff. I don't really care about it, and I don't think the spirits do either. Oh, they'll tell me that someone's going to weather a financial crisis or lose a job or something like that, but they're not predicting lottery numbers or the upcoming average of the Dow.

Bob wanted readings about investments. It began to drive me crazy. All I could say was, "No animal products!" Still, I felt like he thought that I was his hot commodity, his inside secret, his key to wealth and fame.

But I wasn't.

Aboard ship, Bob would spend a lot of time resting in his stateroom. I didn't want to be on a boat just to fall asleep, so I'd wander the decks under the stars in full regalia. One night I felt very lonely, like I was a ghost haunting that ship full of normal people. I went downstairs and lay in the bed next to Bob, but it was all too dramatic and sad. A single tear rolled out of my eye and down my cheek. Why was I in the middle of the ocean with this man? I didn't know.

I didn't want to be a normal person anymore. I wanted to go home. I wanted to go back to Camelot, to the innocent times in the woods with David. He loved the same movies and stories and myths that I loved. He always knew what I was talking about. I felt like I had failed in the real world; I couldn't be a real girl. I needed to be Pinocchio again. I didn't want to be a real girl; I wanted to be back inside of the fairy tale. All the money and financial security in the world doesn't necessarily make you happy.

I had some fantasy that Bob was going to impress my mother. I thought that this was what she had always dreamed of for me when she had been criticizing David for not making more money. But she seemed to disapprove of Bob as much as she had of David. "He's a phony," she said. "I don't like his face." I had some fantasy that Bob was going to impress my mother. I suppose if I'd brought the Pope home—which I wouldn't do because I'm not a big fan of Popes in general, but I'm just saying that if I had—she would have been disappointed. After all, she'd preferred Erik Jasper.

And yet Bob was like my mother in some ways. They were both fearful people, and because of that fear they tried to control everything else around them. They were concerned with what other people thought. Bob was constantly worrying about his own appearance and criticizing mine. I was too fat; I wasn't dressed right; I was behaving strangely. It was all very, very familiar.

Bob and I were functioning less and less well as a couple. He was increasingly frustrated at how little money I brought in and was much fussier than I was about housecleaning. I no longer wanted to pretend that I enjoyed his country music gigs. I started putting colors back in my hair again. I hid chocolate around the house to binge on when Bob wasn't there. One day, in a fit of anger, Bob screamed, "Sometimes I think you're a witch who put a curse on me!" Had it been legal to erect a stake and burn me in New Jersey, I think he would have let them do it that night. I began to suspect that in some other lifetime he'd actually watched me burn. I realized he didn't feel as protected by me as he once thought he would. Being with a psychic didn't make the future more predictable; it just made everyday life more chaotic.

One night back in New Jersey, we had a huge fight about the proper way to close the garage door. We were going out grocery shopping together, and I was loopy from doing readings all day long. Bob didn't understand what it was like, and I tried to explain to him how hard it was for me to pay attention to details like garage door closing.

"All I want from life is a normal girlfriend!" screamed Bob. "Why can't you be normal?"

I heard the voices of the children on the playground taunting me. "What's the matter with you? Are you retarded?" I heard my mother losing her temper in frustration. "Why aren't you normal? Stop being so strange!"

It was such a familiar, terrible place to be. Undervalued. Unappreciated. Unknown.

I had tried so hard to fit in. I felt desperate. If I didn't fit in this time, I never would. I would be on the Island of Misfit Toys for the rest of my life.

Why can't you be normal?

I pictured myself walking the snakes at the Renaissance Faire. I saw myself talking to the dead. I saw the angel before me, an eye on each feather of her wings. I saw Jack.

"No," I told Bob. "I can't be normal. Never."

Cruise ship Suzie and Bob in front of a false moonlit ocean

_____

"Fucker, fucker, motherfucker, shit, shit shit!" I sounded like I had Tourettes, there were so many swear words shooting out of my mouth. It was intense, like machine-gun fire. "Those crap asshole bastards. Fuck them, fuck them, fuck all of you."

The young girl opposite me was totally stunned, but her friend who'd come with her was giggling. "Crap asshole bastard," she snickered. "That's just what your brother always used to say."

"He's really mad," I said, as if it needed to be mentioned. "He wants justice about something, wants you to get the case reopened." It was hard to get more information than that. All I could hear was this torrent of obscenities. I couldn't see anything about this girl's life, about her job or her boyfriend. Just this out-of-control boy.

"Your brother's dead," I observed.

The girl nodded.

"If you don't get the case reopened, he's going to fuck up the boys who did it to him. He wants you know that. He says it's your responsibility."

It came out that a few years ago, the girl's brother had been at a party, and some kids had given him bad drugs that killed him. They'd gone to court, but gotten off on a technicality because they were under twenty-one.

The girl's friend continued to giggle. "That's Bobby all right. I bet he gets those boys. I'm going to keep an eye on the papers and see what happens to them. I bet he makes them have a car accident."

I tried to convince the girl that she was going to have to find some way to calm her brother down, but she was totally over-whelmed. "I couldn't even do that when he was alive," she sobbed.

Now, I've seen kids who have died young in my room, and

they're serene and happy. These are kids who had unlucky accidents and stuff, and they want their family to know that they love them and everything's all right. But this kid? He didn't get enlightened when he died, no siree. He was still a foulmouthed teenager. And he was pissed. Really pissed.

19

The Land of the Freak and the Home of the Vague

My mother was in her nineties and frighteningly out of it. My sister lived with her, but she had a full-time job and no longer felt up to caring for her. My mother was cruel to her, insulting her all day long, and my sister had had enough. She wanted to put my mother in a nursing home.

I was adamantly against it and volunteered to stay with my mother during the day, but my sister knew I also wasn't up to it. Neither of us was. My mother was really difficult. Combative. Violent. Furious.

But the nursing home only made her worse. It was a terrible place. I walked in and I was overwhelmed by the psychic chaos. The old people were reeling from so many unresolved feelings—loss, abandonment, anger, and fear, such terrible fear. The agony made me want to vomit. It wasn't a rest home; there was no rest there.

As for my mother's soul, it was in torment. She was lost and crazed. All of her anxiety, all of her many fears and contradictions had coalesced into one final mass of terror on the edge of death. I don't know if she was possessed or if this was her true self emerging at last from beneath the veneer of everyday life, but when I looked into her eyes I saw two searing black holes, bottomless with rage.

She would slam her wheelchair back and forth against the wall. *Bang! Bang! Bang!* Or she would sit with her head on the table, refusing to look at us or even speak, defeated by her own fury. "She's a tough one," acknowledged the nurses. It was impossible for my mother to have a roommate, and she refused to have anything to do with the other residents. She refused to go to Mass and refused to be blessed by the priest. But every time she saw me, and I went to see her every day, she'd scream at me that I was going to hell.

"Your sister hates you. She's jealous of you," my mother would whisper to me, trying to pit us against each other.

"Your father never wanted you. He wanted you aborted. He wanted you to be an abortion," my mother told me again and again. Whenever she'd said this to me as a child, I'd know she was expressing her own feelings. She was the one who had wanted the abortion. I was the child who proclaimed her infidelity, and even now she couldn't forgive me for it. She looked at me with a pure hatred she had always been able to at least somewhat disguise up until now.

I don't know why I went there every day, except, I suppose, that I hoped we'd find some way to reconcile before she died. She was my mother. I brought healing oils blessed by holy people. I brought sacred crystals. I brought my sweet corgi puppy to her, and he ran out of the room. I brought her only grandson. Bob tried to play his banjo for her. I sat with her and tried to love her. Every time I went to see her, I found myself wishing I knew how to perform an exorcism. I thought that if I could reach her through animals or music or life itself, maybe I could push through the darkness, but it seemed to be hopeless.

Yet I knew from all my many years as a psychic that nothing was ever hopeless. You had to lend a hand to distraught spirits. I knew that if my mother died like this, the work she had to do on the other side would be only that much harder. I wanted to save her soul. I couldn't give up on it. The work you've got to do is the work you've got to do. Death doesn't really change that much. I couldn't tell myself the lie that a lot of bliss ninnies do that somehow she'd go from this tortured state to a place of light-filled peace and love. That's not what I've seen. She'd haunt me; that's what she'd do. I was trying to save us both from that.

I've seen reconciliations happen from the other side. Alcoholics and parents who abandoned their kids and couldn't own the mistakes they'd made when they were alive will finally see and hear the suffering of their children. But it can take twenty, thirty years. It doesn't necessarily happen right away. And I've also seen dead people so trapped in their anger that it was terrifying.

I wanted my mother to apologize to me just once before she died.

I had to stop bringing Gavin to see her; he was too frightened of her. They'd never had much of a relationship anyway. She'd never babysat him, never cuddled him, never even held him on her lap. If I said something about how adorable he was—because he truly was—she'd grimace and tell me to stop making him conceited. In the way she treated him, I saw that she had been honest about not liking children. I wondered if maybe I'd changed my own diapers when I was little.

Bob patted her on the head and smiled at her, but she insulted him and insisted he leave, and finally he decided that he'd had enough.

My father, the self-proclaimed atheist who insisted he prayed to Lucifer, had died in a state of peace. My mother, who considered herself a Catholic, didn't believe in anything at the end.

Steve had been a mess and a failure by so many standard measures, but he had been in love with his life. He had loved women and music and food and people and adventure. He had loved me. And he had been loved. I know he's in heaven, and I know he's got his leg back and he's dressed up as Robin Hood and the angels are all laughing at his antics. But my mother? For my mother, who hated her life and simultaneously fought tooth and nail to keep it, hate and fear had always created her reality. In the end she had no beliefs to offer her consolation. Love, and the practice of love, that's the only thing that saves you in the end.

No matter what sedative they gave my mother, she became more agitated. Sleeping pills would keep her up all night. Valium made her tear her clothes and writhe in her wheelchair. It was so terrible that she wasn't even allowed to eat with any of the other residents. I had to believe she really was possessed. Or at least that's what I told myself. I couldn't accept that this might be who she really was.

Even more terrifying was the possibility that this was the fate that might be waiting for me. My mother's mother had been similarly deranged in her last days. I shivered at the thought. The fear of mental illness in my life has been very real.

My grandmother had also been a frightened person, but when I was twelve she had gone berserk and begun ripping up Bibles and breaking her rosary beads. My aunts had called in a Catholic priest to do an exorcism on this eighty-year-old woman. No one would let me in the room. "Grandma's not really Grandma anymore," they told me. Could that possibly have been true?

I do think that at the end of our lives we become more open than we have been since childhood. The angels and demons are ready to fight for our souls again. It's the last fight of good and evil. If we don't have real faith, a true belief in goodness, the demons can claim our souls. But it's not our outward professions of belief that matter in the end. It's how we've lived and loved.

My mother kept telling me I was going to hell for being a fortune-teller, but she was already there. That nursing home was hell. Her dementia was hell. Every choice she made in her life, and probably in her past lives, had brought her to that particular inferno, and she was burning in it. It was a terrible thing to witness.

Hell is being stuck in our own karma. My mother was ending this life just like she had ended her last one—in an asylum, alone. But she wasn't really alone. My sister and I were with her, and we wanted to love her. I'd always wanted to love her. She could have claimed her joy with Steve, with me, with my sister, in so many different ways, but she didn't and she was in hell.

What had happened to my mother in this life, in her last lives, to bring her to such a place of demented terror?

I wanted to understand her, but over the years whenever I'd tried to talk to her about her family and her childhood she'd gotten defensive.

"Why do you want to talk about things like that?" she'd say if I tried to get her to open up. "I'm your mother, not your friend."

She wanted to talk about what people were wearing, who was fat and who was thin, and the color of my hair. She was obsessed with appearances and how other people might see you. It all felt like some vast cover-up of, well, something.

Maybe that's why I entered the truth-telling business, to say fuck you to that camouflage of conventionality.

The daily indignities of nursing home life, of simply growing old and helpless, were too much for my mother.

She got a bad urinary tract infection a few months after she was in the nursing home, and I was with her when the doctor arrived. As he tried to pull up her gown to examine her, she became hysterical, thrashing and screaming, "Don't touch me down there! Get your hands off of me! Don't touch me there!"

At that moment I felt more pity for her than I have ever felt for another human being on this planet. She was like a wild animal, using every part of herself to fight him off. Hell on earth isn't an idea; it's real suffering, such terrible suffering.

How could she look at me and say that I was going to go to hell?

Maybe she wanted me to join her there. But I wouldn't. I just wouldn't.

The more I resisted my mother's efforts to bring me down, the more unhappy I was with Bob. He was disappointed in me because I hated the real estate class he'd made me take out of some ridiculous fantasy that we'd go into business together. "You're just a piece of shit," he said to me one night in a fit of frustration.

How dare he? In the midst of my mother's final cruelties I just couldn't take this. At least David had never called me names.

Bob and I threw a big Halloween party but ended up getting into yet another terrible fight—over the decorations. Halloween is a sacred holiday for me as a psychic. It's Samhain, the Celtic "Festival of the Dead." It's the time when the veil between life and death is at its thinnest. I hated that Bob thought of it only as a time to put goofy cutout paper witches and ghosts in the windows and get sick on candy corn. I wanted a *real* Halloween. I wanted to honor the dead and commune with the spirits and the ancestors.

"Can't I just put up my Halloween decorations, Suzie?" Bob begged.

"No!"

I hated ugly, warty green witches. Witches are real, and they should be respected. Besides, a lot of them are very beautiful. The way Americans celebrate Halloween is all about denying what that night is really about—trivializing it, making that energy small and manageable. It's not that Halloween should be scary. It just ought to be real.

As a kind of apology, Bob offered to take me to Sleepy Hollow a few days later. It was a beautiful November day, crisp, with the leaves still bright red and orange. Bob wanted to find the legendary Headless Horseman, and there sure were plenty of postcards and tchotchkes in every quaint little shop in that suburban town. But there wasn't that much to do there, and yet again the adventure revealed the rifts between Bob and me instead of reconciling us. He had no idea what I was really about.

I'd just clicked on my seat belt for the drive back to New

Jersey when words unexpectedly shot out of my mouth. "I wanna go to Woodstock," I announced.

"What?" said Bob.

"Let's go to Woodstock."

My voice was speaking, but the words were coming from behind that trapdoor that opens in the back of my brain when I'm doing readings.

"What's in Woodstock?"

I had no idea.

I had no idea where Woodstock was, how far it was from Sleepy Hollow, or why I had just suggested we drive there. I knew it was connected to hippies and sixties music, but I'd never been a hippie, and I'd never even liked American rock and roll. I wasn't into the Grateful Dead, and I thought *The Last Waltz* was about a dance. When I was a teenager, I'd been longing for England and listening to old folk ballads about medieval times.

"You really want to go to Woodstock?" Bob was scratching his head.

I nodded, almost despite myself. "I want to go to Woodstock."

"Was the concert there?" asked Bob.

"I don't know," I answered. "I guess so."

Bob was programming the town into his GPS. "It's about an hour and a half away," he said.

"Okay," I answered. "Let's go."

"Why not?" said Bob, pulling out of our parking spot.

We didn't talk much on the drive north on the thruway. Huge mountains loomed in the distance.

I began to feel these familiar prickles up and down my arms when I saw them.

We turned off the highway and onto a rural county road that led us past furniture stores and gas stations and more and more trees. I was feeling increasingly giddy, like a little kid, jumping up and down in my seat.

"What are you so excited about?" asked Bob.

"I don't know," I answered.

"Welcome to Woodstock," announced a sign at the cross-roads. Next to it was a cutout wooden sculpture of a guitar and a peace sign. The huge mountain I had seen on the highway was right beside the town. It felt protective, as if it was holding the little village close to its heart.

Inside my own heart something sang out in recognition and reunion. I'd made it. I'd crossed over some invisible finish line in a race I hadn't known I'd been in. I felt a release of energy within me. I was here.

We followed the sign and turned left towards Woodstock. The spire of an old-fashioned white church rose before us, and there were lots of little shops and restaurants arranged along either side of one simple street. You could hear the sound of rushing water from nearby streams and rock music coming from the shops and drumming from the flower-filled village green. I felt a sparkling electricity, a serpentine energy emanating from the ground that I had only felt once before—at Glastonbury.

"What a lot of freaks," said Bob.

Strolling along the sidewalk was a very tall man wearing pink fairy wings. Most of the women had long hair, the men had scraggly beards, and one of the women had a beard. A lot of people were actually wearing tie-dye. This old guy with a long white beard was dressed in a patchwork dress and carrying what looked like a wizard's staff. There were dogs everywhere.

Bob parked the car and we got out to walk around, and a man in worn jeans and a ratty sweater pressed a small rock into my hand and gave me a thumbs-up. I looked down at the rock and it was covered in a symbol I would later learn said "Om."

The strangers passing me on the street were smiling and waving at me.

"Hey!" said a punked-out young woman with a dog.

"Hey!" I found myself answering.

There were a lot of young people milling around. Ordinary teenagers on skateboards, stoned-looking boys lolling on park benches on the green, and a lot of kids who looked like they'd put on costumes that morning.

"The people around here all look like you," said Bob.

Bob, however, looked completely out of place in his bright polo shirt and pressed pants, like the whitest slice of Wonder Bread you've ever seen.

For lunch we went into the Joyous Lake, a famous old restaurant where a lot of music greats had gotten their start. We sat out on a deck looking out over the town, and a pretty blond with streaks in her hair just like mine came over and pressed a CD into my hand. "I think you're going to love my music."

A handsome-looking guy, clean shaven, leaned over to me as he passed our table. "Who *are* you?"

It was strange and wonderful at the same time. I felt like I had arrived in the fairy realm at last.

"Are you a rock star?" asked a large, blowzy woman covered in rhinestones.

"Not yet," I joked.

I was used to attracting attention in New Jersey. I was used to people pointing at me, or snickering, or pulling their kids away when they got too close. This was different. I felt welcomed.

My whole life I had been a fish flopping on the dry boards of the dock, and now I was back in the ocean. I was back in the water again. I could feel it. I could breathe here. This was my element.

"They like you here," said Bob with a note of surprise in his voice.

A couple with cameras around their necks came over and asked for my autograph.

"Can I get a photo of you with my husband?" asked a woman.

After lunch Bob and I went window-shopping, checking out stores filled with jewelry and leather goods, upscale clothing and novelty T-shirts. There were a lot of art galleries. We crossed a stream that burbled through the center of town. There was a shop filled with statues of fairies and old icons, another with Tibetan mandalas and Hindu posters. We passed a head shop or two and a wine store and then came to an old white Victorian building that announced it was a dance and drumming studio. There was a "For Sale" sign on a small patch of green grass.

Bob and I stopped and looked at it. Both of us were drawn to it.

After a short silence, Bob turned to me. "Do you want me to buy this for you, Suzie?"

I was startled. "Why?"

"You once said you wanted a store. . . ."

"I talked about it once, that's true."

"This would be a good place for you to have a store. This is a good town for you."

"How far are we from New Jersey?"

Bob shrugged.

Neither of us said anything else, but I realized at that moment that Bob was as exhausted by our relationship as I was. This was his way of putting me out to pasture. He was done, and he was going to give me a store as a good-bye present. I had failed at normal. Miserably. But it was also something else. He was right. This was my town. I belonged here.

Almost immediately Bob put in a bid for the store, but it turned out it was already contracted to somebody else who wanted to turn it into a restaurant. I found myself praying fervently that the restaurant deal would fall through and Bob and I would be able to buy the building after all. I was already collecting fairy dolls and punk clothing that I wanted to sell in my shop. But most of all, I wanted to move to Woodstock. I had to move to Woodstock. I couldn't stop imagining myself there in that store.

My friends were stunned. "You don't belong up there with all those hippies. What about your readings?"

But I didn't want to do readings anymore. I wanted a little shop filled with clothes and jewelry and crystals. I was losing my mind from doing readings. I was done with readings. I let people know that I was going to retire. Though I promised that I'd still do a reading here and there for my regulars.

A few months later, Bob got a call saying that the other person had backed out of the deal and had decided not to buy the building after all. Bob put a down payment on it at once.

Around this same time David got evicted from his apartment. Out of the blue, Bob invited David to live with me in Woodstock. Over the years, as Gavin went back and forth between us, David and Bob had unexpectedly become friendly.

But he didn't ask me if I wanted to move back in with David; Bob just decided that I was going to.

Over the years I'd remained close to David, not just because he was Gavin's father, but also because he was my oldest friend. But I knew then that Bob really wanted to be done with me. He didn't want me going back and forth to New Jersey to bring Gavin to see his dad. Bob wanted to put me away up in the mountains, just like my sister had put my mother in the nursing home.

Except that to me Woodstock felt like heaven.

David moved into our condo while we were waiting for the closing and Bob moved back in with his parents. While David and I were organizing our things for the move, I started looking through my old photo albums. In one there was a picture of me at the baby shower my girlfriends had thrown for me just before Gavin was born. I was wearing a T-shirt, which was unusual enough, but when I looked closely I could see what was written on it. "Woodstock: Peace and Love."

It was then that David remembered what the angel had told me. "Remember? She said you were going to move to the Catskills, that you would be safe there."

"I'm not moving to the Catskills. I'm moving to Woodstock."

David laughed. "Those mountains you saw? Those are the Catskill Mountains."

"You will be safe there," I heard the angel saying.

Safe from what?

The night before the closing, the car was all packed and I was ready to do my last reading for five people. As usual, I needed the money. I brought my cards and my tape recorder and sat down with the women around a coffee table. I shut my eyes for a moment, and when I did I saw a red velvet curtain, one of those theatrical curtains with golden tassels you see at a Broadway show, softly beginning to close. I opened my eyes and still I saw it. The curtain was closing. Something was coming to an end.

The women were getting restless.

"I can't see anything," I said. The curtain before my eyes had shut.

A closing? The closing on the shop? The closing of my psychic life? What was closing?

When I got home, David was waiting for me. "Sit down. I need to talk to you."

"What?" I said, instantly concerned.

"I went on the Internet tonight. Jack Wild just died."

A small stone dropped into my heart and sent ripples outward. I'd known he was going to die since I'd met him. Still, it felt significant to have his death align with this huge transition I was making.

Three days later my mother also passed away.

———

The spirit of an older woman appeared in a reading I was giving that turned out to be my client's mother. In the crook of each arm she was cradling a baby. One was her own miscarried child. And the other was her daughter's. She was so happy to be holding them. Her daughter was weeping as I described how happy these unborn babies were to be in her mother's arms. They were all reunited.

20

How Not to Die

I was still visiting my mother every day in between packing when, just as I was about to say good-bye to her and move, I noticed a new smell coming from her body. I remembered that smell from when both Daddy and Steve had died. It wasn't so much the odor of decay as the sweet, sickly smell of funeral lilies. My mother smelled like flowers. Death was coming.

She was conscious and her eyes were open, but her breath had begun to rattle in her throat. She stared straight ahead, rigid and terrified. She was over ninety-five years old then, and her heart was still strong, even though every other part of her had begun to collapse.

I knew that she didn't want to go. She was afraid that heaven wouldn't take her because of her adulterous affair, because she was "dirty." Or at least that's what I thought.

I desperately wanted my mother to experience some kind of peace before she left. The hard thing was, I know from my readings how little changes for the dead. They take with them their rage, their confusion, or their joy. It's not so much death itself that should frighten us, but who we are when we arrive at the moment of death.

My sister and I sat with her, each of us holding one of her hands. "You do know that there's an afterlife, don't you?" I whispered, trying to soothe her.

"No," she rasped.

"You've seen what I do. I talk to the dead. We'll still be able to talk after you go. We're not really saying good-bye."

"No," she said again. "I don't believe in anything."

I knew it was defensive. I knew that what she believed in was the judgment of a cruel and unforgiving God. I knew that she was sure she was going to hell. But I wanted her to be done with hell, to let go of it at last and open up to the possibilities of love and forgiveness. I really thought that it could happen for her at the end. Sometimes it does.

Even my crazy old grandmother, the one everyone thought was possessed, finally let go of her demons just before she passed away. My aunts said that when my grandmother had taken her last breath, her eyes had opened wide and her face had been transformed by an expression of wonder and joy. She died smiling.

"Do you see angels?" I asked my mother. I had been praying that they would come to comfort her.

"No."

"Do you see your mother or your father?"

"No."

Each breath she dragged into her body seemed like it would be her last. But she would not give up. Her fury and rage at life, at death, at her very soul seemed to keep her going.

I wanted to be gentle and comforting and loving. I was

sure I was the right person for the job. I had my crystals and my feathers and my sacred oils. I anointed her third eye and at one point even climbed onto her bed and waved my arms to clear away any obstructions her etheric body might be experiencing.

Leave it to a priest to walk in at exactly that moment. There I was with my rainbow-colored dreadlocks, standing on the bed of this little old Catholic lady, flapping my arms like a lunatic. He stood in the doorway staring at us. My mother managed to turn her head away from him. She hadn't let a priest come near her in years.

He left without saying a word.

I thought maybe I could bring somebody through from the other side to help my mother. But no one wanted to come. I called on Daddy, on Steve, on Aunt Mary, on Tatum, our dog. *Please come and help her do this in peace*, I begged them. But no one wanted to be in that room with my mother. I've never been in a place that was so empty of spiritual activity as my mother's room as she died.

It's only in retrospect that I realize that I was trying so hard to create peace for her because I so desperately needed it for myself. I wanted a word of forgiveness from her before she died, some gesture of understanding, of love. I held her hand in mine for days, but she never once squeezed it back.

Hour after hour, day after day I watched her breath, sure that each one would be her last.

I wanted her to be free, but she had never wanted to be free.

On the third day, exhausted, I picked up a book and let my attention wander away from her deathbed. That was the moment she chose to die. She didn't want me with her. She hadn't wanted the reminder of her sin at her passing.

"She's gone," said my sister.

The undulating line of the heart monitor had gone flat.

My mother was dead.

I didn't feel anything at that moment, neither sorrow nor relief. I had been waiting for something, and I hadn't gotten it.

The room was empty. I couldn't feel my mother's spirit anywhere.

An old nurse came in and murmured clichés like, "God bless her. Now she's with the angels. At last she's at peace."

But I wasn't so sure.

Had she just disappeared and become a glob with everything else? What happened to a consciousness like my mother's at death? What had she experienced? I had no idea.

I wanted to see an angel come for my mother. I wanted to see an expression of bliss or happiness or simple peace on her face at the end. But nothing happened. I tried to feel the energy in the room, I was alert to it like a cat, but I couldn't feel anything, not a prickle of an otherworldly being in the room. When my dog Milo had died, all kinds of other creatures had arrived to welcome him home—fairies, other corgies, even Saint Francis. A huge rainbow had spread out across the clouds at the moment of Milo's death. But when my mother died, nothing happened at all.

Nothing had changed in our relationship.

I suppose it shouldn't have surprised me. My mother left the same way she had lived, in denial of love, in denial of anything truly spiritual. Nothing changes with death. The story isn't over. There was just more work to do, for the both of us.

My sister let out a long sigh, stood up, and began cleaning out the drawers of my mother's bureau. The nurse started filling out paperwork. From the room next door, a television blared a soap opera. There was nothing sacred about my mother's death.

Her body was lying there on the bed, and I had no ritual and no sacraments for that moment.

I wanted some kind of ceremony. I wanted prayers, but I didn't know which ones. I needed a way to close off the big gap in the veil torn by my mother's death. But I had no idea what to say or do. At last I sang to myself the words of Sarah McLachlan's "Angel":

"You're in the arms of the angel,
May you find some comfort here."

When Daddy had died, I had wept. When Steve had died, I had cried my heart out. When my animals passed away, I always shed tears. But when my mother died, I felt nothing. It was as if nothing had changed between us. She had withheld love from me in life, and she refused to love me even at her death. But at least it was over.

My mother has never once visited me as a spirit. She never even visits my dreams. Other people's mothers and fathers are always showing up in my sessions with last things they need to say, bits of advice, life tips, apologies. Daddy even came through to me once and told me that he'd always known I wasn't his daughter, but it hadn't made any difference at all because he'd loved me. He also told me to stop cooking with Teflon pans, that they give people cancer.

Steve visits me all the time, particularly in dreams. I often hear his laughter and feel his presence. I know he's watching out for me, sword in hand. He's one of my protectors. Just like Jack. Jack is always close.

But where my mother went, I have no idea.

My sister arranged the simple funeral. There was a wake with an open casket, and I felt compelled to take death-mask photos of my mother's waxen corpse. My cousins were aghast, but people used to always make castings of the dead, and I couldn't see why I shouldn't do the same. I didn't develop the photos, though.

My mother was cremated and my sister brought her ashes home. I guess cremation is okay for some people, but I've been burned in so many past lives that, in this one, I want for once just to let my body crumble and my bones turn to dust.

The priest who delivered my mother's funeral mass was from India and had a heavy accent. My mother had always been very racist and judgmental about foreigners.

"Grandma wouldn't have liked this guy at all," whispered Gavin to me. We both started giggling and couldn't stop.

"It serves her right," said Gavin, and I agreed.

"Do you think Grandma is in the bad heaven or the good hell?" asked Gavin as we filed out of the church.

"Does it matter?" I said. "Wherever she is, she's still unhappy, isn't she?" But I think that was his point. Wherever she is, she's waiting with her arms crossed, dissatisfied. What did she want? I'd always wanted to know and now I never would. At least that's what I thought at the time.

A few weeks after the funeral, I asked my sister about my mother's will. Was there going to be a reading? I guess I still thought it would be like in the old movies where all the relatives sit down in some oak-paneled lawyer's office. But my sister just sent me a copy of it.

I wasn't even mentioned.

My mother left everything to my sister. She gave Gavin a few thousand dollars, but my name was nowhere in the document.

Bob said that legally I could challenge it, that she couldn't completely cut me out of an inheritance without observing numerous legal formalities. But it didn't matter. I didn't exist to her. She didn't want me to exist. She never had.

When she died, she aborted me at last. I was in shock.

It wasn't until she was dead that I realized the only way I could have made her truly happy was if I had destroyed myself. But I didn't. I had a life. I got married. I traveled. I had a child. I even found a man to take care of me financially. But none of it mattered. My very existence had taunted her. She was a woman whose life was filled with secrets, and I was not only the evidence of her biggest deception; I was also uniquely gifted to see through all of her lies.

Many years after her death, I exchanged sessions with a woman who did something she called Violet Alchemy Healing. She chanted over me in some strange language and waved incense around, and I actually saw a circle of spirits around me. Outside of that circle, far beyond it in the shadows, I had a glimpse of my mother, her eyebrows arched, her mouth scowling. "Come join us!" I called to her, but she wouldn't.

Jack was there, though, and he smiled at me. He was young again and dressed like the Artful Dodger. With a great sweep, he took off his top hat and bowed to me. "I'd do anything, for you, dear, anything," he sang.

I wondered if in the world of spirits he'd put in a good word for me with my mother. He probably did.

————

At first, the middle-aged woman who showed up for a reading was skeptical. "How do you do this? What's your technique? Can you explain to me how this works?"

"I'm sorry," I told her. "I have absolutely no idea. None at all."

Still, she decided to sit down in my room and let me take a look at her life.

"There's a man standing behind you." I saw him at once. "He's short but strong. He died quickly of an aneurism. But he's still with you. He's very close to you. He's standing right behind you and he's wrapping his arms around you like they were wings."

The woman gasped. "Wings?"

"Yes," I said. "That's what they remind me of, cupped wings."

It turned out her lover had bought, just before he had died, a painting of golden wings that he hung above their bed. The wings weren't outstretched but folded inward in an embrace, just the way I'd seen him holding her.

Usually, when people have just died, I have to help them move on and understand that their loved ones can't exist in the same realm with them anymore. But this man didn't want to move on. He was right there with her, and he was going to stay there for the rest of her life. He wanted to. She was never going to have another boyfriend or husband. But she would always feel this man close. She never had to think he wasn't there. He was.

"You don't have to learn how to live without him. You have to learn how to live with him in this new way."

21

By the Time I Got to Woodstock

A few days after the funeral, in the middle of a March snow-storm, Bob and David drove me up to Woodstock. On the drive up the thruway I decided I needed a new name. My mother had christened me Suzan, but I was ready to leave everything about her behind in New Jersey. I decided to call myself Fiona, after my devoted cat.

Bob and David unpacked two cars' worth of stuff. They painted the walls; they set up a jewelry tree I'd found and racks for clothes. They built a large cage for my two cockatoos and Amazonian parrot. I put my four-poster bed in the front room of the second-floor apartment looking out on the mountains. I painted the room pink, and I hung fairy dolls from the bedposts. I made everything as feminine as possible. It was a girl's room, a no man's land. David moved a few of his things into the attic, and Bob staked out the back room on the first floor of the shop.

I know how strange it seems, a dysfunctional Oreo with

me as the creamy center. But I was done with them both, and I was friends with them both, and I loved them both. I was grateful that they were willing to be there for me and that they had found a way to get along with each other.

David told me that Bob had called him up to say that he wanted to "pass the torch."

"What torch?" asked David, baffled.

"Suzie," said Bob.

It made me feel like an inanimate object. I was furious at Bob and more determined than ever to be done with him, although Bob wanted us to evolve into some other kind of modern family.

He decided we all needed to go on a cruise together to heal. Bob, Gavin, myself, and David. Needless to say, it was awkward. What I discovered, though, was how much I'd missed David. He loved nature the way I did and would swim out in the deep water while Bob splashed around in the shallows. At dinner Gavin got dressed up in a suit and tie, David dug into the buffet, and Bob seemed strangely jealous of how easily the rest of us got along. I was stressed out and ready to return to Woodstock and a room of my own that I wasn't going to share with anyone again, ever.

I still feel that way.

I am done with romance. There is just none left in this girl, let me tell you. I don't want to call myself a crone, I still think I look pretty good, but let's face it, that's where I am. I love my animals. I love my son. I love my friends. I even have a lot of affection for Bob and David, but I'm just not anyone's wife anymore.

A friend told me that the Oracle of Delphi in ancient Greece was always a woman who was done with marriage and children. She was usually over fifty. That's the new phase I'm headed towards, I think. Freedom. I have women friends who are still desperate to find men, to hook up with boyfriends. They are in their sixties and seventies, and they're still on the prowl for that perfect guy. Maybe it's easier for me because I met my soul mate in this life, so I can let that all go.

These days I'm married to me.

After moving me in, Bob and David drove back to New Jersey to be with Gavin, who was going to finish up the year at his school and come up to Woodstock on the weekends. They left me alone in the building with three birds, two rats, and Milo, my Welsh corgi.

I was in my late forties and this was the first time I had ever lived by myself.

The mountain was shrouded in snow and absolutely beautiful. I felt like I was finally home.

People had been dropping by while we were moving in. Apparently, the building had a lot of history. It had once been a vegetarian health-food store in the sixties run by a commune of hippies; after that it had been a magic shop. Once it sold only kaleidoscopes. An old woman had supposedly fallen down the stairs and died just after the turn of the century. But if so, I've never seen her. Bob Dylan was rumored to have written a song in what was going to be my bedroom.

In all, the energy in the house was calm and settled. I was surprised when that first night I wasn't lonely at all. I was so used to feeling separate from everyone and everything in New Jersey, but in Woodstock I felt surrounded by my people. The man with the fairy wings had popped in that first day to see if I had any evening dresses he could buy. I sold him one for ten dollars.

My first morning in Woodstock, Milo and I went out for a walk to get some breakfast, and everyone who passed us waved and said, "Hi." Families stopped to pet Milo; people on the street introduced themselves. In New Jersey I felt like people were always checking each other out to make sure they were fitting in, and I, of course, never did. But in Woodstock I could step outside with my purple hair, and people would come over to me to say hello. I felt like I was in some cheesy fifties musical, and in an instant everyone would start dancing and break into song.

And there were all kinds of people, not just hippies. What I liked best were the artists—the musicians, the painters, and the writers—who've been coming here since the turn of the last century, long before the famous music festival. A lot of people don't realize that this area has been calling out to spiritual types for a long, long time. Even the Esopus Indians considered it sacred grounds. The ley lines that lie beneath Woodstock are so similar to the ones at Glastonbury. But Glastonbury was the past and Woodstock was the future. I was so happy I was here.

That morning I passed a bush in front of a local convenience store, and it called out, "Hello!" I thought I might be having some kind of biblical moment where even the plants were starting to talk to me when a small, sinewy old man with a grizzled beard emerged from the shrubbery.

"You look like my ex-wife," he said. "She was one good-lookin' dame."

"Thanks."

"I'm Rocky," he said, holding out his hand.

"I'm Fiona."

Later I found out that the bush was only his temporary

home. He'd been a famous featherweight boxer, had once served time for manslaughter, and was now a town fixture, one of many homeless people who wandered the streets of Woodstock—hippies, drug addicts, dropouts, wandering musicians.

The man who had given me the stone with the symbol on it turned out to be a spiritual ascetic who rarely spoke and went around town painting blessings on rocks and bits of paper he found. Someone explained that once upon at time he'd been a successful New York patent lawyer, but he had dropped out of that world to paint and meditate.

Another fellow I learned later was called Puppy John tipped his hat to me as I passed. "Good morning, Suzan," he said.

I was startled. I'd been telling everyone my name was Fiona, but I was to discover that many of the street people in Woodstock had psychic powers. They were very attracted to me, it seemed, which would at times become problematic. I've never been able to do readings for the mentally ill; their egos are too shattered for me to get a clear line on any information. But the people in Woodstock were different. There was a charged spiritual energy that seemed to flow up from the ground and touch everyone in some way.

I was to find out that the area had been spiritually sacred to the Lenape Indians long before the arrival of the Dutch and English. The town attracted religious characters of all types. There was a Tibetan monastery at the top of the mountain, and red-robed monks often smiled at me as we passed on the street. There was a Greek Orthodox monastery down the road and a Zen Buddhist monastery where two streams converged a few miles to the west. There was a Sufi center, five Christian churches, a lively synagogue, and countless other meditation, channeling, and yoga groups. The Dalai Lama was coming to visit in May. Half the people in town had names given to them by their gurus.

On the way back to my own store after a walk one day, I noticed a small shop across the street with a sign covered in familiar Wiccan symbols. It was a tiny little place, selling sage and candles and the usual witch gear. I talked to the owner, an attractive young woman with a mass of long red hair who, predictably, had grown up in a repressive family of Baptists down south and come to Woodstock to find her freedom. I knew exactly what she was talking about. She invited me up to a full-moon circle on the top of the mountain in a place called Magic Meadow.

"It's a beautiful hidden bowl surrounded by peaks and filled with apple trees and mountain laurel," she told me. "When they're in bloom, it's like being inside of a cloud. You'll have to come up with us. We drum and sing under the stars and make wreaths for our hair. It's a very holy place."

She began reciting an old chant in praise of the goddess I knew from days at the Church of the Mystic Light, "Isis, Astarte, Hecate, Demeter, Kali, Lianna."

I'd dabbled in Wicca long ago when I was with Erik and hadn't really been taken with it because it felt like it was too skewed to the feminine, but this woman was so gentle and so genuinely friendly I found myself wanting to get to know her. "That sounds really nice," I said, surprised that it did.

An older woman with crooked teeth and gnarled hands came into the shop. She was wearing an odd assortment of tattered skirts and scarves that somehow worked together to give her an oddly stylish look. She reeked of patchouli oil, which I was beginning to discover was the official scent of Woodstock.

"Angel Nicole, meet Fiona; she's just arrived in Woodstock," said the red-haired witch. "You should show her some of your drawings."

Out of her pocket Angel Nicole produced a wad of postcard-sized copies of what were clearly larger paintings—all of angels. They were some of the most beautiful and truest portraits I had ever seen.

"You see angels, don't you?"

"Oh yes," she said casually, as if it were the most ordinary thing in the world.

"I saw an angel once," I said. "In England. The feathers of her wings were covered in eyes."

Angel Nicole beamed. "I know her! Sometimes I see her with Jesus."

"You know Jesus?"

"He comes and talks to me sometimes," she admitted shyly. "Here's a picture of him I did." She pulled out another small painting.

When I saw it, I realized that she was probably telling the truth.

Angel Nicole lived in a van with her dogs, and I started letting her come to my apartment to take showers or to stay there when it was too cold.

When Bob came up and met her, he nearly keeled over.

"This is your new friend?" He was appalled. He couldn't understand how I could even talk to such a person. In New Jersey, she would've been hauled out of the condo complex by the police. What Bob couldn't get through his head was that I had a lot more in common with Angel Nicole than I did with some overstuffed suburbanite on a cruise ship.

I put her full-sized paintings of angels up in the store.

One day she brought me a special painting she'd created just for me. It showed a giant eye rising like the sun over the ocean. There was something Egyptian about it. I put it up in my bedroom and felt it keeping watch over me.

The day after I put up that painting, though, while I was cleaning out the birds' cage like I did every morning, somehow a perch dislodged, stuck out through the bars, and pierced my eye. I heard the hollow *plonk* as the dowel went right into my eyeball. The pain was so immediate and intense that I passed out.

I came to on the floor, and I was sure that I was blind in that eye. I couldn't see anything. I was in excruciating pain. Somehow I managed to get out my cell phone and call David. "Call 911!" he yelled at me.

I dialed 911, and then I called Bob. I was terrified. Nothing like this had ever happened to me. I'd never had an accident before.

"You called an ambulance?" said Bob. "Don't you think you're overreacting?"

But the police and the EMTs were already at the shop by then, and they put me on a stretcher and raced me to the hospital. Which was a good thing, it turned out.

The nurses and doctors were mostly concerned about the bacteria on the perch from the birds.

I told them that Bob seemed to think I was overreacting.

"Let him put a stick through his fucking eye and see how he feels," said one of the nurses.

It turned out my cornea was badly scratched, and I needed antibiotics for a possible infection. Worst of all, I had to wear an eye patch over the eye, and I couldn't wear my contact in the other eye for six weeks. I was blind again, like I had been as a little girl.

Some people say that Woodstock makes you more of what you really are. If that's so, then this was the first step in the heightening of my psychic powers. Once again I couldn't see the outside world, but the spiritual world was clearer to me than it had ever been. I was basically walking around blind, but I was sensing all kinds of spirits. I was feeling like I was on the edge of experiencing all kinds of new realities.

In Woodstock I'm not really that special. There are astrologers and mystics, monks and shamans, Buddhists, Wiccans, Christians, Jews, Sufis, and pagans. It's as if the whole town is the Church of the Mystic Light. I began to feel more confident in my abilities, and my sight seemed to grow more powerful because of that.

My intention had been to retire, but it was strange not doing readings anymore. Still, no one in Woodstock knew I was a psychic. I felt restless. My shop, which Gavin had named the White Gryphon after our cockatoos, wasn't doing much business yet, and a lot of the locals explained to me that things would be slow until the summer tourists started coming into town. Because I needed a little extra money, I decided to put up a sign in the window for Psychic Animal Readings.

I was thinking that now and then someone might show up with their dog, and I'd pat its head and tell its owner if it was sick or if it missed its littermates. That kind of thing. Nothing too heavy or serious or intense. I was imagining the occasional old lady with a mutt she'd picked up at the pound, wondering where he'd come from.

I had no idea what totally insane animal lovers Woodstockers were.

There was a special pet parade every fall where people dressed their animals up in costumes. There were two different sanctuaries for liberated farm animals. Every other person was a vegan. Almost at once, people began pouring into my shop with their dogs, cats, guinea pigs, and even hedgehogs. I was suddenly Saint Francis.

But the really big problem was what the animals were telling me. They weren't just talking about dog food or needing to go to the vet. They were talking about the spirits of the dead, and they were inviting those spirits to speak through me to their owners.

A couple showed up with a depressed dog who turned out to be in mourning for a young girl who'd died. It was the couple's daughter and she had a lot to say to them. Now other parents who had lost children started coming to the store.

The dark underside of Woodstock was drug abuse, and so many people came in who had lost loved ones to overdoses.

I was seeing all kinds of people—shop owners, teenagers, cops, hairstylists, lawyers, businesspeople, old people, the devout, the atheists . . . everybody was coming to me for readings. People began driving up from New Jersey; weekenders from the city told their friends about me. Canadians were arriving. I couldn't even answer my phone anymore. Sometimes I had to hide upstairs because there were so many people in the shop wanting to meet with me. I had taken down the sign about being an Animal Psychic within days, but it didn't matter. Word had gotten out.

I had never been so busy.

A lot of people don't need to see me. Either they're not going to listen to what the spirits are going to tell them or they know it already, like the characters in *The Wizard of Oz*. Of course when the dead come through, that's different. When people are dealing with issues of life and death, of grieving and loss, that feels important. But if you want to know if your boyfriend is cheating on you, don't come to me. You know he is. You're just hoping I'm going to tell you that he's not. I get so bored with those kinds of petty concerns.

When I got overwhelmed by the visitors, I would often go hide in the Artists Cemetery. Woodstock has a bunch of cemeteries, but the most beautiful one is hidden on a soft slope behind a grove of hemlocks minutes from the center of town. All kinds of musicians and painters and writers are buried there, as well as the ordinary people who have known and loved them. Long before the sixties rock concert made it famous, artistic types had been flocking to the town to put on performances and set up utopian communities. No one super famous is buried in the Artists Cemetery, but it's a special place filled with misfits and seekers. It's dark and quiet there, and a lot of the old tombstones are covered in thick, green moss.

I had always thought that when I died I'd be buried somewhere near Glastonbury, but after I came to Woodstock, I knew at last that I had found a place where I could truly rest. Only it sure looked like it wasn't going to happen until after I was dead.

———

The moment this woman walked into my room, I wanted to vomit. Sometimes I'll feel the twinge of someone's arthritis or the dull pounding of a headache, but this was an overwhelming sensation. I was going to throw up.

I put my hand over my mouth and tried to keep it together. "How are you feeling?" I asked her as waves of nausea rolled over me.

"Terrific!" she said. But I could see a black, hideous energy permeating her entire body. Was it AIDS? Was it cancer? Was it catching?

"I think you need to go to a doctor," I told her.

"I take supplements," she said. "I'm in great health."

"Excuse me for a moment," I managed to mutter before I had to rush out of the reading room. I barely made it to the bathroom before I vomited.

"Please," I said when I returned. "Go get a checkup. You need a checkup."

"I'll be fine. Really."

"No. You won't. You need a doctor. This is something very serious."

I tried and tried, but she wouldn't listen to me. That happens sometimes. A few months later I saw her obituary in the paper.

22

I'm Not Going Anywhere!

Gavin was impressed by the Dalai Lama, who spoke on the local baseball field to everyone in town about kindness, but other than that he didn't love Woodstock. Our home was smaller; his school was meaner. None of the warm hippie vibes had seeped into the regional middle school where he started going in September. It was a cold place lit by green fluorescent lights, and each day that Gavin got off the bus he looked sadder and sadder.

I asked him what he thought about the place, but he'd just shrug. Another mother, though, told me what was really going on. The new kid, Gavin, was being bullied by some of the local rednecks for his long hair, his big words, and his quiet ways. It made me feel insane and brought back all my own rage at the cruelties I had endured in school. I was trying to figure out what to do when I got a call from the school nurse asking me and David to come in at once. Gavin had been beaten up in the woodshop.

David and I drove as fast as we could to the middle school. Gavin had actual finger marks on his throat. He had been picked up by the neck and slapped across the face by a group of eighth-grade hoodlums. I flipped. I totally flipped. I felt insane. How could something this horrible happen in a school? I stormed into the middle school office demanding to know what was going to be done about this. Were the bullies going to be expelled? How was Gavin going to be helped to feel safe from this day onward?

An administrator listened to me from behind his desk, nodding as if he understood me. "Well," he finally said. "The real issue is how Gavin is going to learn how to stand up for himself and fight."

I was stunned. "My son does not come to school to learn to fight!"

David and I took Gavin home and withdrew him from the public school. There was no way we were sending him back to such an emotionally clueless place. In the following months and years I cannot tell you how many parents have come to me about the bullying their children have experienced at that school. Gavin loved his public school in New Jersey, but this place had a terrible, dead energy.

David and I started talking to everybody in town about what we should do and kept hearing about a private school that was very gentle and sweet. One day, I was buying a bottle of wine in the liquor store, and I saw a man I instantly recognized as Donovan's son. I remembered him from the concerts in England. But now he was grown-up. He looked just like his father and was standing at the checkout counter.

"Donovan?" I asked, because that was his name also.

"Yeah?" He turned to look at me, clearly wondering how I knew him.

"I knew your dad in the eighties," I explained. "I was friends with Pat and Margaret."

Coincidentally, both he and his father lived locally. I asked where his kids went to school, and he also mentioned the private school everyone else had. I figured if the grand-child of the man who'd written the score for a movie about Saint Francis went there, it was good enough for Gavin. That was the sign I needed. With my sister's financial help, we en-rolled him in the Woodstock Day School the following week.

Gavin was just beginning to settle in when it was time for us to go and have our first parent-teacher conference night. David and I were impressed by how thoughtful and warm Gavin's teachers were and were talking about it on the ride home. But as we drove through town, we began to hear sirens. Fire trucks whizzed past us, followed by a police car and an ambulance. People were running down the sidewalks ahead of our car. We came around the curve of the main street through town and saw flames shooting up from the roof of the White Gryphon. The windows were bursting from the heat, and the entire top of the building was on fire.

"Oh my God, oh my God!" I was screaming. "Gavin! Gavin!"

David and I abandoned the car in the middle of the road and leapt out.

"I'm going in!" I screamed, running towards the building. But firemen held me back. "My son's in there! My animals are in there!"

The whole top floor of the building caved in. And sud-denly it was gone. There were firemen everywhere with their axes and hoses. People were coming up to me, but I didn't know what was happening. I had to get in there to find Gavin.

More windows popped. People in the street were screaming and crying. It was like some scene from a horror movie, only it wasn't a movie. It was really happening. It was a parent's worst nightmare, to go out for a simple evening and to come back and find your child in a house on fire.

The policeman wouldn't let go of me, but a moment later a neighbor was beside me, letting me know that Gavin was in her house. He was okay. Not only that, he'd called 911, shut the fire door to the shop below, and heroically managed to rescue all of the animals on his own.

"Do you have any enemies, ma'am?" asked a burly fireman coming over to me.

"What do you mean?" I asked, too distraught to understand the question.

"This is no ordinary fire. It's like a bomb went off up there."

"Really?"

"Three-alarm fire that fast? Awfully strange."

"I don't even know anyone here! We just moved to town!"

By the time they got the fire out on the top floor, the attic of the building was a charred, smoking catastrophe.

We lost everything we owned. Our clothes, our furniture, our books, our records, our artwork, everything. Luckily, I had most of my photo albums downstairs in my reading room, so they were all right, and except for some smoke damage the store itself was unharmed. Still, it was a devastating, heartwrenching experience.

I walked around the black, empty remains of our apartment in a daze an hour later. I sat down on the floor. It was still hot. There were no walls anymore, just blackened beams.

"I'm just going to sleep here tonight," I said to David.

"You can't sleep here, honey," said one of the firemen.

"I'm okay. I'm staying here." My bed was gone; my fairies were gone; my pink room was gone. Still, I could see the mountain out of the window frame.

Eventually David and one of the firemen had to carry me out of the building.

A woman who owned a motel around the corner let us stay in one of her cabins with all of our animals. The families and teachers at Gavin's school were amazing, taking up a collection for clothing, bedding, and kitchenware. Shops around town put out cans so people could donate to help us out. We became the Cratchits, the local charity case. "Oh, you're the family who lost everything in that fire," is what people said now when they met us.

One of the parents at the Day School had a small cottage on the Hudson River that he let us live in for the next six months. I was strangely disoriented. I couldn't eat. I couldn't think. I certainly couldn't do readings. It felt like I had been personally attacked and had barely survived. But by what, and for what reason, I had no idea.

The insurance investigators discovered that there had been some problem in the internal wiring of the refrigerator, which had literally exploded like a bomb. It was a total fluke; it was amazing that anyone had survived.

Even though I had lost everything I owned, I became oddly fixated on a single Betsey Johnson coat I had just bought and never worn. It was the one loss I truly mourned. *It's just stuff*, I kept saying to myself, *just stuff*. Still, I wished

I'd worn the coat at least once. Why save anything? You never know what's going to happen next.

The cottage was in the middle of nowhere. David drove Gavin to school and then met up with Bob at the building. The two of them were renovating it together.

I lost myself in books. I walked down to the river. I found an old cemetery on the edge of the woods and visited it every day. But I wasn't in my body. Everything was gone. My life in New Jersey. My mother. Jack. The new life I had tried to make for myself. Everything.

One night David and I were watching a horror movie when a strange thought struck me. The main character was about to walk into some room she clearly wasn't supposed to go into. I knew she wasn't supposed to go into it, everyone watching the movie knew she wasn't supposed to, but still, there she was, opening the door and stepping inside. She had no business going in there. She should have known better. How could she be so stupid?

That's when it hit me. Was this the mistake I was making?

In doing my psychic readings, was I walking down the wrong hallways, jimmying the locked doors, wandering into the forbidden forests? Might I not be opening myself to some onslaught of darkness and plain old creepiness because of what I do? Was the fire a message for me to stop?

Bob certainly thought that was the case. He'd been reading *The Secret*, and he was sure that through "the laws of attraction" I'd brought the fire on myself. Bob thought the house had burned because I watched too many horror movies. He didn't really think it was my psychic powers, though. He still liked those. He was always calling me up to help him find misplaced checks. He still couldn't get that I could never see that kind of thing.

Friends in New Jersey were sure I was going to move back. "You're not going to stay up there after that, are you? You can't possibly be supposed to stay. Isn't the fire a sign? Shouldn't you come back?"

I thought about it a lot, those months by the river. I wasn't scared, but I was curious. Something had tried to burn me out of town. Some old force didn't want me in Woodstock, but it wasn't *of* Woodstock, that force. No. It was angry that I was there—that somehow, despite everything, I had made it to my home. I could sense that. I knew it. Lifetime after lifetime I have been silenced. I have been dismissed, ignored, and burned. Again and again I have been burned. Wasn't I always being burned by Popes and Puritans? Weren't they always threatened by what I might see?

What was it they didn't want me to see, didn't want me to say, age after age?

"You're not going to stay in Woodstock, are you?" phoned another New Jersey friend.

"Yeah, I am," I decided. "This is my home. I'm not going anywhere."

I invited some of the Tibetan monks I ran into on the village green to come on over to the building and say some blessings over it. They circled the property in their red and orange robes, cheerfully chanting. First clockwise, then counterclockwise. It felt good.

David had made friends with a man who was Native American. He sculpted us two white gryphon statues to serve as guardians. He also brought over some of his friends to remove whatever curses might be lurking on the property. They lit sage and smudge sticks and waved feathers and chanted at each of the four corners of the building.

Driving back and forth from the store to our cottage, I often stopped at a little grocery store that specialized in English teas and cookies. The owner of the store was a tall man with long gray hair. He felt like he was caught somewhere in between being a man and a woman, like the old Greek seer Tiresias, though I didn't mention this to him. One day, however, when I was paying for a package of chocolate biscuits, he asked me completely out of the blue, like he was suggesting I try a new marmalade, what I knew about the Black Madonna.

"The *Black* Madonna?"

"Everyone always thinks about the White Madonna, which is really just the version of Mary the Church wants us to accept. You know, the Pure Blessed Virgin in her white robes. But there is another Madonna and she is dark—like the earth. There are statues of her all over Europe and always have been. Her face and skin are usually black. The Church is always claiming they were blackened in fires, but they weren't. They are all at ancient sites, places where the Goddess has always been worshiped. Those statues started out black, like the statues of Isis. A lot of those statues were just statues to Isis that were taken over by the Church. The Mary everyone knows? She's just a whitewashed version of the Goddess."

"*Really?*" This was all news to me. It was one of those very strange moments I sometimes have in my life. Here I am, buying English tea cookies, and suddenly I get the feeling that I'm about to experience some major revelation in my life. The little hairs on my arms were all electrified.

"She is Isis, actually. And Aphrodite. And Mother Earth."

"Yeah?"

"That's why she's black, like rich soil along the river deltas. She's the fertile earth beneath our feet."

"Isis, Astarte, Demeter, Hecate, Kali, Lianna," I said, remembering the chant of my Wiccan friends and trying to make some sense of what the man was telling me.

"That's right." The man was beaming at me expectantly.

"Is there anything else I should know?"

"We don't take credit cards, I'm afraid."

I handed him a five-dollar bill, left the shop in a stunned state, and got back in the car with David.

On the ride home, I couldn't stop thinking about how my whole life there had been something that enraged me about the Blessed Virgin. Mary had always seemed prissy to me, and something about her celebrated purity, all of that immaculate virginity and everything, had never felt right. She'd always felt like my blond-haired mother, pretending that she was perfectly proper and denying that she had a body with needs and desires. *Ha!* I thought. Underneath the pastel blue veils was really a Black Madonna, earthy and alive. I saw Isis with her wings outstretched to hold the world and a bare-breasted Kali, skulls hanging around her neck, sticking out her tongue. A Black Madonna wouldn't behave like some long-suffering martyr to her life. She'd say what she really thought. She'd do what she really wanted.

Ever since I was a little girl I had sensed there was another Mary, hadn't I?

A familiar onslaught of fury grabbed hold of me. I wanted to shake those poor pathetic nuns from my childhood and tell them that they had been wrong. It didn't matter how long our skirts were or if we were good girls or sluts. I'd known it all along. They were wrong. Their Mary was wrong. I wanted to take that old statue of my mother's and hurl it onto the ground and break it forever. I wanted to scream at the pastel-wearing psychics who tried to pretend there was no darkness in the spiritual world, who thought everyone was just bathed in white light and there was no evil as long as you pretended that there wasn't. Most of all I wanted to yell at my mother, "Stop worrying about what the neighbors think!" All that fear about fitting in and behaving properly had made my life with her such a misery.

I'd always felt that prissy Mary looking down at me, smug, blond, perfect, and untouched. She didn't want to look at dead people; she didn't wear lipstick that was too red; she didn't think about the things that happened *down there*.

"Don't touch me down there!" I heard my mother screaming at the doctor in the nursing home.

I felt a cold chill deep inside of me. I got out of the car, and instead of going inside to the cottage, I walked through the woods to the old cemetery.

No one had been buried there in a long time. Many of the gravestones were crumbling and the names were hard to read. Still, I could feel the dead all around me. Women who had died in childbirth, children taken by disease, grandmothers, grandfathers, the lonely, the blessed, the suffering, the forgotten. My people.

I could see everything about them, even now, but I had missed the one true thing about the person closest to me. My whole life I had avoided seeing it, until this moment with the Black Madonna at my back.

How had I never seen it before? It had always been there right in front of me, in plain sight, and yet somehow I had never before let myself witness the one thing my mother had most feared that I would know about her. Her whole life she must have been frightened that I knew.

I sat down by a gravestone trying to take in what I had just seen.

She was a little girl in a red dress, and she was hiding in a closet beneath the stairs of her house. Her heart was racing; she was trembling. She was terribly frightened her brother might find her. Again. A wave of revulsion swept over me, and I knew. Her brother had been so much older than her, hadn't he? And my mother never spoke of him, at all, and she wouldn't let my sister and me even talk to him at family reunions. I remembered my aunt Mary refusing to see him and hissing that she wished that he would die.

It was as if my whole life I had deliberately chosen not to see what I knew must be true. I couldn't see it until my mother was dead because if I had, it would have killed her. My mother had been molested as a little girl by her older brother. I knew it. I didn't have any proof other than what I'd seen, but I knew it.

I also knew that there was no one I could talk to about this. My mother and Aunt Mary were dead. My own sister was committed to maintaining my mother's idea of herself. There was no reason to seek out my cousins and talk about it with them. This wasn't information that mattered to anyone else. It was between my mother and me, between us and the Madonna whose name I had not known until this day.

A wave of pity flowed through me, not just for my mother but for all of the abused women told that if they weren't virgins they were whores. My poor mother. Poor veiled, submissive

Mary. If only they'd had a Black Madonna to fight for them, to tell them that it hadn't been their fault, that their bodies were not shameful no matter what had been done to them. I wanted a goddess who would tell that little abused girl that she was still perfect, still beautiful, and still powerful, and I wanted her to lift up her foot and squash the man who had hurt her like a bug. Instead, my mother had Mary telling her to be quiet, settle down, and keep herself covered up, for goodness' sake, or *everyone will think you're asking for it.* Mary was the wrapped-up goddess men had given to women to keep them in their place. No wonder she had always made me so angry.

My mother's hell had been so much deeper than I had realized.

Her relationship with my father made sense for the first time, too. She was so uncomfortable with her sexuality that she gave herself to a sexless marriage. But she couldn't get rid of her natural passions. Still, they had to be a secret, let in undercover. I knew I'd always embarrassed her, but I had no idea until this moment just how much. I was a symbol to her of everything that was dark and wrong and bad. I was even dark and brown eyed instead of comfortingly blond.

I was not Mary's daughter; I was the handmaiden of the Black Madonna. I was defiant; I asked questions; I saw things I wasn't supposed to. I wouldn't be tamed.

Knowing all of this didn't excuse my mother for who she'd been, however. Let me be clear about that. Just because I understood her in a new way didn't mean she still didn't owe me an apology.

Everybody has terrible things happen to them, if not in this life, then in past lifetimes, but suffering doesn't let us off the hook. We've got to decide what to do with it. My mother could have chosen to accept having a psychic daughter as a gift. Maybe it would have helped her to contact the other side, to explore her own past lives, to discover other kinds of spirituality that might have healed her. She could at least have gotten into therapy.

I was also given a lot of suffering in my childhood, but I've been determined not to let it hold me back, because I know that life doesn't ever stop. Every day is a chance to start over. We are given new days and new births and new lives at every moment. There's no death and there are no dead ends, and when we can truly realize that we are always standing at the crossroads, life becomes a lot more interesting and enjoyable.

I felt a renewed defiance from what I had seen. The most important thing I could do was not leave Woodstock. I wasn't going to let myself be burned out of town. My mother had given in, she was always a victim, but I wasn't going to be. I was going to fight back, keep asking questions, and keep speaking up for the darkness and the dead.

These days I sometimes wear a cross and sometimes an Egyptian ankh around my neck. I don't think the Black Madonna cares which one I have on.

Eventually, we moved back to the White Gryphon, and because Bob and David's renovation had been so successful, Bob decided to buy another house up the street and fix it up with David.

It was late one night, and I was about to shut off the television when David announced that he was going to do some work on the house.

"Now?"

"Yes," he answered. In retrospect, he wasn't behaving like

himself. He was almost robotic, possessed. But I was tired and I went back to bed with my book. What I didn't realize, since it was only just past midnight, was that it was now officially Friday the 13th.

I was just drifting off to sleep when I heard a neighbor pounding on the front door of the shop and screaming, "Come quick! Fiona! Fiona! Come quick! There's been a terrible accident."

I flew down the stairs and out the door. There were police cars and ambulances racing up the road. Lights were flashing. People were screaming. I ran up the street to the house where David had been working.

"Don't go in the garage!" someone screamed as I approached.

"Stay back! Don't go in there!" pleaded a policeman, grabbing my arm.

It felt like the fire all over again.

Policemen with flashlights were searching the ground in front of the house. Blood was splattered everywhere.

"What happened? What happened?" I yelled.

"Don't let her in here! Don't let her see me!" David was screaming as the EMTs brought him out on a stretcher.

David had cut off all the fingers of his left hand with the table saw.

A neighbor drove Gavin and me to the hospital behind the ambulance, but by the time we got there they had already decided to airlift David to New York City. The neighbor brought Gavin and me back home, and the moment we walked in the phone rang from the hospital. They needed to see if we could find the one finger the police hadn't been able to locate. We found it, we put it on ice, we got it to the hospital in the city, but ultimately it didn't make any difference.

After seven operations, one of them more than twenty-four hours long, David still wasn't able to keep any of his lost fingers.

When the hospital called to tell me that it wasn't going to work, I let out a primal scream from the deepest place of my being. I think I could have handled it better if it had happened to me than to sweet, gentle David. After all, I don't need my fingers to do readings. But David used his hands all the time. He made things. That's who he is. Whether he's crafting an elfin sword or a beautiful piece of crystal jewelry, he's a craftsman. A left-handed craftsman. His fingers were always busy. He fixed things. But it was even deeper than that.

David had always been my rock. No matter what happened, he was there and steady, the one making everything safe and comfortable in his own odd, eccentric way. I live in the ether, but David is practical. He does the driving and the cooking. I realized in that moment that David had always been my protector. No matter where I had roamed, he had been there for me. What did it mean that he had been attacked? Was it because of me and what I did?

David was in terrible pain, both physically and emotionally.

He looked like a Civil War soldier in the hospital, covered in bloody bandages. They were even using leeches at one point to try to get the blood flowing between his reattached fingers and his hand. I kept thinking it was like something that had happened to one of King Arthur's knights. It was a mythic wound to take away David's hand.

Were we supposed to leave Woodstock? I had to ask that question again. I asked the spirits, Jack, my father, the universe, the ground beneath my feet, and I listened hard and the answer I got was always the same.

No. *You belong in Woodstock.*

Whatever was trying to get me to leave town should have known that I can be pretty obstinate about doing things my way. I was staying put, and I knew that if I did, some new kind of destiny was going to open up for me.

A tall, bearded priest from a tiny ramshackle chapel up near the top of the mountain stopped by the store one day. I think he was Russian Orthodox. He'd heard about David; he'd been there for the fire.

"There's a war being fought here between good and evil," he told me. "You should know that, but you should also know that you are good, so good, powerfully good. This is an old fight, the oldest fight of all, and you're a part of it. I'm glad you're here. We need you. Big changes are coming soon."

I don't know if he was talking about things we can see in the real world or the forces of angels and demons. Or maybe both.

I was so out of it, I couldn't really take in what he was saying. Long ago the angel had told me I would be safe in the Catskills. What a joke! Could she have been kidding? Was she setting me up? How was I possibly safe in this town?

I had the monks come back, and also the Native Americans, and everyone did a lot more chanting. Another spiritual teacher in town told me that whenever the demons arise to attack, you know you are on the right path. I wish I had felt more reassured.

To fight back, I decided to get my back tattooed with my own protective demons. I had the tattoo artist create a wild-looking vampire woman with bared teeth—gorgeous but lethal. I wanted her to have my back. She's one part Kali, one part Anne Rice, one part gargoyle. My rats, too, are part of the tattoo, curled together in the symbol of yin and yang, light and darkness. It's an empowering tattoo; it makes me feel safer, tougher. I felt very open when I came to Woodstock, caught up in the lighthearted fairy magic of the place. But I've become much more armored since I've been here. Powerful forces are on the move.

Soon after all that, a beautiful, statuesque blonde wandered into the store. I noticed that she had Celtic knot work and seraphim angels tattooed on her arms. She made me feel like Gollum, what with my vampire lady and rodents crawling over my scrawny back.

The blonde noticed my tattoos. "Rats?" she said. "Do you like rats?"

"I love them," I said a little defensively. "I have two for pets."

"So do I!" she exclaimed. I was surprised.

We started talking about rodent care and tattoos. She was not the kind of person I had first imagined. She was completely open to rats and bats and all the supposedly ugly things in the world that most people reject. When I looked at her more closely, I saw that she, too, had darkness within her. But it didn't overwhelm her. At one point I realized she was studying my face.

"You don't have any wrinkles at all, do you?"

"That's because I'm an immortal from Transylvania," I joked.

And just like that, she took me in her arms and gave me a real, beautiful, motherly kiss on the side of my face.

No one had ever kissed me like that before.

I felt acceptance and love. From a total stranger.

I never saw her in Woodstock again. I don't know who she was.

I think some of my clients imagine that the spiritual life doesn't have any darkness in it. They imagine that if they say the right prayers and do the right meditations, nothing will ever be hard for them again. They'll always walk in the light. But sometimes the demons are as important as the angels. Sometimes the demons lead us to the angels. Don't ever take away my demons, because if you do, you might take my angels, too.

———

"I'm looking for a real psychic," announced a brash woman with toxic city energy who barged into my shop towards the end of the day. I was sitting by the cash register, reading a novel, The Evolution of Bruno Littlemore. It's about a talking ape.

"There's the lady at The Golden Wishes down the street," I answered without looking up. She'd opened a store a few months earlier next to an art gallery, scrawling the name in gold lettering across the window with an illustration of a crystal ball.

"She's not real," said the woman staring at me.

"No, she's not," I agreed. I turned the page and kept on reading.

"I'm looking for a real psychic. Someone said there was a real psychic in this town. At one of these stores."

I shrugged. "Good luck finding her," I said, and went back to my book.

———

Nothing I said seemed to move the old woman sitting in front of me. She acknowledged the things I saw about her, but remained stern and unemotional throughout her entire reading. She'd had a tough life. I could definitely see that. Just as she was about to go, however, I noticed a goat curled up by her feet.

"This may sound strange," I said to her. "But did you ever have a goat? A white goat with tan markings?"

For a moment the woman just stared at me, amazed. I noticed tears were beginning to spill out of her eyes. "You're good, aren't you?" she whispered.

"That goat loves you," I told her.

"Shema," she said softly, with tenderness. "That was her name."

"The goat says you helped her. You loved her."

Now the woman was openly weeping. "She helped me. She saved my life!"

More than sixty years earlier when the woman had been a little girl, her family had been starving to death in Poland after World War II. But Shema the goat had kept the children alive with her milk.

"I loved her so much," sobbed the woman.

And the goat loved that little girl enough to return to visit her as an old woman. Honestly, I'm not sure Shema had ever left her. I think Shema the goat had always stayed close. Guardian angels can look very different than we imagine.

23

My Reading Room

My reading room is a small alcove off of our store not much bigger than a closet. I have filled it with the faces of the dead. My father, dressed as Robin Hood, smiles down at me from a photograph. He looks very handsome. There's a photo from Jack's movie-star days that he signed for me in California. Daddy's on the wall, and my mother, too, frowning. I have a photo of myself hugging my cat, Fiona.

When I look at her, I know that I am not Fiona. And I'm not Suzan or Seretta or Suzie. I have no name. I am whoever I always was. I'm not sure I've ever really had a name. I'm whoever I will be. I am the oracle. That's why it's always been so easy to change my name.

On the other side of the room I have photographs of the spirits that have come through me. People bring me photos and Mass cards of their mothers, their husbands, their children, their pets. I put them all up on the wall. I've never known these people in life, I've only known them in death, but it's not so different, really.

A spiritual healer once visited and thought he might help me clean out the lingering psychic energy of the room, but when he entered it he said he felt like he was standing in the rushing waters of a mountain stream. So many souls pass through that room, they're always on the move. He told me it was a beautiful place, a place of healing.

I keep ashes in the room, too—of my own pets who have passed, of the dead my clients bring to me. A friend bequeathed to me the ashes of her Great Dane because she was moving around and wanted someplace holy to keep them. I wished my sister would let me have the ashes of my mother. I didn't like the idea of them stuck in a box in a house. It felt wrong, sacrilegious. No one should be stuck in a cardboard box for eternity. My mother didn't leave me anything in her will, but I wish she'd left me her bodily remains. I like to think I would have known what to do with them. They weren't really her anymore, but spirits complain about their final resting places to me all the time. They want to be somewhere special. It should have a little thought put into it. They need to be somewhere sacred and healing.

Particularly if they've been upset and unhappy in their lives.

I continue to wish I had more knowledge of my mother and her mother. I wish my mother had opened up to me more. It's important to know where we come from; it's the only way we know where we are. I put up plastic bats in the room for my Transylvanian grandmother. I wish, too, that I'd known her better. The older I get, the more I feel like her. I always picture her out in the middle of a storm.

When I lived in New Jersey, I started going out each night,

no matter the season, without a coat and barefoot. I would run around our condo complex, first clockwise and then counterclockwise. The neighbors must have thought I was out of my mind. When the monks came to bless our house, it reminded me of what I used to do. I needed to feel the ground beneath my feet and the stars above my head. I feel like I am a creature of the night, of the darkness, of the dead.

I have a friend who is writing a book now about the Black Madonna, and he tells me that I am very close to her and she to me. She is the darkness we come from and the darkness we return to. She is the darkness between the stars and the darkness of the dirt. Everywhere I went in Woodstock I began to find out more about her. I'd go to a sale at the library and would suddenly find a book that was about her connections to Mary Magdalene, my old friend from childhood, the other Mary I'd always preferred. A local musician turned out to be leading tours to the Black Madonna's shrines in Europe. A woman who came to me for a reading was having visions of her. One day I, too, had a vision of a young woman with wild hair kneeling on the ground at the center of a vortex. In one hand she held earth and in the other bones. I think it was her. I think I have always been close to her. She is my true mother.

Two years ago a giant hurricane blew up the Hudson Valley, bringing down the grid and turning off the lights. Woodstock was plunged into total darkness. The winds were howling; fat raindrops had begun to fall; the trees were swaying back and forth. As the storm grew stronger, I felt an urgent need to go out in it, just like I had in London years ago.

I took off my shoes and, wearing only a simple cotton dress, headed outside. I didn't tell anyone I was going. I put my headphones on to listen to Nightwish, this sweeping symphonic folk music that matched my mood. I headed into the woods.

The birds and other animals had all hidden themselves away. Branches were falling, but I didn't feel afraid. I came to the creek and the waters were furious, already spilling over the banks. I didn't know that all around me floods were washing away bridges, cars, friends' homes. I followed the curves and twists of the creek. I walked and walked, ecstatic as the wind roared around me. I didn't have any sense of danger, only of freedom. I wasn't aware of my feet squishing through mud; I wasn't aware that I was drenched to the bone; I wasn't aware of the trees crashing all around me. I wasn't aware of anything but the cleansing power of the wind. I reveled in the wildness of the storm.

Nothing in nature could hurt me. That's what my grandmother had said.

I was as happy as I had ever been, walking through the hurricane.

I didn't see a soul as I walked. I emerged at an old farmhouse, but there were no cars on the road. But, then, I didn't want to see people or cars. Nightwish was still playing. I turned around and made my way back home the way I'd come.

As I walked up the steps back to the shop, I realized that I should have told David and Gavin where I'd gone. I'd been out for hours and hours in a hurricane. They must be so worried about me. But when I walked upstairs, David was reading and didn't even look up when I came in.

"I'm back!" I announced.

"Were you checking on the birds in the shop?" asked David.

"I've been out in the storm for hours!"

"What are you talking about?" said Gavin. "You were just here a few minutes ago."

"What?" I was totally confused. That's when Nightwish clicked off. It was only forty-five minutes of music. But how could I have been gone for only forty-five minutes? It was over three miles to the farmhouse driving on the road. Walking through the twists and turns in the woods, it was over twice that. I couldn't have walked seven miles in forty-five minutes. No one could. But somehow I had.

When I was in England for the first time, standing in the garden with the fairies, I had felt similarly out of time. That night, listening to the storm rage, I felt something in the earth waking up again. It could only return in the darkness when the lights were off, the computers were useless, and the grid was completely down.

The storm was devastating. It would be weeks before the power returned. The next day in town, as people emerged, they shared their stories of flooded basements and trees that had slammed through living rooms. There were other stories, too.

A reclusive artist who lived by himself in the woods came into the shop and whispered to me, "The mythical creatures are back."

I'd have thought he'd been holed up in his cabin too long, if I hadn't felt it myself.

A client who was usually very businesslike and often skeptical assured me that, after the storm had finally passed, she stepped outside to look at the damage in her yard and saw a small creature crouching under her porch. When she came closer, he scrambled away.

"I don't know what he was. An elf? A fairy? A leprechaun? I don't know, but he wasn't anything I'd ever seen before. Do you know what he was?"

I didn't, but I thought probably many people were seeing

things they'd never seen before, now that they weren't looking at the television and the Internet all the time.

I was sitting outside on the steps of our shop, talking to passersby. David had gone to find some dry ice at the fire station. I'd had a reading scheduled for that afternoon with a new client, but I was sure she wouldn't show up. There were still roadblocks everywhere. Trees and power lines were down. Whole highways had been washed away.

A pretty teenage girl I'd seen around town from time to time was walking up the street by herself. She had a cup of coffee in her hand, so I knew the local café must have its generator on. She caught my eye and came over to sit beside me. I have a fondness for these local kids. I can't believe they enjoy being with me, but they do. I was so unpopular at their age, and now they treat me like one of the cool kids. Still, I dread it when they ask me for advice about their love lives.

The girl took a sip of her coffee. I could tell she had something big to tell me, and I was gearing up to let her know I wasn't up to a reading when she said softly, "I saw this . . . this guy last night."

"Is that so?" I was pretty sure I'd never done a reading for this girl before. I had no idea whom she was talking about. But I'm terrible with faces and names, except in my reading room.

"I was wondering if you might have seen him before?" She glanced at me expectantly. "I don't know. I thought maybe you of all people might have. I've heard about you. My friend Laura's been to you. You told her all about her ex-boyfriend. And my friend Ellen. You helped her talk to her dad."

I didn't recognize either of these names, but now I had begun to pay more attention to the girl sitting beside me. She was small and fair and fine boned. I could see the blue lines of veins twining up her arms. She was an old soul. How do I know that? It's information that comes to me in a flash, a stream of images from past lives cascading backwards in time. But I could also see the enormity of the girl's spirit barely contained by her tiny body.

"Who are you talking about?" I asked, finally giving her my full attention. Every hair on my body prickled, like it does when I'm about to receive a revelation from the other side. "Who did you see?"

The girl shivered. There were goose bumps on her arms, too.

"I used to see him when I was little, but I haven't for a long time. Until last night. He came again. Right in the middle of the storm, after the lights had all gone out and it was really wild out. I'm frightened of him."

"Yeah? Well, what does he look like?" I asked her, already preparing myself for what she was going to say. I remembered who I had seen at the height of the hurricane in London so long ago. I felt a bottomless terror in the pit of my stomach, familiar from childhood. I'm not afraid of much, but I was afraid of this.

"He comes to my room when I've just fallen asleep. He's a tall man in a wide-brimmed black hat. He looms over my bed. His eyes—"

"—are on fire," I finished for her.

We both shuddered.

All around us were the sounds of the village struggling to return to normal. Chain saws buzzed; generators whirred; neighbors called out to each other. The sky was a brilliant turquoise blue. The storm had passed. But in that moment, the girl and I were enveloped in darkness together.

"You've seen Ankou, too," she said. "I thought so."

I didn't know this name, and yet I did, in every cell of my body, in some lost place in my soul. The name plunged me back in time. I was in a cave. Waves crashed across rocks. I could see enormous gray stones stuck upright in the ground, stones that were older than Stonehenge.

"*Ankou?*" I repeated. "He has a *name?* That's his name?"

"My parents say so," said the girl. "They told me to call him by his name. They said that would make him less frightening. But I can never remember anything, much less his name, when he appears. It's overwhelming."

"It is," I agreed.

"My friend Matthew saw him once. He'd been taking too many drugs and he was really messed up one night. He passed out in his room and when he woke up he saw this coil of smoke winding out of his abdomen—"

"His etheric body," I said.

"He saw the coil and then he saw the man in the wide-brimmed black hat in his room. He knew he'd come to take him, that this was it. He was going to die. Only he didn't. He hasn't done any Ecstasy since then, and he's getting his shit together now. But I've always seen . . . Ankou . . . ever since I was a little girl. I even used to hear his cart coming up the driveway."

"He has a *cart?*"

"In Brittany he drives a cart, yeah. That's how my dad figured out who he was. That and the hat and the eyes."

"Who are your parents, and how do they know all of this?" I was feeling disoriented all of a sudden and slightly woozy, as if someone had spun me around and around and I didn't know what direction I was headed in anymore.

"They do a lot of research for their work. That's how they found the stories about him. They figured it out." She sighed heavily. "I guess."

"What do you mean, 'I guess'?"

The girl narrowed her eyes. "Just because you can explain something doesn't mean you understand it."

"Who do you think this Ankou is?" It had been so many years since I had last seen him in London, but the cold fear this discussion of him inspired in me was immediate and powerful. In a life filled with many strange experiences, he had been one of the few visions to ever truly frighten me. Even talking about him in the light of day unnerved me.

The girl had a distracted, intense quality. She picked at her cuticles; she twisted a strand of her hair. She had a lot going on inside of her. And she was seeing all kinds of things that most people didn't. I could tell. She reminded me of myself at her age.

"Who is he?" I asked her again. My whole life I had wanted to know and feared the answer. Was he the one who had engineered the attacks against me in Woodstock?

The girl stared at me. She was terrified, too. I could tell that she didn't want to tell me, but that she had to. She took a breath. "He's the King of the Dead," she said at last.

"What?"

I was astounded. Was that all? The King of the Dead? The dead aren't frightening to me. Death isn't frightening to me . . . or at least I didn't think so. "If he's the King of the Dead, how come he's got this name I've never heard of before?"

"Oh, he's got lots of names. He pops up all over the world. Ankou is just what they called him in Brittany, where he drives a cart when he comes for the dead. It's an old Celtic name. But he's also Charon, the ferryman from Greek mythology who takes the souls to Hades on his boat, and Jizo, in Japan. But what I want to know is *why* I see him." She took another breath and stared at me defiantly. "Is it because I'm about to die?"

The Lord of Death. Could this being I thought of my whole life as the embodiment of malice and evil only be the ferryman between this world and the next? Was that who I'd been afraid of all these years?

But that would make sense. Terrifying as he was, he was only the navigator, the messenger, the guide. Of course I saw him. Only he didn't just take souls away—he brought them *back.*

I thought of the mothers, the boyfriends, the children, the snakes, the dogs, all the spirits who, through me, had come back over the years. Ankou had brought them to me. I always used to sense his presence in the mirrors when the voices would flow like a river towards me. I had seen him, too, the night of the London hurricane, but that was also the night I had seen the angel. Ankou had been her guide. Still, as a child I must have thought, like this girl, that his appearance signaled my own personal death. No wonder I'd been terrified. Death is terrifying. But would I have been so terrified if I had known even one of his many names?

Was that why some people, my own mother among them, were so frightened of *me*? Because I commune with the dead? Most people don't want to think about death at all. Our old people disappear into nursing homes; we're not washing the corpses of our loved ones and laying their bodies out in our own parlors to pray over; we don't dig their graves. Sometimes we don't even give them graves. We've lost so many of the meaningful rituals connected to death, the dying, and the dead.

The dead are right here. If I have one message that I want people to hear, that's it. They aren't scary, they aren't ghouls, but they would like us to acknowledge their presence. The dead are everywhere.

We try to pretend we're not going to die. But we are. At any moment. And we should be ready to meet that moment. If I have learned anything over the years, it is that.

We're frightened of death, of the night, and of the darkness, of the earth, and of our graves. An image of the Black Madonna arose in my mind. She'd been taken out of the darkness and put in the sun and wrapped in pastel robes and made white and infertile and inaccessible . . . and lost her power. But like Ankou, she was originally a figure of darkness, the womb we come from and go back to in the end, which is also the beginning. Backwards and forwards. It's not a one-way journey. If Ankou leads us to death, he also leads us to life.

"Why don't you come into the shop?" I invited this girl whom the hurricane had blown to my steps to answer a lifelong mystery. I stood up, collecting myself. I was light-headed but also strangely relieved, exuberant even. "You're not going to die for a long time," I said to the girl, because she wasn't. "But together maybe we can figure out why you're seeing this Ankou. I think children do because they are close to the spirit world. Writers and poets do, I'm sure of it, and musicians, at least when they let themselves be channels. And people like me do. . . . Let's go to my reading room and I'll tell you what I can see about you."

———

A new client called up to announce that she was canceling her appointment.

"That's fine. Do you want to reschedule?"

"No."

"Okay then."

"All right, all right, I'll be there." I could hear her sighing heavily over the phone and muttering to herself.

"Whatever," I said. "I'm not filling your appointment time."

About an hour later, a very old women peeked through the door. She was dressed all in black and had three different crosses hanging from around her neck. She was clutching rosary beads. I was surprised she wasn't dragging a huge wooden cross behind her. She looked like she was walking into a nest of vampires.

"I came," she said. She was visibly trembling.

"Okay then." I led her into my reading room and she sat down tentatively on the edge of her chair. She looked liked she might bolt at any moment.

"Who is Joseph?" I asked her. "He's standing right beside you."

"That's my father!" She started to cry.

"Everything's all right, he wants you to know. You don't have to be so frightened."

"I was afraid to come here. My daughter made the appointment for me, but I thought it might be evil. I go to church every Sunday, you know. This is against my religion. It's forbidden."

"There are prophets in the Bible; people have visions; two psychics recognize Jesus when he's a baby."

"Do they?"

"Anna and Simeon. They're the ones who welcome his mother at the temple."

"That's right. They were psychics, weren't they?"

"They were."

"Is my father really next to me?"

"He is. He's always with you. He loves you very much. He wants you to know that."

"You're not evil, are you? You're really a very nice lady to show me that. Is there anything else I should know?"

24

After the Apocalypse

All of my clients were getting so worked up about the Mayan Apocalypse. Was it going to happen? When? Was it really going to happen in 2012? Should they get canned goods or would canned goods be pointless? A small part of me couldn't help wondering if the end might not be coming.

You don't need a psychic to tell you that the Earth is in a sorry state, and that technology is interfering with the natural order of things. We've become obsessed with our computers and our cell phones and our YouTube videos and our music and our buttons for this distraction and that amusement, and we've stopped paying attention to what's happening right in front of us.

The Earth has been raped, and not enough people are listening to her weeping. The birds hear it and they drop from the sky, filled with sadness. The whales and the dolphins hear it and beach themselves on the sand in despair. We have forgotten that everything in nature is divine. The animals we eat (or choose not to eat), the trees, the flowers, and especially the ground beneath our feet. People used to know that the mountains were goddesses, that the rivers were gods, that fairies were the souls of nature. There was a sense of divinity, not as something out there or up in the sky, but all around us and within us.

The Earth is shuddering in horror these days. Hurricanes, tornadoes, floods, fires—we all know what's coming. I have this yearning for some kind of primordial dragon to erupt out of the ground and set the world right again. But I fear that nobody would respect it. They'd kill it or, even worse, ignore it. I feel cynical about the human race and all that we've destroyed.

People come to me and so often they know in their hearts what I'm going to say, or their dead relatives are going to say, before I say it. Is some kind of big reckoning with nature coming? You tell me.

Maybe that's what the angel had meant when she had said I would be safe in Woodstock.

Around that time I had a dream about Jack. He drove up to my shop in one of those psychedelic old sixties buses all covered in graffiti and Day-Glo paint. The bus was packed with souls I knew were dead, but Jack opened the door and leaned out to me. He was young again and had long hair down to his shoulders. "Don't worry, but the end is coming!"

"Jack! It's you!" I cried.

"Sure, it's me," he answered in his thick Cockney accent. "I just wanted to tell you, my little sister, that even though the end is coming, you are going to be all right."

I reached out and touched his hair. "You have hair like Jesus," I said for some reason.

"We're all Jesus, little sister," answered Jack. "We're all the saviors of the world if only we knew it."

The door closed. He was happy. He was young.

Just before the big end-time catastrophe that didn't happen, I went down to Mexico with some girlfriends. People were making pilgrimages to pray to the Mayans or their spirits or something to save us. All of this talk about some final reckoning was filling me with doubts. What was I doing with my life anyway? Did it matter? So what if I could see dead people? What difference did it make in the world?

I guess everyone has doubts about their work from time to time. But this was bigger than that. I was feeling empty and lost in a way I never had before. A lot of it was because I couldn't connect to my mother in the spirit world. She just wouldn't show up. All my long-gone pets were always coming to visit. My father visited pretty regularly. Everybody else's great-aunt Margaret traipsed through my reading room. But my mother wouldn't even visit me in dreams.

I suppose she was angrier at me now more than ever for the things I'd seen about her. Maybe I should have just let her go, but I couldn't.

We were staying in a run-down resort close to the ocean. The name of the beach was La Luna, and I went out at night to walk under the moon. I was feeling lost in the universe that night. I wasn't really sure why I was there. I had no real reason to be in Mexico. I didn't care one way or another if the apocalypse happened. I wasn't looking for anything—except some kind of sign about, well, something. It was very dark on the beach with no lights anywhere. No one else was out, even though the night was balmy and still. The waves lapped softly at the shore.

As I was walking I found myself saying the old chant to the goddess, "Isis, Astarte, Hecate, Demeter, Kali, Lianna." Over and over again I repeated these names, so many different names, all for the Black Madonna. I wanted to see her for myself. "Show me I'm on the right track," I begged. It was a prayer from the deepest part of my soul.

It was close to midnight.

I sat down in a beach chair that had been left in the sand. I listened to the surf. The night was black, and the sky was filled with thousands and thousands of stars.

My hand fell over the side of the chair and touched what I thought at first was a boulder. Until I heard it breathing. A giant flipper flopped onto my leg. Once. Then again. And again. Some enormous creature was there beside me, touching me. I couldn't breathe. Quietly and very slowly, I turned to see what it was. Illuminated only by the moon and the stars was the hugest sea turtle I have ever seen in my life. She was right beside me, touching me, trying to get my attention.

I looked at her, and she looked back up at me with the darkest, deepest almond-shaped eyes. I touched her head gently, and she patted me again with her flipper. "You're my sign, aren't you?"

I started to cry.

She made whooshing noises, in and out, as she breathed. There were no other turtles on the beach; she wasn't laying eggs. There was no reason for her to be there. I got out of the chair and lay in the sand in front of her so I could gaze directly into her eyes.

It was easy to understand how an older, more observant people had imagined a sea turtle as the Great Mother carrying the weight of the whole world on her back. She was ancient and wise. She was heartbroken.

The turtle reached out and tapped me once more with her fin. It was the strangest thing. Me and this giant turtle alone on the beach together. She came right to me and touched me.

Whoosh! Whoosh, she answered me. Then, slowly, she turned herself around and dragged herself back into the sea.

I had a vision that night of the saints returning, not just the Catholic saints but also the holy ones of the old religions from all over the world, from the ancient times, from all times. They were coming back because we needed them. I realized I had met some of their incarnations already in my reading room—young people with urgent questions and old eyes. They were ready to take their place on the side of the Black Madonna and fight for the life of the planet itself. I remembered the long-ago words of my grandmother that we must return to the old ways.

My job going forward is to speak for the dead so they can help us find our way again. They know the old ways. They remember. They'll guide us through whatever's coming.

Soon after I got back from that trip, some friends introduced me to an ancient oak tree they had discovered on the side of the mountain looming over Woodstock. The tree must be five or six hundred years old, my friend told me, old enough to have remembered a time before airplanes soaring overhead and electric lights and paved roads and too many people crawling over the earth. It has a huge trunk with a heart-shaped boll that I can just barely touch if I stand on my tiptoes.

This oak tree reminded me of the old trees I had met and hugged on my many visits to England. Long ago people used to put statues of the Black Madonna in the hollows of such trees, which they worshiped. Long before people went to church, they went out into groves of trees to commune with the spirits.

My friends who consider themselves followers of the Black Madonna found a replica of one of the old French statues of her, made out of silver. One day in the spring we brought it to the tree together. There was a small hollow at the base of the trunk that was exactly the same shape and size as the metal figure of the Madonna holding the child up against her left shoulder, close to her heart. She fit into the tree perfectly. The tree had been waiting for her. Something was in place at last in my life.

I had never felt at home in any church, not even among the Wiccans, really. But out here on the side of the mountain, I had faith in the trees and in Her.

When I got home that day, my sister called out of the blue. She had decided that day to sell my mother's house.

"Yeah?" I said. It didn't really have anything to do with me. I didn't live there. I didn't even visit it, and I certainly didn't own any part of it.

My sister sighed. "We have to do something with her ashes."

"Oh," I answered. My inheritance at last.

"Do you know what we should do with them? Do you want them?"

"I do."

On a hot summer day, I drove with some friends and my sister to the side of the mountain. We blessed ourselves with water from a mountain spring, and then we climbed up a steep embankment until we came to the tree. I knew already that I was going to tell everyone my mother's secrets in the book that I was writing. But I also knew at last that this was, finally, the only thing that could really heal her, wherever she was hiding.

Hadn't my whole life been a testament to the healing power of communication, of speaking the truth no matter what?

It was time to give my mother back to the earth, back to the Mother who would accept her exactly as she was and let her begin to grow again. My mother had told me long ago that if she ever could come back, she would want to be a tree next time. We dug a hole close to the trunk, and I tore open the plastic bag holding the small weight of my mother's ashes.

I laid my mother to rest on hallowed hippie ground. The people of my town would have appalled her, but they were also the people who were going to heal her. "You're in my land now, at last," I said to her. "This is my world. You're on my turf, and you know what? It's going to be good for you, so get used to it."

For a flash I had a vision of her, holding out her hand to me, a little reluctantly, a little limply, it's true, but she was there. It was the first sight I'd had of her since she had died.

"There's no rush," I said to her. "We've still got a lot of work to do. But we've got all the time in the world. We all do."

I spread her ashes in the hole and covered it over with dirt and moss. Thunder began to rumble and soon rain would come and bring what was left of her closer to the tree's roots. I looked up to wipe away a bead of sweat and saw a flash of indigo in some nearby brambles—they were the feathers of a blue jay. Its body was gone and all that was left were its wings.

My mother is not exactly happy about this book. Sometimes when I wake up in the middle of the night to go to the bathroom, I'll sense her just outside the door, wearing a bathrobe, her arms crossed, frowning. She's not saying much, but she's there. She's not very happy that I've revealed all of these things about her.

"This is good, Mommy," I tell her. "We need to talk about this stuff. We really do."

I came into this world a little old English lady, but these days I am beginning to feel younger and younger, released from centuries of suffering. More and more I am beginning to recover the old ways and the old ways are making me young. I'm Benjamin Buttoning it, despite my crow's-feet. Things are going to work out, if we reach out to the dead, if we help them, if we let them help us. If we remember that they are all around us.

Things are going to work out.

The journey goes on, the story goes on . . . and we go on.

There aren't really any endings.

My mother

A little old Italian man came to see me last week. He was dying. He knew it. I knew it. He had absolutely everything wrong with him, including pancreatic cancer. He had tubes sticking out of his arms and his neck, and every time he talked his false teeth nearly jumped out of his mouth. He was divorced, childless, and alone. His name was Apollo.

Apollo, the god of prophecies and oracles. You can't make this stuff up. I am constantly surprised by the universe's sense of humor.

"I took a chance you'd be here. People told me I'd never be able to get in to see you, but here you are," he said to me. "I don't have anybody to love and nobody loves me. I need to find somebody to love."

I could see his apartment. It was small, dusty, and lonely.

There was another vision, though, beyond that one. I saw him sitting in a vineyard wearing an elegant suit, a glass of wine in his hand. His hair was slicked back. He was healthy. He didn't have any tubes in his neck. He was waiting for someone. I told him so, and he started to cry. I didn't tell him that it wasn't in this lifetime. But I think he knew.

"And my soul mate?" he said. "Is my soul mate there? That's all I want to know. I'm looking for my soul mate. Is she there?"

I am always amazed at how people never give up. Never. Here he was, weeks, maybe days, from death, and he was still hoping to meet that special eighty-year-old girl. What could I say to him? He was going to find her, I could see that clear as day, but not in this lifetime. First he was going to have to die, and then he was going to have to be reborn and struggle through the business of living again. The spiritual adventure has so many twists and turns.

On the table where I do my readings was an iridescent stone heart that someone had once given me as a present. I wasn't sure why I'd left it in the room—until now. "Take this, Apollo. Sleep with it. It'll be all right. You'll see. Just hold it until you meet her. It won't be long now. I promise."

"You're really giving me this? God bless you. Bless you. Let me pay you for this. What do I owe you? Let me give you a few dollars so you can buy something for your pet cockatoos."

"Nothing, Apollo. No money. This one's on the house."

Haunted, at 24

Acknowledgments

During the writing of this book, we became more than friends. We have shared a fondness for marzipan and a taste for Kahlúa. We have celebrated holidays together and fallen in love with each other's dachshunds. We confided to each other our worries, our dreams, our deepest secrets, and our everyday wonders. Barely a day passes now that we don't feel the need for a bit of a chat. In the midst of figuring out how to tell this remarkable story, we discovered a great deal about ourselves and the universe, but the most important thing we found out was how much we meant to each other—that we are, in fact, however it works, soul sisters.

We met because Perdita was desperate for help. Her daughter was sick with a mysterious illness, and a friend at the gym, Jo Schwartz, to whom we owe an incalculable debt of gratitude, suggested that she needed a reading with Suzan. That reading changed both of our lives forever.

One day, early in our friendship, Perdita noted the signed

photo of the child actor Jack Wild in Suzan's store. "Did you
love him as a kid, too?" she asked. "Oh yes," said Suzan mysteriously. "He was my chum." That question led to a wealth of
stories shared over blueberry smoothies and vegan quesadil-
las at Woodstock's beloved Garden Café. To the patient
waitresses and the cruelty-free cooking skills of chef Pam
Brown, we owe many thanks. The hours we spent sitting in
the sun at the front table, recording the sessions that became
this book, were filled with laughter and revelations for us
both. Jack always seemed to be there—in memories and in
dreams. Once he actually seemed to materialize when a local
teenager, who bore an uncanny resemblance to him, showed
up wearing the Artful Dodger's top hat. "Who is he? I mean
really?" Perdita has asked Suzan repeatedly. Suzan asked
Jack himself this question, and he answered that he was one
of the "gentry," an old-fashioned word for the fairy folk.

Fairies, angels, saints, and all manner of supernatural beings have guided us during the writing of this book. And ferry-
ing them to us across that open channel was the dark figure
of Ankhou, the Lord of the Dead. With each day that passes
we understand a little more about his strange role in our lives.
When we started the book, he told Suzan how important it
was that people realize that the "dead are right here." Then
he added, "but tell them this in a way that's entertaining." We
can only hope we have fulfilled our mission.

To the legions of the dead, we owe everything. Perdita
thanks her mother and her father, both of whom dramatically appeared in that first session, and Suzan thanks Steve,
her beloved Robin Hood of a father, always at her side. Again
and again, he offered signs and encouragement to let us know
how happy he was that his story was being told at last.

On this side of the veil, there were many souls offering practical help. First and foremost we have to thank our powerhouse of an agent Gail Ross and the incredibly talented team at Ross-Yoon Agency, including Howard Yoon and Anna Sproul-Latimer, who offered insightful editing. Through it all, Gail has created opportunities and adventures for us that we could never have imagined. She is a blessing—as is her long-gone "white dog" who arrived at our first meeting together and convinced Gail that Suzan was for real. We thank Kenny Wapner for passing along our manuscript to her.

At St. Martin's we have been fortunate to have the wise and experienced hand of Jennifer Weiss gently opening up the hidden heart of this story, and we have enjoyed her assistant Sylvan Creekmore's thoughtfulness and enthusiasm.

Many friends read the manuscript early on and offered counsel. We thank Robert Burke Warren, Beckie Kravetz, Babs Mansfield, Diana Cobbold, Violet Snow, Linda Dickey, and Karin Miller-Lewis especially.

Sara Reilly contributed irreverence and friendship and is one of those rare people who can appreciate Suzan's gifts without ever having to make use of them.

To our own Dr. Who and Rose, Michael, and Alana Ellick, thank you for the past, thank you for the future, and thank you for sharing with us this wild ride on the TARDIS.

We thank our families—human and animal—for the healing powers of their love.

Our children—Gavin, Sophie, and Jonah—were in turns encouraging and skeptical. They kept us honest and productive and serious about this project. May it bring to them many rewards both spiritual and practical.

Perdita thanks her husband Clark Strand for everything,

BP 1.17

but most of all for helping her accept her own spiritual insights, and for sharing with her, lifetime after lifetime, the journey of the heart. Clark listened to every word of this book from the very beginning. He offered invaluable editing and encouragement. But more than that, he was this book's spiritual midwife. He and Suzan are both intimate friends of the darkness, of each other, and of Our Lady.

Thank you to Bob for getting Suzan to Woodstock.

Thank you to Luna the dachshund, Babyhead Willie and Sweetie Poo the cockatoos, Scully the Rat, and all the many animals who have helped Suzan create a family.

And to David Saxman, who has been more patient, more stoical, and more enduring than Stonehenge, Suzan owes so much. He has risked grave psychic and physical harm to be her lifelong knight in shining armor. He cares for the animals, he talks to the trees, and he makes sure there is always a home to come home to.

Finally, Suzan owes a belated "thank you" to Madame Florence from New Jersey. Suzan didn't believe her when she said that one day a woman would walk into her shop and help her write a book. Not everybody believes what a psychic tells them—even a psychic. But here's the proof that what she said was true.